THE ILLUSTRATED ENCYCLOPEDIA OF THE

PRESIDENTS OF AMERICA

THE ILLUSTRATED ENCYCLOPEDIA OF THE
PRESIDENTS OF AMERICA

AN AUTHORITATIVE HISTORY OF THE AMERICAN PRESIDENCY,
SHOWN IN MORE THAN 460 PHOTOGRAPHS AND ILLUSTRATIONS

PROFESSOR JON ROPER

HERMES
HOUSE

CONTENTS

INTRODUCTION

On 4 November 2008, Barack Obama was elected as the 44th president of the United States. Among his predecessors, 25 held the office between 1788 and 1900. While the names of George Washington, Thomas Jefferson and Abraham Lincoln still resonate in the nation's history, others, such as Millard Fillmore, Franklin Pierce, Chester Arthur and Benjamin Harrison have drifted into timeless obscurity. John Quincy Adams and Rutherford B. Hayes are remembered more for the controversial circumstances of their election than for their achievements in office. Andrew Jackson was synonymous with the age in which he lived, but most presidents remain among those to whom history pays scant attention.

Below: George Washington sees the first American flag made by Betsy Ross.

For James Madison, the architect of the United States Constitution, that is how it should be: executive power in America's republican government was best checked, balanced and contained by other institutions of government. The presidency was never intended to be the focal point of the political system. Neither was the vice-presidential office to become a natural stepping stone to winning the White House. Between 1788 and 1900 John Adams and Martin Van Buren were the only vice presidents to fulfil that ambition.

By refusing to hold on to office for longer than eight years, George Washington established an important precedent for his successors, most of whom felt constrained by his example. Yet his self-imposed limit proved more of an aspiration than an achievement. Only six presidents elected in the

Above: The bald eagle became the national symbol in 1782, during the American War of Independence.

19th century completed eight years in office. Two more – Lincoln and William McKinley – were re-elected to a second term, but both were assassinated soon afterwards. James Polk was the first to retire voluntarily after four years in the White House, becoming one of the seven 19th-century presidents who completed only a single term.

William Harrison, following a tradition established by James Monroe, gave his inaugural address outside. Soon afterwards he succumbed to pneumonia. Zachary Taylor also died of natural causes. Lincoln and James Garfield both fell to an assassin's bullet. John Tyler, Millard Fillmore, Andrew Johnson and Chester Arthur were the four vice presidents who entered the White House in tragic circumstances, following the death of the president. They each served out their predecessor's term in office but were never elected to it in their own right.

Until the Civil War (1861–5), presidents struggled to keep the United States together in the face of sectional tensions, such as those caused by the issue of slavery that threatened to tear

Above: The White House has been the president's official purpose-built residence since 1800.

it apart. Of the 14 presidents preceding James Buchanan, who left office in the year the war broke out, nine came from the slave-holding South. After the war ended, for the remainder of the century,

nobody from the former Confederate States ran for executive office, let alone occupied the White House. At the same time, President Ulysses S. Grant and his successors surveyed a new and challenging political landscape as

Below: The Oval Office, here occupied by Kennedy, is the heart of the White House.

America experienced a period of rapid economic and social change. (In an era of technological innovation, in 1879 the first telephone was installed in the White House.) Among those elected during this time, Grover Cleveland remains unique: he is the only president to have been elected to two non-consecutive terms in office.

Below: The Fourth of July is the annual celebration of the colonies' Declaration of Independence from British rule.

In the 20th century, as the United States became a global superpower, the scope of presidential power correspondingly increased. Nevertheless, among the 19 presidents elected since 1901, only Theodore Roosevelt, Woodrow Wilson and Franklin Roosevelt thus far have established historical reputations that match the most distinguished of their predecessors.

Indeed, it was Franklin Roosevelt who rewrote the political rulebook. His unique achievement was not only his

Above: The presidential seal of the USA.

longevity in office (he occupied the White House for just over 12 years); he was also the architect of the modern presidency. Yet Roosevelt's example created the paradox of contemporary presidential power: while its potential has increased, his successors have struggled to use it successfully. His legacy has yet to be surpassed.

Between 1904 and 1932, Republicans won five out of seven presidential elections: Theodore Roosevelt served out William McKinley's second term before winning one of his own, William Taft and Herbert Hoover were one-term presidents and Calvin Coolidge inherited the presidency from Warren Harding, the first 20th century chief executive to die from natural causes while in office. Since Franklin Roosevelt won his four consecutive elections, Democrats have not enjoyed much greater success than they had before he entered the White House: in the 15 presidential contests held since 1948, when Harry Truman achieved an upset and an unanticipated victory, they have won on only six occasions.

Like Truman, Lyndon Johnson inherited the White House following the death of his predecessor (John F. Kennedy) and was then elected in his own right. His presidency was another political watershed: he was the first chief executive from a former Confederate state to win election. Four of the eight

THE FIRST FOURTH OF JULY

Above: Uncle Sam, who personifies the government of the USA.

PRESIDENTIAL ROLL CALL

George Washington, 1789–1797	Benjamin Harrison, 1889–1893
John Adams, 1797–1801	Grover Cleveland (again), 1893–1897
Thomas Jefferson, 1801–1809	William McKinley, 1897–1901
James Madison, 1809–1817	Theodore Roosevelt, 1901–1909
James Monroe, 1817–1825	William Taft, 1909–1913
John Quincy Adams, 1825–1829	Woodrow Wilson, 1913–1921
Andrew Jackson, 1829–1837	Warren Harding, 1921–1923
Martin Van Buren, 1837–1841	Calvin Coolidge, 1923–1929
William Henry Harrison, 1841	Herbert Hoover, 1929–1933
John Tyler, 1841–1845	Franklin Roosevelt, 1933–1945
James Polk, 1845–1849	Harry Truman, 1945–1953
Zachary Taylor, 1849–1850	Dwight Eisenhower, 1953–1961
Millard Fillmore, 1850–1853	John F. Kennedy, 1961–1963
Franklin Pierce, 1853–1857	Lyndon B. Johnson, 1961–1969
James Buchanan, 1857–1861	Richard Nixon, 1969–1974
Abraham Lincoln, 1861–1865	Gerald Ford, 1974–1977
Andrew Johnson, 1865–1869	Jimmy Carter, 1977–1981
Ulysses S. Grant, 1869–1877	Ronald Reagan, 1981–1989
Rutherford Hayes, 1877–1881	George H. W. Bush, 1989–1993
James Garfield, 1881	Bill Clinton, 1993–2001
Chester Arthur, 1881–1885	George W. Bush, 2001–2009
Grover Cleveland, 1885–1889	Barack Obama, 2009–

presidents elected after Johnson have come from the South: Jimmy Carter from Georgia, Bill Clinton from Arkansas, the Texas-based George H. W. Bush and most recently his eldest son. Indeed, George W. Bush was the first member of Abraham Lincoln's party raised in the former Confederacy to become president of the United States of America.

Eight of those elected since 1900 have been former state governors. Seven, including Gerald Ford who was appointed to the office and who inherited the presidency on Richard Nixon's resignation, were former vice presidents. Six had served in the Senate. Three – William Taft, Herbert Hoover and Dwight Eisenhower – had not held elected office prior to entering the White House.

John F. Kennedy was assassinated, and Ronald Reagan narrowly survived an attempt on his life. The president's security has become a perennial problem and a paramount concern. While some may be tempted to cut themselves off from their fellow citizens, contact between politicians and voters remains the air that breathes life into American democracy. Nowhere is this better demonstrated than in the small towns of states such as Iowa and New Hampshire as the nominating process begins anew every four years and aspirants to the office meet potential supporters of their cause.

The presidency combines constitutional authority and political power, focusing attention on the personal qualities and character of its incumbent. Over the past 200 years it has become the most important institution of America's federal government and is at the centre of national political life. In the 21st century, who may join Wilson and the two Roosevelts, together with Jefferson, Lincoln and Washington, the most outstanding among the 44 who have become president of the United States of America?

Left and below: The Republican party symbol is the elephant, while that of the Democratic party is the donkey.

PART ONE

EARLY PRESIDENTS
1754–1901

The American Revolution led to the birth of the United States of America, a new nation, with a new and innovative system of government. The United States was the first country in the world to create the elected office of president to serve as its head of state.

Left: Mount Rushmore has immortalized the greatest American presidents in stone. From left to right are George Washington, Thomas Jefferson and Theodore Roosevelt.

CHAPTER ONE

GEORGE WASHINGTON, JOHN ADAMS

AND THE FOUNDING OF THE UNITED STATES OF AMERICA, 1754–1801

THE AMERICAN REVOLUTION HAD COMPLEX CAUSES, BUT ITS CHIEF RESULT WAS THE SETTING UP OF THE WORLD'S FIRST SUCCESSFUL FEDERAL GOVERNMENT. AT THE TIME OF THE FIRST CONTINENTAL CONGRESS IN 1775, NONE OF THE PARTICIPANTS KNEW WHAT FORM THEIR NEW CONSTITUTION WOULD TAKE, SHOULD THEIR STRUGGLE AGAINST THE BRITISH BE SUCCESSFUL, BUT THEY KNEW THAT IT MUST BE BASED ON A NEW SET OF PRINCIPLES. THE COLONISTS' DISCONTENT HAD BECOME FOCUSED ON THE MONARCHY, AND THEY WERE SETTING OUT TO REJECT NOT JUST BRITISH RULE BUT ALSO THE BRITISH PATTERN OF GOVERNMENT. THE CONSTITUTION AGREED IN PHILADELPHIA IN 1787 WAS DESIGNED TO PREVENT THE ACCESSION OF AN AUTOCRAT IN THE MANNER OF THE BRITISH MONARCH. THE SOLUTION LAY IN THE ELECTION OF A PRESIDENT WITH EXECUTIVE AUTHORITY, HELD IN CHECK BY THE JUDICIAL AND LEGISLATIVE BRANCHES OF THE GOVERNMENT.

Left: The Declaration of Independence (1776) was part of a revolution that paved the way for the Federal Constitution (1787).

THE ROAD TO REBELLION

1754–1775

What were the events that turned the man who would become the first president of the United States into a rebel? George Washington began his military career fighting alongside the British to prevent the French settlers from encroaching upon land in the Ohio Territory west of Virginia. He ended it against all odds as the general who forced Britain to give up its North American colonies. Along the way, he hastened the course of history.

In 1754, as a freshly promoted lieutenant colonel in the Virginia regiment, the 22-year-old Washington ordered his men to fire on a detachment of French forces. It proved to be the first engagement in what escalated into the French and Indian War. The following year he returned to the Ohio Territory with Major-General Edward Braddock, the commander-in-chief of British forces in America. This time he experienced a heavy defeat at the hands of the French defending the strategically important Fort Duquesne. The fighting became part of a wider conflict between the

Below: George Washington and his followers raise the British flag at Fort Duquesne in 1758.

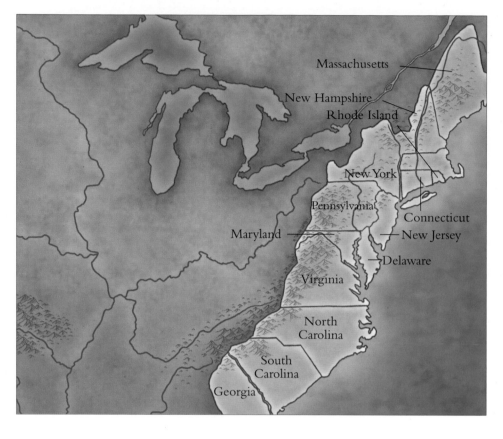

European powers – the Seven Years War (1756–1763) – which would end with French defeat, leaving the British as the dominant European power on the continent of North America.

During the struggle the Native American tribes, then the most numerous group living in the American

Above: In 1775, 13 of the British colonies that had been established in the New World rebelled against British rule.

interior, maintained a series of shifting alliances with France and Britain in the hope of postponing what would soon become inevitable: their displacement by the European settlers who were flocking to the New World. When, in 1758, the British took control of the upper Ohio valley for the first time, with Washington once again involved in the campaign that culminated in the capture of Fort Duquesne, the tribes in the region switched their allegiance to the winners. By the end of 1760 France's influence was waning and it had surrendered Quebec, Montreal and Detroit. Fighting ended with the signing of the Treaty of Paris (1763). France ceded New Orleans and the Louisiana Territory west of the Mississippi River to Spain and the rest of its mainland North American territories to Britain.

THE COST OF WAR

The cost of fighting the Seven Years War in both Europe and America had more than doubled the British national debt. Britain argued that its American colonies had benefited from the war, since they were no longer threatened by France's imperial ambitions in the New World, and they should now show their gratitude for their greater sense of security by accepting a number of new taxes imposed on them to help ease the burden of Empire. The Americans naturally disagreed. Repeated attempts by Britain to increase revenue from its colonies in the decade following the signing of the Treaty of Paris created a widening political chasm.

In 1765, the British parliament approved the Stamp Act, which put a tax on any printed paper used in the American colonies, including legal documents, contracts, newspapers and playing cards. The revenue raised in this way was to pay for the expense of maintaining British troops in the colonies. The act was passed without consultation with the colonists.

Below: Paul Revere, an express rider, alerted the people of Lexington to the imminent arrival of regular army troops.

In Massachusetts, John Adams, a lawyer who would become the second president of the United States, was drawn to the radical cause. Prompted by his opposition to the Stamp Act, he first entered the public arena in 1765, arguing that such taxes should be agreed to by those who would pay them, and not simply imposed: this had been a constitutional principle since the signing of Magna Carta, but was now being denied to colonists, though they were still British subjects. The Stamp Act proved unenforceable. It was repealed in 1766, though not before it had provoked the memorable slogan of independence: "No taxation without representation." Adams would become one of the leading advocates of American independence as resentment against Britain grew in the colonies.

QUARTERING ACT

In the same year that the Stamp Act was passed, the Quartering Act was extended from Boston throughout the colonies. It allowed for British troops to be billeted and provisioned in private homes without charge. Most colonies had accepted such terms in war, but in peacetime it was an imposition many Americans found unacceptable.

IMPORT DUTIES

Two years later, the Townshend Acts attempted to finance colonial administration through the imposition of taxes on a range of goods imported to America, including glass, paint, oil, lead and tea. In retaliation, Americans refused to order supplies from Britain and transatlantic trade suffered.

The relationship between Britain and its North American colonies continued to deteriorate, and it was the event of

MINUTEMEN

The Minutemen were volunteer rapid response units of the Massachusetts militia, formed during the 17th century to act as the first line of defence when emergencies arose. Although they lacked a centralized command, they were typically well trained and organized, selected from the younger, fitter members of the militia.

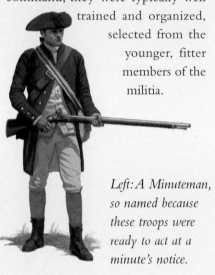

Left: A Minuteman, so named because these troops were ready to act at a minute's notice.

Rome might seek to claim it. They now saw the religious toleration for Catholics in Canada incorporated in the Quebec Act as a cynical manoeuvre intended to keep what Americans regarded as 'the fourteenth colony' loyal to the Crown. Some argued that this was an attempt to undermine the Protestant faith in North America.

The Quebec Act achieved its desired result: Canada would remain loyal to Britain, despite the American colonists' later attempt to capture Quebec. It would also become a sanctuary for American Loyalists, who fought for the Crown against the Patriots in what would be a civil war as well as a struggle for colonial independence.

Massachusetts became the front line in the confrontation between the colonies and Britain. The British forces, massed in Boston, were targets for American hostility as New England prepared for war. On 18 April 1775, Paul Revere, a New England silversmith who supported the call for rebellion, rode into American history when he travelled from his home in Boston to Lexington to warn the local militia that the British were on their way to search and destroy military supplies being hoarded by the colonists. Forewarned, the Massachusetts Minutemen confronted the British troops at Lexington and Concord, in the opening battles of the American War of Independence.

1773 known as the Boston Tea Party that came to symbolize the extent of American discontent. In its aftermath, the British government closed the harbour in March 1774 and in May Parliament approved the Coercive Acts, aimed at punishing Massachusetts. These additional measures tightened British control over the colony and effectively suspended its governmental charter, the origins of which could be traced back to the establishment of the Puritan colony in Massachusetts Bay in 1630.

THE CANADIAN COLONIES

Meanwhile, with increasing unrest in the south, the British government tried to secure the allegiance of the French Canadians, who were the overwhelming majority of those living in Quebec. The Quebec Act, passed in December 1774, reformed the governance of the area and added to the displeasure of New England colonists. Many of them were descended from those Puritans who had come to the New World to counter the prospect that the Church of

THE BOSTON TEA PARTY

The British East India Company monopolized the tea trade between India and the colonies, but the high tax levied on the product encouraged Americans to boycott it and buy cheaper tea smuggled from Holland, which affected the company's profitability. In May 1773 the Tea Act was passed, permitting the company to sell directly to the colonies free of British duty, undercutting American wholesalers. For the colonists it was another example of arbitrary rule. In protest, in December 1773 men disguised as Native Americans boarded ships moored in Boston harbour and unceremoniously dumped the tea they carried overboard. The act of defiance dramatized the colonists' increasing hostility to British policies and rallied support for the patriot cause. John Adams, the future president, confided in his journal: "This destruction of the tea is so bold, so daring, so intrepid and so inflexible, and it must have so important consequences and so lasting that I can't but consider it an epoch in history."

Below: The Boston Tea Party was an act of rebellion that shocked the English king.

WASHINGTON TAKES COMMAND
1775

In December 1758 George Washington had resigned from the Virginia regiment. He had sought a commission in the British Army, but this had been refused. Although he was the regiment's commanding officer his military reputation counted for nothing: British officers in North America, who had gained preferment through royal patronage rather than by merit, were contemptuous of the colonial militia, and indeed regarded most Americans as little more civilized than the Native Americans with whom they shared the continent. So he abandoned his military career and in January 1759 married the widow Martha Custis. Her wealth helped him to enter Virginia's colonial aristocracy and develop his estate at Mount Vernon, but he soon found that his prospects were tied into an imperial system that controlled the market price of tobacco, his principal source of income, upon which he relied to sustain the expensive lifestyle his social position demanded. Washington, like many Virginia planters – Thomas Jefferson was another – became consistently and chronically indebted to his London mercantile house.

In 1763, with the war with France over, a royal proclamation made the Ohio Territory part of an extensive Indian reservation. Further colonial settlement was banned. For Washington, who himself had interests in land there and who considered America's westward expansion inevitable, it symbolized yet more unwarranted British interference in the future of North America.

Resenting his British military superiors, his financial dependence on London merchants and his suspicions that the king would ultimately grant land rights in the interior to British rather than Virginian aristocrats gave Washington good reasons to support the cause of independence as it became the major issue in mid-18th century American politics. For more than a decade, in common with others in the colonies his resentment against British rule grew.

THE CONTINENTAL CONGRESS
In 1773, Benjamin Franklin, one of the most famous Americans of the day, suggested that all the colonies should meet to discuss their grievances against the British. Initially there was little support for the idea, but in September 1774 twelve colonies (Georgia stayed away) sent representatives to the first Continental Congress. Washington was among them. Meeting in Philadelphia,

Below: The Continental Congress was funded and directed by the Thirteen Colonies, and unified them for the first time under a provisional representative government.

the Congress agreed to rally support for a boycott of British goods. It also composed the Declaration of Rights and Grievances, addressed to King George III.

Early the following year, the British parliament passed an act restricting New England's trade to that with Britain alone. Determined to back its legislation with force, it met with equally defiant resistance from Americans.

At its second meeting in May 1775, with Georgia this time represented – the Continental Congress would create the Continental Army with George Washington in command. While he may not have anticipated the full magnitude of the task before him, he was at least prepared for the challenge. When he had journeyed from Virginia to Pennsylvania to attend the Congress he had packed his military uniform.

THE THIRTEEN COLONIES

British settlers had begun to establish colonies in eastern North America in the late 16th century, and by 1763 there were 20 British colonies on American territory north of Mexico. Thirteen united to fight against British rule and formed the original United States. Of the loyalist colonies, the five in the north would later form the Dominion of Canada, and East and West Florida in the south would be ceded by the British to Spain in 1783.

VIRGINIA

First colonial settlement: 1607
Colonial history: Jamestown established by the London Company.
Total population in 1790 census: 747,550
Total number of slaves in 1790 census: 292,627
Electoral College votes in 1789: 12
(2 votes not cast)

NEW JERSEY

First colonial settlement: 1618
Colonial history: Dutch settlement; British control (1664).
Total population in 1790 census: 184,139
Total number of slaves in 1790 census: 11,423
Electoral College votes in 1789: 6

MASSACHUSETTS

First colonial settlement: 1620
Colonial history: Plymouth Colony (1620); Massachusetts Bay Colony (1630). Colony united (1691), annexing Maine.
Total population in 1790 census: 378,556
Total number of slaves in 1790 census: 0
Electoral College votes in 1789: 10

NEW HAMPSHIRE

First colonial settlement: 1622
Colonial history: Originally part of Maine; separate colony (1629), annexed by Massachusetts (1641–3). Separate colony 1679 onwards.
Total population in 1790 census: 141,899
Total number of slaves in 1790 census: 157
Electoral College votes in 1789: 5

PENNSYLVANIA

First colonial settlement: 1623
Colonial history: Settled by Dutch and Swedes; British control (1664), granted to William Penn (1681).
Total population in 1790 census: 433,611
Total number of slaves in 1790 census: 3,707
Electoral College votes in 1789: 10

NEW YORK

First colonial settlement: 1624
Colonial history: New Netherland; British control (1664): renamed New York.
Total population in 1790 census: 340,241
Total number of slaves in 1790 census: 21,193
Electoral College votes in 1789: 8
(none appointed in time for election)

MARYLAND

First colonial settlement: 1634
Colonial history: Charter granted by King Charles I to Cecil Calvert.
Total population in 1790 census: 747,550
Total number of slaves in 1790 census: 292,627
Electoral College votes in 1789: 12
(2 votes not cast)

CONNECTICUT

First colonial settlement: 1635
Colonial history: Settled from Massachusetts and other colonies.
Total population in 1790 census: 237,648
Total number of slaves in 1790 census: 2,648
Electoral College votes in 1789: 7

RHODE ISLAND

First colonial settlement: 1636
Colonial history: Settled from Massachusetts; given royal charter (1663).
Total population in 1790 census: 69,112
Total number of slaves in 1790 census: 958
Electoral College votes in 1789: Constitution not ratified in time for the election

DELAWARE

First colonial settlement: 1638
Colonial history: Settled by Swedes; Dutch control (1655); British control (1664).
Total population in 1790 census: 59,096
Total number of slaves in 1790 census: 8,887
Electoral College votes in 1789: 3

NORTH CAROLINA

First colonial settlement: 1653
Colonial history: Carolina settled from other colonies; separated from Virginia: land granted to private company (1663).
Total population in 1790 census: 395,005
Total number of slaves in 1790 census: 100,783
Electoral College votes in 1789: Constitution not ratified in time for the election

SOUTH CAROLINA

First colonial settlement: 1670
Colonial history: Separated from North Carolina (1712) with appointment of separate governor; became crown colony (1729).
Total population in 1790 census: 249,073
Total number of slaves in 1790 census: 100,783
Electoral College votes in 1789: 7

GEORGIA

First colonial settlement: 1733
Colonial history: Private company granted land by King George II of England.
Total population in 1790 census: 82,548
Total number of slaves in 1790 census: 29,264
Electoral College votes in 1789: 5

THE FLAG OF THE UNITED COLONIES

Above: The Betsy Ross flag dating from 1777 shows 13 stars, each representing a colony, on a blue background. The 13 red and white stripes also each represent a colony. The stars are arranged in a circle, symbolizing perpetuity, and together they represent a new constellation. Five-pointed stars were revolutionary in flag design.

Above: The Francis Hopkinson flag (1777) shows the 13 stars staggered in alternate rows. Both flags were in use at the same time.

THE WAR OF INDEPENDENCE

1775–1782

John Adams, one of the founding fathers and a driving force in the battle for independence, like Washington, attended the first two meetings of the Continental Congress, and he later took credit for nominating Washington to command the Continental army. Whereas the colonel from Virginia was the unanimous choice for leader, in the confused atmosphere of the time there was still a debate over the need to raise a Continental army, rather than relying on separate forces from each colony to confront the British on American soil. When that issue was resolved, Washington accepted the commission.

Now a rebel fighting against the British Crown, Washington faced his greatest political, personal and military challenge. The odds on victory were long, but the consequences of defeat were profound. Even if he survived the war, on the losing side, he could be hanged as a traitor. Moreover, this was not yet a fight between nations. Thirteen colonies, each protective of their own interests and prone to rivalries among themselves, were taking on the world's most formidable military power.

Washington's war with the British began with the Siege of Boston and ended six years later with another siege at Yorktown, Virginia. After its surrender, the British army marched out of the town while their band played 'The World Turned Upside Down'. It had been. Despite losing more battles than he won during the long campaign, and although he did not believe it at the time, Washington had achieved America's independence. It was the persistence of the Patriots, coupled with the fact that their successes came at critical times in the conflict, and ultimately with the support of the French, that had earned them their victory.

VALLEY FORGE

In 1776, in New York, Washington confronted General William Howe, who commanded the greatest military force ever seen on the North American continent. Not surprisingly, the British forced the American troops to retreat into Pennsylvania. On Christmas night, however, Washington took the fight to the enemy. Crossing the Delaware River in the depths of the New England winter, he launched a successful surprise attack on the garrison at Trenton, which was manned by mercenaries recruited by the British from Hesse in Germany. This, together with his victory at Princeton just over a week later, revived what had been dangerously close to a lost cause.

During 1777, Washington lost important battles at Brandywine Creek and Germantown in Pennsylvania. In October, however, his generals, Horatio Gates and Benedict Arnold (later to become America's most notorious traitor) defeated the British General Burgoyne's forces at the Battle of Saratoga in New York.

The year ended with Washington moving his army into winter quarters at Valley Forge. It was a harsh winter. The general's stoicism as he, together with his troops, endured cold, disease, and a lack of food, symbolized American resolve in a war that Washington realized could be won through such heroic perseverance. It was at Valley Forge that Baron von Steuben, who had served in the Prussian army, made a vital contribution to America's war effort. He trained Washington's troops to such a professional standard that they were able to fight on equal terms with the British forces, now commanded by General Sir Henry Clinton, and the Americans avoided defeat during the Battle of Monmouth Court House in May 1778.

THE TIDE TURNS

On 10 July 1778 France declared war on Britain, exploiting its rival European power's problems in the New World. France's promised international aid was of little immediate help to America, as the French military contingent took time to arrive. For two more years

Left: The Battle of Lexington marked the start of the American revolution.

Right: More than seven years after fighting broke out, Washington returned to New York triumphant in 1783. He had secured independence for the colonists and would be the nation's first president.

Washington's army hung on in the north, suffering increasingly from lack of resources and eventually verging on collapse. Meanwhile the British waged a successful campaign against the southern colonies. When Clinton captured Charleston, South Carolina, in May 1780, it was America's worst defeat of the war. He then withdrew to his New York headquarters, leaving General Lord Charles Cornwallis in charge of British forces in the south.

The following year America's fortunes changed. Throughout the south, General Nathanael Greene used guerrilla tactics to harass the British, and in February 1781 another of Washington's generals, Daniel Morgan, inflicted a heavy defeat on Cornwallis's troops at Cowpens in South Carolina. In March the Americans won the Battle of Guilford Court House in North Carolina. With the British still threatening Virginia, Washington was now able to draw on French support and turned his attention from New York to his home state.

SURRENDER AT YORKTOWN

Cornwallis had moved his army to the Yorktown peninsula. Mistakenly believing that Clinton wanted him to remain there, instead of trying to break through the French and American lines, he stayed where he was. Meanwhile Washington and the French commander moved their combined forces south. On the way, Washington entertained his French ally at Mount Vernon, the first time he had seen his home in six years. On 15 September the American and French forces laid siege to the British

Right: Benjamin Franklin and Richard Oswald discussing the peace treaty between Britain and America in Paris.

army and on 19 October it was over. Cornwallis's surrender at Yorktown precipitated America's triumph.

The following year negotiations between the two sides began in Paris. The peace treaty was finally signed in September 1783. On 22 December Washington arrived in Annapolis, Maryland, to celebrate the victory. In a final heroic gesture, he resigned his commission. He was the most famous rebel in America.

THE DECLARATION OF INDEPENDENCE
1776

By 1776 American resentment against the British was becoming increasingly personal, with profound consequences. It focused on King George III and the institution from which he derived his power: the monarchy. In January, Thomas Paine published *Common Sense*, whose many readers included George Washington. Paine's arguments were persuasive: "But where ... is the King of America? I'll tell you Friend, he reigns above, and doth not make havoc of mankind like the Royal Brute of Britain. Yet that we may not appear to be defective even in earthly honours,

let a day be solemnly set apart for proclaiming the charter ... by which the world may know, that so far as we approve of monarchy, that in America THE LAW IS KING."

To become truly independent, the colonies would have to accept the need to reject not only British rule, but also the British system of government. John Adams and Thomas Jefferson (who became the second and third presidents) took the lead in moving the Continental Congress towards this radical vision. Adams drew up widely read guidelines for creating a republican

government and was largely responsible for the passage of a congressional resolution in May, encouraging the colonies to draft their own constitutions. At the same time Jefferson, also in Philadelphia to attend the Congress, was involved in discussions about a constitution for his home state. On 11 June, however, following the tabling of a resolution proposed by Virginia and seconded by Massachusetts: "That these United Colonies are, and of right ought to be, free and independent States", both men were distracted by a fresh task, that of presenting for Congress's approval America's Declaration of Independence.

THE DECLARATION

John Adams, who thought the more important job would be to advocate its adoption by Congress, left the writing of the declaration to Jefferson. A few days later, Jefferson had finished. He showed his work to Adams and to Benjamin Franklin, the author, inventor and statesman, and the most famous American of his time. They were the two colleagues whose opinions he most respected, and he accepted their minor amendments. He was less happy when Congress insisted on some major changes and revisions, which cut the Declaration of Independence to three-quarters of its original length, but on 4 July 1776, after Adams' articulate and impassioned speech in its favour – Jefferson called him "our Colossus on the floor" – the final version was agreed.

At the time, few realized that it was a decisive moment in American history. The cause of independence had been articulated in the language of revolution. It was Jefferson's concise and elegant expression of the philosophy of

Left: The Declaration of Independence was signed by congressmen from each of the Thirteen Colonies.

Left: King George III, whom Jefferson held to be personally responsible for the course of events that had led to America taking the irrevocable step of declaring its independence from Britain.

in shaping America's future. Like Adams, Jefferson believed that citizens should agree the form of government under which they lived, rather than be subjects of a monarch imposed on them by an accident of birth. The king had embroiled his nation and its American colonies in war. The desire to prevent such abuses of executive power would influence Americans – not least Jefferson's great political ally, James Madison – when they turned their attention to designing a constitution for a nation and to creating the office of president of the United States.

Below: Benjamin Franklin, John Adams and Thomas Jefferson drafting the Declaration of Independence.

natural rights and his vision of America's future as a democratic republic that meant that his words not only spoke to his contemporaries but would also become an inspiration for future generations: "We hold these truths to be self-evident, that all men are created equal, that they are endowed by their Creator with certain unalienable Rights, that among these are Life, Liberty and the pursuit of Happiness – That to secure these rights, Governments are instituted among Men, deriving their just powers from the consent of the governed – That whenever any Form of Government becomes destructive of these ends, it is the Right of the People to alter or to abolish it, and to institute new Government, laying its foundation on such principles and organizing its powers in such form, as to them shall seem most likely to effect their Safety and Happiness."

The remainder of the declaration, including Jefferson's long diatribe against George III, was also significant

THE FRAMING OF THE CONSTITUTION
1787

When James Madison (who would become the fourth president of the United States) joined Virginia's delegation to the Continental Congress in 1780, the war against the British king had yet to be won, but thanks to the arguments of Adams and Jefferson, monarchy was already only a memory for the Americans. As Francis Lightfoot Lee from Virginia, who had signed the Declaration of Independence, had observed in 1776: "Constitutions employ every pen."

With the Declaration, the colonies – now states – had become politically sovereign. They worked to 'institute new government' to replace the one they had rejected. More accurately, they created new governments, acting as if independent of each other as well as of Britain. The question remained as to the state of the nation: indeed, was there a nation at all?

THE ARTICLES OF CONFEDERATION

By 1777 the Continental Congress had drafted the Articles of Confederation. These allowed it to direct the war effort and to frame a co-ordinated foreign policy on behalf of all the colonies, but by the time Madison arrived in Philadelphia to represent Virginia in the Congress, not all states had ratified them. It was not until March 1781, a mere six months before Washington marched on Yorktown, that the last state (Maryland) agreed their terms.

Even though the Articles referred to "The United States of America", they committed the states only to "a firm league of friendship with each other for their common defense, the security of their liberties, and their mutual and general welfare". They envisaged a confederation of sovereign states, rather than the creation of a nation.

Each state had one vote in the representative Congress, and there was no mention of an executive office to provide political leadership. Having identified the monarch's abuse of power as the provocation for taking up arms, Americans remained suspicious of any constitutional and institutional arrangements that might lead to similar results once they had freed themselves of British control.

After the war, there was a similar suspicion of executive authority in the newly independent states. The state legislatures became the principal seats of political power, but their members were often elected annually, and control oscillated between competing factions. The result was political instability.

Below: George Washington was a natural choice to preside over the debate at the Constitutional Convention.

By the mid-1780s, there were some, like Madison, who worried that internal division between the states and political unrest within them would undermine not only the independence George Washington had fought for but also the revolutionary thinking about republican government that Adams and Jefferson had advocated.

Moreover, Washington, the former rebel, had now retired from public life, and the two revolutionaries were abroad: Jefferson had gone as American ambassador to France in 1784; Adams had remained in Europe after the Paris peace negotiations and was appointed ambassador to Britain the following year. When Jefferson visited Britain, he and Adams attended the court of George III, and the king made a point of publicly snubbing them: testament to the importance of their roles in achieving American independence. They were both still in Europe when Madison, the architect of the Constitution of the United States, arrived at the centre of the political stage in order to help preserve it.

In August 1786 Daniel Shays, who had fought at the battles of Bunker Hill and Saratoga, led a rebellion in Massachusetts of farmers who were suffering from debt as a result of the

state's high taxes. The following month, at a meeting in Maryland, Madison and Alexander Hamilton agreed the need for a Constitutional Convention that would seek to remedy the perceived deficiencies of the Articles of Confederation. A stronger national government might help the states avoid such political turbulence. It would, as Madison realized, "decide forever the fate of republican government".

Above: The Constitution, agreed in 1787, created the office of president of the United States.

THE CONSTITUTIONAL CONVENTION

Once again, Washington left Mount Vernon to travel to Philadelphia. In May 1787, as one of 55 representatives from the 13 states, he took his place as president of the Convention, which promptly ignored the task with which it had been charged – revising the Articles of Confederation. Instead it considered the Virginia Plan, proposed by Madison. This was a radical idea for a new national government.

For Madison, the opening words of the eventual document embodied its true political significance. "We the people" rather than "We the states" were the sovereign authority that instituted the government of the United States. This was again revolutionary. 'The people' – however that term was defined – would agree the powers of

Left: Independence Hall in Philadelphia, the meeting place of the first Continental Congress and a national landmark.

the United States government rather than, as had been the case, have the states define what it might do. The federal government could act independently, although it would preserve a political relationship with the states, the exact nature of which would become a matter of continuous negotiation.

It followed that, like the states themselves, the United States needed a set of institutions that would allow it to exercise its independence without abusing its power. Here Madison adhered to the conventional wisdom that had been best summarized by John Adams in 1775: "A legislative, an executive and a judicial power comprehend the whole of what is meant and understood by government. It is by balancing each of these powers against the other two, that the efforts in human nature towards tyranny can alone be checked and restrained."

This was what the Constitution tried to achieve. In a series of political compromises, the Convention created "separated institutions sharing powers"

Above: The Constitution was signed on 17 September 1787. Two years later, George Washington became America's first president.

within a federal system in which both the people and the states had a political stake. The first article set up the Congress. The popularly elected House of Representatives, initially with 65 members, and the Senate, in which each state had two senators chosen by their legislatures, had to agree what could become law. The third article provided for a Supreme Court in which judicial power was invested.

Article two, though, was just as significant for the nation's future. It stated that "the executive Power shall be invested in a President of the United States of America" who would hold office for a term of four years.

THE FEDERALIST PAPERS
In September 1787, as the Convention finished its work, Benjamin Franklin was asked what it had achieved.

FEDERALISTS AND ANTI-FEDERALISTS
As they fought the battle for its ratification, supporters and opponents of the Constitution that had been agreed at the Philadelphia Convention identified themselves as Federalists or Anti-Federalists (those who supported ratification of the Constitution and those who did not). One important intervention in the argument by the Federalists came when Alexander Hamilton, James Madison and John Jay collaborated in writing the Federalist Papers to persuade doubters of the merits of the plan for a national government. In the end the Anti-Federalists obtained a significant concession: in order to achieve ratification of the Constitution, the Federalists accepted the Anti-Federalist argument that a Bill of Rights should be added to the document in order to guarantee that essential individual freedoms were preserved.

His answer was simple: "A Republic, if you can keep it." A more fundamental question was whether the states would accept the new Constitution and the powerful federal government that Madison and his allies had proposed. It would come into effect once nine of the 13 states had ratified it, but reality dictated that if important states – among them New York – rejected it, the design for a national government would be in tatters. The Federalist Papers, written by Madison with Alexander Hamilton and John Jay, aimed to persuade the people of New York to accept the plan. As future generations tried to interpret the language of the Constitution, this collection of essays became important in explaining what those who framed the Constitution had in mind, the problems they faced and the ways in which they thought they had overcome them.

In July 1788, New York was the eleventh state to ratify the Constitution. It was eventually agreed unanimously, but not before the Anti-Federalists had argued for the addition of a Bill of Rights. This, again designed mainly by Madison, was incorporated as the first ten amendments to the Constitution. Agreed in 1791, it established a stockade of individual rights, including freedom of speech and religion, into which government should not be allowed to enter.

THE OFFICE OF PRESIDENT

Despite their distrust of executive power, those discussing the office of president in Philadelphia were not too prescriptive as to its form. They accepted that the president should have a role both as a politician (with a limited veto on congressional legislation) and as head of state. The chief executive was designated commander-in-chief of the nation's armed forces, but was given few specific powers: principally those of pardon, treaty-making and appointment – notably of Supreme Court justices. The president was also required to keep the Congress informed "of the State of the Union" and to "recommend to their consideration such measures" as were judged "necessary and expedient". In cases where the president might be charged with "Treason, Bribery or other high Crimes and Misdemeanors" there was the sanction of impeachment and removal from office.

The Convention made progress because it had a candidate in mind. George Washington was once again to be trusted with a critical role that would shape America's future. But there was to be no coronation. In keeping with the principles of a democratic republic, the presidency was open only to those who offered themselves for election to it.

Below: The construction of the Capitol building, the home of Congress and seat of government, began soon after the Constitution was ratified. President Washington laid the cornerstone of the building in September 1793.

THE ELECTORAL COLLEGE
CHOOSING THE PRESIDENT

According to James Madison's notes of the proceedings, when, on 4 September 1787, the Constitutional Convention meeting in Philadelphia discussed how the president should be selected, James Wilson of Pennsylvania confessed that he thought the matter to be "in truth the most difficult of all on which we have had to decide".

Of the many ideas that were considered, three that were rejected pointed the way to the political compromise that was eventually reached. First, the president was not to be selected by the federal Congress: it made the office dependent on the legislature, and thus compromised the essential principle of a separation of powers. Second, the state legislatures were not to choose between candidates because this would upset the delicate balance between state and federal power that was the basis of the principle of federalism. Finally, direct election was opposed, not only because it gave too much influence to the most populous states – who by merely voting for their own candidates would be able to outnumber the voters of small states, whose interests would therefore not be reflected in the outcome – but also owing to a distrust of democracy and the electorate's capacity to make such an important decision.

The matter was decided on 8 September, when the electoral college came into being, though the term itself was not used in the Constitution. The electoral college became perhaps the least understood institution, but in political terms it was the most significant factor in shaping both the character of presidential campaigns and the outcome of presidential elections.

VOTING PROCEDURE
The Constitution outlined the workings of the college. Each state was to be allocated a number of electors equal to the number of representatives it had in the federal Congress (though the representatives themselves were barred from appointment as electors). The electors would then meet in their respective states. Each would have two votes and would cast these for their two favoured candidates. When all the votes from the states were counted, the person who topped the ballot would become president and the runner-up would become vice president.

There was one other requirement. If it happened that no candidate gained an outright majority of electoral college votes, then the federal House of Representatives would determine who was to become president, choosing from among the five nominees who had received the most support. In this event, each state delegation in the House would have one vote to decide the outcome of the election.

The electoral college system was complicated, and in practice it did not work in quite the way that had been intended at the outset. The idea was that each state would select members of the community who could be trusted with the responsibility to decide who would be the best candidate to serve as the nation's president. Initially, it was the state legislatures that determined who became a member of the electoral college. Gradually, however, the institution was given an injection of democracy, and the electors began to be chosen by popular vote in each state.

THE PRESIDENTIAL TICKET
Sometimes the elections of college members were held in districts, but as political parties developed and electors were pledged to vote for particular party nominees, the result was that a state's electoral college votes could be divided among candidates. Large states therefore moved towards a 'general ticket' electoral system. This meant that the winner of the state's popular vote gained all that state's electoral college votes. The smaller states followed this lead, not wishing to diminish what little influence they had over the outcome.

The principle of federalism was preserved as the states became the focus

Left: George Washington taking the oath of office on 30 April, 1789. His inaugural address established an important precedent.

FOR PRESIDENT · FOR VICE PRESIDENT

WM. McKINLEY. · THEO. ROOSEVELT.

of presidential elections. Candidates now had to put together a winning coalition of states in the electoral college. Depending on the patterns of political support, however, the system meant that it was possible for the candidate with the most popular votes not to gain a majority in the electoral college, and for the president to be elected without winning most people's support.

In the presidential election of 1800, another problem arose. The newly formed political parties were orchestrating matters – but one did not do so well enough. Thomas Jefferson and Aaron Burr, who were running as president and vice president respectively, each received the same number of electoral college votes. Under the election rules, it was the House of Representatives that eventually decided that Jefferson would become president. Once that matter had been resolved, a

Constitutional Amendment was agreed that separated the election of president and vice president to ensure that the situation could not happen again.

In the 1824 presidential election, no candidate gained an outright majority in the electoral college. Congress exercised its constitutional powers to place John Quincy Adams in the White House. The electoral college 'misfired' again in 1876, when, amid allegations of fraud and corruption, an Electoral Commission awarded disputed electoral college votes to Rutherford B. Hayes, who became president despite the fact that his opponent, Samuel J. Tilden, had won the popular vote.

More recently still, in 2000, the Supreme Court intervened to decide the result of the election, because George W. Bush and Al Gore contested the legality of votes cast in Florida, which were critical to the outcome of

Above: Presidential and vice-presidential nominees run on the same ticket and are chosen to appeal to different voters.

the contest. There have also been over 150 instances of 'faithless electors' – individual electors who for some reason have failed to vote for their party's designated candidate.

When such controversies occur, voices are raised in favour of reform. More usually, however, Americans seem still to be persuaded by Alexander Hamilton's view, writing in *Federalist 68*: "If the manner of it be not perfect, it is at least excellent. It unites in an eminent degree all the advantages, the union of which was to be wished for." That remains the hope, and indeed appeared to be the case when, on 4 February 1789, the electoral college met for the first time and unanimously elected George Washington as president.

GEORGE WASHINGTON
1789–1797

George Washington's family came from Essex, England. John Washington, his great-grandfather, was a clergyman, but was asked to resign when his fondness for alcohol affected his ability to spread God's word. He decided to start a new life in the New World, and settled in Virginia in 1657. He soon acquired a different reputation among the local Native Americans, who called him 'town-taker' after he exploited legal technicalities to deprive them of their land. In contrast, his most famous descendant, George Washington, born on 22 February 1732, would be regarded as a paragon of integrity. Nevertheless, Washington inherited some family traits, including his physical presence and height and an abiding interest in the ownership of land.

Washington was 11 years old when his father died. His half-brother, Lawrence, his elder by 14 years, looked after him through his adolescence, but at the age of 34, after a trip to Barbados hoping to cure his tuberculosis (during

Below: George Washington being sworn in as commander-in-chief of the newly formed American army in 1775.

WASHINGTON'S CABINET

During his first term in office, George Washington devolved responsibility for important areas of the new administration's activity to his principal advisors, who became members of his Cabinet. The key positions, established in 1789, were secretary of state, secretary of the treasury, secretary of war and attorney general. As the range of executive and federal government activity grew, other portfolios were added, but the president still had the final say in any major policy decisions that had to be made.

---

which Washington, who accompanied him, contracted smallpox), Lawrence succumbed to the disease. Mount Vernon, Lawrence's 1,000ha (2,500 acre) plantation, became part of George Washington's inheritance.

Washington did not have a college education. After his initial military career, his marriage to the wealthy widow, Martha Dandridge Custis, brought with it a family when he became stepfather to her two children,

Jack and Martha. He had no children of his own. Washington's involvement with politics began when he entered the Virginia House of Burgesses in 1759, the year after he had resigned his commission in the militia. His military experience led to the Continental Congress appointing him to command the American army during the War of Independence and his political stature was confirmed when he returned to public life to chair the Constitutional Convention in 1787.

While often maintaining a pose of indifference towards politics, Washington cultivated his reputation and disguised his ambition with displays of reticence. It was his military contribution to the cause of independence, the political legitimacy his presence gave to the Constitutional Convention, and the trust that his contemporaries placed in him that led to him being chosen, inevitably, as the nation's first president.

Born: 22 February 1732, Westmoreland County, Virginia
Parents: Augustine (1693?–1743) and Mary (1708?–89)
Family background: Farming
Education: Not formally educated
Religion: Episcopalian
Occupation: Soldier, plantation owner
Slave owner: Yes (in his will he freed his slaves)
Political career: Virginia House of Burgesses, 1759–74
Continental Congress, 1774–5
Chairman, Constitutional Convention, 1787–8
Presidential annual salary: $25,000 (Washington refused payment)
Political party: Federalist
Died: 14 December 1799, Mount Vernon, Virginia

Right: George Washington was the natural choice as first president of the newly formed United States of America.

PRESIDENT WASHINGTON

Washington took office on 30 April 1789, delivering his inaugural address in New York. Washington was initially both cautious and judicious in his approach to the use of executive power in a government that was still regarded with suspicion by many contemporaries. His first task was to define the shape of the office that he held. Everything he did established a precedent for the new republic. As he observed: "I walk on untrodden ground."

Washington's Cabinet, which, like its British counterpart, had no formal constitutional basis, was one in which politicians from Massachusetts, Virginia and New York held the key positions. John Adams was vice president. The first secretary of state – overseeing the new

THE VIRGINIA HOUSE OF BURGESSES

In 1619, the Virginia Company in London – concerned to attract more emigrants to the colony it had established in Jamestown, Virginia, in 1606 – agreed to devolve political power to an assembly. The governor, selected by the company, appointed a council of six members. Two representatives from each of the 11 plantations established there became members of the Virginia House of Burgesses, America's first elected legislature. As the colony grew, representation would be based on county divisions. The laws passed by the House were subject to the approval of the council, the governor and the company in London. Nevertheless it provided a forum for political discussion in which, 150 years later, prominent colonists such as George Washington, Patrick Henry and Thomas Jefferson would argue the case for American independence.

nation's foreign relations – was John Jay. He left to become the first chief justice of the Supreme Court, and was replaced by Thomas Jefferson. Alexander Hamilton from New York served as secretary of the treasury.

Reconciling such formidable political talents proved difficult. The major antagonism was between Hamilton and Jefferson and resulted from their fundamentally opposed visions of America's future: one in favour of a strong national government, and the other in favour of strong state government. Hamilton took advantage of the initial lack of political organization in Congress to create a coalition of like-minded supporters there. He was opposed by James Madison, now a member of the House of Representatives, who ensured the Jeffersonian persuasion also gathered support in the legislature. Two parties emerged: the Hamiltonian Federalists, in favour of strong central government,

and the Jeffersonian Republicans who saw the states as the nation's bedrock.

In Washington's first administration, the scale of the presidential office was small: he had more people working for him at his private estate at Mount Vernon than he employed to help him in New York. Early in his presidency he made visits to all the states then in the Union: in 1789 he went to New England, and then journeyed south the following year. His main duties were ceremonial, but he walked a political tightrope. Critics hinted that he was attempting to recreate the trappings of monarchy, and Washington had to be careful not to give the impression that King George III was about to be replaced by George I in America. He tried for as long as possible to maintain a role 'above politics', but as the partisan divisions emerged in the Cabinet and then in Congress, the president was forced to take sides.

MARTHA WASHINGTON

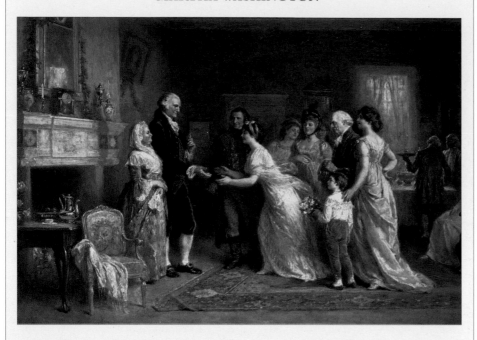

Martha Dandridge, 'Lady Washington', was born on 2 June 1831 in Virginia. Aged 19, she married Daniel Custis, who was 20 years her senior. He died in 1757, leaving her with two young children and a large tobacco-producing estate. It was there, two years later, in a mansion known as 'White House', that she married George Washington. During his presidency, she established a pattern of formal dinners and public receptions, attracting unfavourable criticism from those who thought their style too monarchical. Nevertheless, she remained

Above: The Washingtons entertained in style. Some accused them of thinking they were American royalty.

popular, especially among war veterans, who remembered her sharing their privations in winter quarters, notably at Valley Forge. For 40 years she supported her husband in Mount Vernon, on the battlefield, and in New York and Philadelphia while he was president. Before she died in 1802, she burnt their letters, preserving the privacy of her marriage for ever.

Washington agreed, but the controversy was further evidence, if any was necessary, that his presidency was becoming increasingly involved in the political battles of the time.

POPULAR RE-ELECTION

In the 1792 presidential election, only six of the 15 states chose electors by popular vote. The qualification to take part in the election in those states varied widely: in the event, only 13,000 popular votes were cast. (According to the 1790 census, the United States had a total population of 3.9 million.)

Although Washington was identified more and more with the Hamiltonian Federalists, Jefferson recognized that his fellow Virginian still had the capacity to unite the nation. "North and South will hang together," he told the president, "if they have you to hang on." The electoral college vote confirmed this: again it

POLITICAL PARTIES

When Alexander Hamilton organized the Federalist party in support of his plans to create a strong central government, the opposition, led by Jefferson and Madison, called themselves Republicans. They sometimes accepted the label of Democrat-Republicans as a term of approval, in contrast to their opponents whom they characterized as aristocrats and quasi-monarchists. The Federalists used the same expression, Democrat-Republican, as a term of abuse, associating democracy with the excesses of mob rule in the French Revolution. After 1800, Jefferson's party dominated the political scene and the Federalist cause collapsed. During the 1820s and 1830s, as party competition re-emerged, Andrew Jackson's supporters appropriated the name of Democrat. Later on, the successors to their main opponents, the Whigs, once more became known as the Republican Party.

THE NATIONAL BANK

In 1791, Hamilton proposed the establishment of a national bank to hold deposits of federal funds, issue paper money, provide loans to the government and capital for investment. Congress passed the Bank Act that would set it up. Washington questioned whether or not he should veto this measure on the grounds that the Act was unconstitutional, and asked his secretary of state and his treasury secretary for their written opinions on the matter.

Jefferson based his argument on the Tenth Amendment, part of Madison's Bill of Rights agreed by Congress that

year, but yet to be ratified. He believed that "all powers not delegated to the United States, by the Constitution, nor prohibited by it to the States, are reserved to the States or to the people". For Hamilton, however, "if the measure … is not forbidden by any particular provision of the Constitution, it may safely be deemed to come within the compass of the national authority … A bank has a natural relation to the power of collecting taxes – to that of regulating trade – to that of providing for the common defense." Hamilton said Congress was right to approve the establishment of the National Bank.

STATES ENTERING THE UNION DURING WASHINGTON'S PRESIDENCY:

VERMONT	KENTUCKY	TENNESSEE

Entered the Union: 4 March 1791
Pre-state history: Acquired by Britain (1763)
Total population in 1790 census: 85,341
Total number of slaves in 1790 census: 0
Electoral College votes in 1792 election: 3

Entered the Union: 1 June 1792
Pre-state history: Not a territory: the area was part of Virginia until achieving statehood
Total population in 1790 census: 73,677
Total number of slaves in 1790 census: 12,430
Electoral College votes in 1792: 4

Entered the Union: 1 June 1796
Pre-state history: Ceded by North Carolina to Federal government as Southwestern Territory (1789)
Total population in 1800 census: 105,602
Total number of slaves in 1800 census: 13,584
Electoral College votes in 1796: 3

was unanimous. Washington, unopposed in the election, reluctantly agreed to serve a second term.

Shortly after Washington had reassumed office, in April 1793, war broke out between Britain and France, which was itself in the throes of revolution. Washington declared the United States' neutrality, keeping the nation out of the European conflict. However, the hostilities remained a threat to peace in the United States because Britain had maintained a military presence on American soil after the Treaty of Paris.

As tensions escalated, the president sent John Jay to London. His mission was to negotiate the removal of the British troops and put trade relations between Britain and the United States on a better basis. Jay succeeded in his first objective, but his American critics argued that he had been diplomatically out-manoeuvred by Britain, and had made a trade deal that was unfavourable to the United States. Jay's treaty, otherwise known as the Treaty of London of 1794, was passed by Congress only after the president had committed his considerable prestige to the battle.

FAREWELL ADDRESS

Washington left office at the end of his second term, establishing a final precedent that lasted 144 years. However, before stepping down, on 17 September 1796 he published his farewell address. In it he warned "in the most solemn manner against the baneful effects of the spirit of party" that had progressively impacted upon his administrations. He also advised the nation to "observe good faith and justice toward all nations. Cultivate peace and harmony with all … It is now our true policy to steer clear of permanent alliances with any portion of the foreign world." If his warning was ultimately in vain, his advice became a guiding principle for the nation's foreign policy for the next 150 years.

FINAL DAYS

Washington was 65 when he returned to Mount Vernon. His retirement was short, but one final act remained. He had become convinced that slavery, the South's 'peculiar institution', was morally wrong. If the principles of the Declaration of Independence were to

have any meaning, it had no place in a democratic republic; he felt that it threatened the nation he had helped to create. In 1798 he reportedly observed: "I can foresee that nothing but the rooting out of slavery can perpetuate the existence of our union."

His end came on 14 December 1799, but even in death, once again, he led by example. By a simple act, George Washington ensured that he added a lasting lustre to his military and political achievements. Ever mindful of his place in history, he made provision in his will for his own slaves to be freed.

Below: Mount Vernon, the ancestral home inherited by George Washington, and the house to which he retired.

ALEXANDER HAMILTON
FOUNDING FATHER

Alexander Hamilton has a unique place in American political history: he was a former secretary of the treasury and was killed in a duel by an incumbent vice president. It was one of the most famous duels recorded, and the final act in a controversial life, during which Hamilton made immense contributions to the causes of independence, revolution and the development of the United States of America.

John Adams called Hamilton "the bastard brat of a Scotch pedlar" which, although he may have intended it as libel, was an accurate description of Hamilton's origins. Born in 1755 on the Caribbean island of Nevis, he arrived in New York in 1772 and joined the Patriot cause. During the War of Independence, he served as Washington's aide-de-camp and at Yorktown he led an infantry charge against the British.

Below: Burr and Hamilton prepare to fight. Duelling was an established way of resolving matters of honour, although it was condemned by Washington and Franklin, and was being outlawed in some states.

In 1787 Hamilton issued the call for the Philadelphia Convention, which would agree the Constitution of the United States. There he outlined his vision of a national government, according to which the president and senators would hold office for life and Congress would have extensive influence in determining the laws of the land.

Left: Alexander Hamilton, author of many of the Federalist Papers, in which he argued for ratification of the Constitution.

This plan, radically different from Madison's idea of a federal republic, illustrated the competing philosophies that ultimately opened the political divide between them. Nevertheless, Hamilton accepted the compromises achieved in Philadelphia and collaborated with Madison in writing *The Federalist*, helping to persuade New York to ratify the Constitution.

COMPETING PARTIES

As secretary of the treasury in Washington's government, and a powerful influence in the Federalist party, Hamilton's main achievements, which were the financing of public credit and the federal government's assumption of the war debts of the states, were hardly calculated to seize the popular imagination. However, he realized that political independence and the future success of the United States depended upon its economic vitality. The Republicans accused him of favouring the industrial and commercial interests of the North over the agricultural concerns of the South. With Jefferson's election in 1800, Hamilton's influence and that of the Federalist party in national politics was largely eclipsed.

When Vice President Aaron Burr ran as an independent candidate in the 1804 race for governor of New York, Hamilton was his implacable opponent. His reported remarks at a dinner party were taken by Burr as a slight, sufficient to challenge Hamilton to a duel. Afterwards, Burr escaped to South Carolina despite being indicted for murder in two states: New Jersey, where their fatal meeting took place, and New York, where, on 12 July 1804, Hamilton had died from his wound.

JOHN ADAMS
1797–1801

Born: 30 October 1735, Braintree
(now Quincy), Massachusetts
Parents: John (1691–1761) and
Susanna (1709–97)
Family background: Farming
Education: Harvard College (1755)
Religion: Unitarian
Occupation: Lawyer
Slave owner: No
Political career: Continental
Congress, 1774–8
Commissioner to France, 1778
Minister to the Netherlands, 1780
Minister to England, 1785
Vice president, 1789–97
Presidential annual salary: $25,000
Political party: Federalist
Died: 4 July 1826, Braintree,
Massachusetts

John Adams's political misfortune was to become president after a widely respected and wildly popular incumbent had left office. He had served as Washington's vice president for eight years, and it was inevitable that he would remain in his shadow. As president, he faced some formidable challenges. Political divisions and party rivalries threatened domestic stability. France had interpreted Jay's treaty as creating a potentially hostile alliance between the United States and Britain and so there was also the prospect of war. Adams's major achievement was to preserve the peace, thereby ensuring that the nation survived a hazardous period of political turbulence.

LIFE BEFORE THE PRESIDENCY
Like George Washington and Thomas Jefferson, with both of whom his career was entwined, John Adams traced his

Right: John Adams, the first president to live in the newly completed White House.

family's roots in America back to the 17th century. He was the first president to graduate from Harvard, which was then a college rather than a university. His father had expected him to become a minister but, like many of his successors, he instead became first a lawyer, then a politician. He was not only a leading supporter of colonial independence but also an advocate of republican government and fiercely patriotic.

After serving in the first and second Continental Congress, and playing a critical role in the events leading to the Declaration of Independence, Adams spent time in France, Holland and Britain before returning to America and becoming the first vice president of the United States. He disliked his eight years as Washington's understudy, moaning to his wife Abigail: "My country has in its wisdom contrived for me the most insignificant office that ever the invention of man contrived or his imagination conceived." Finally, in 1796, it was his turn to be president.

THE ELECTION OF 1796
His contemporaries recognized that Adams was irascible, cantankerous and argumentative, but since, like Washington, he had become identified

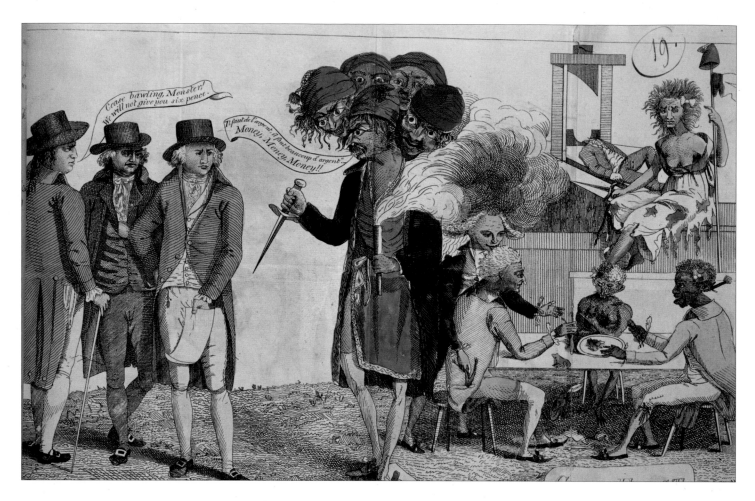

Above: A contemporary cartoon satirizes the French request for bribes before America's statesmen were received.

with the Federalist cause he was the party's preferred candidate. When the electoral college met in 1796, however, Alexander Hamilton tried to influence the southern states to support Thomas Pinckney from South Carolina instead of Adams, thinking he would be less independently minded. Hamilton's efforts misfired however, and merely led to the New England states refusing to vote for Pinckney. Thomas Jefferson, the Republican party's candidate, was the beneficiary: he gained only three fewer votes than Adams, beating Pinckney, and as a result Jefferson became vice president.

It fell to Adams, in his constitutional role as president of the Senate, to announce his own victory. He was inaugurated as president on 4 March 1797. Jefferson returned home: like Adams he placed loyalty to his political beliefs above the friendship that stretched back 20 years to the days when both men had argued for revolution.

ADAMS IN OFFICE

Adams's four years in office were dominated by the impact that the threat of war had on both domestic and foreign policy. In 1797 Adams sent three envoys to France in an attempt to secure peace. The outcome was the 'XYZ Affair', so called because these were the initials used for the three French agents who demanded a substantial bribe before any negotiations with the French foreign minister could take place. In 1798, when Adams made this public, it caused outrage in the United States.

ALIEN AND SEDITION ACTS

Rumours circulated of an imminent French invasion. In 1798, Federalists in Congress hastily passed four pieces of legislation, collectively called the Alien and Sedition Acts. The first lengthened the time before residents in the United States could apply for American citizenship. The second gave the president power to deport non-citizens – aliens – who were considered "dangerous to the peace and safety of the United States". The third permitted aliens whose loyalties were thought to lie with an enemy power, namely France, to be arrested and deported. The Sedition Act defined treason as including the publication of "false, scandalous and malicious writing" and was used to imprison editors of Republican newspapers.

In February 1799, Adams split the Federalist party and effectively destroyed his prospects for a second term when he announced he was making renewed diplomatic efforts to resolve the continuing 'quasi-war', which had involved American and French naval forces, by sending another delegation to France. A treaty was agreed, but Adams failed in his bid for re-election and the Federalists also lost control of the legislature. In 1802, the Republican-dominated Congress repealed the first of the Alien and Sedition Acts, which had aimed to deprive the party of its strong electoral following among recent arrivals from Europe. The remaining three acts had already been allowed to lapse when, during the two previous years, they had become due for renewal.

LIFE AFTER THE PRESIDENCY

Adams became the first incumbent president to be turned out of office. His defeat signalled the beginning of the end for the Federalist party, which never managed to win the presidency again. He retired to his farm in Quincy, Massachusetts. With his wife Abigail acting as go-between, he and Jefferson rehabilitated their relationship through a long and fascinating correspondence. If Adams's last words, "Thomas Jefferson survives", were a question, the answer was no: his friend had died in Virginia a few hours earlier on Independence Day, 1826.

Below: Adams Mansion in Quincy, the home of John and Abigail Adams.

ABIGAIL ADAMS

Abigail Smith, born in Massachusetts in 1744, married John Adams in 1764. Four of their children survived to adulthood (a fifth, a daughter, died aged two) and their son John Quincy Adams would later become president.

Although Abigail was separated from her husband for long periods, between 1784 and 1788 she joined him in France and Britain, returning to the United States when he became vice president. Her correspondence survives. She was unafraid of giving her husband forthright advice. While he took part in discussions leading to the Declaration of Independence she admonished him to "remember the ladies and be more generous and favourable to them than your ancestors. Do not put such unlimited power into the hands of the husbands." But he forgot and he did. She was a passionate Federalist; her critics complained she wielded too much influence, calling her 'Mrs President'.

Above: Abigail Adams is famed for her support of women's rights.

Following Adams's election defeat, the couple retired to Massachusetts, where she was instrumental in reviving his friendship with Thomas Jefferson. She died in 1818, three days after their 54th wedding anniversary.

CHAPTER TWO

THOMAS JEFFERSON TO JAMES MONROE

1801–1825

THE 'VIRGINIA DYNASTY', PRESIDENTS JEFFERSON, MADISON AND MONROE, DOMINATED AMERICAN POLITICS IN THE EARLY YEARS OF THE 19TH CENTURY. EUROPEAN POWERS STILL HAD IMPERIAL AMBITIONS IN NORTH AMERICA, BUT IN NEGOTIATING THE LOUISIANA PURCHASE, JEFFERSON ENDED FRENCH TERRITORIAL INTEREST, AND MADE POSSIBLE THE UNITED STATES' MOVEMENT WESTWARD ACROSS THE CONTINENT. FOR HIS SUCCESSOR, THE THREAT FROM BRITAIN REMAINED AND IN 1812 MADISON WAS FORCED TO FIGHT WHAT WAS REGARDED AS A SECOND WAR OF INDEPENDENCE WITH THAT COUNTRY. INTERNATIONAL RELATIONS ALSO DOMINATED MONROE'S PRESIDENCY. HIS DOCTRINE, PROMULGATED IN 1823, WOULD DEFINE THE CONTOURS OF AMERICAN FOREIGN POLICY. THIS, THEN, WAS THE FORMIDABLE POLITICAL LEGACY OF THE 'VIRGINIA DYNASTY', FORMED IN THE CRUCIBLE OF A CRITICAL ERA IN THE DEVELOPMENT OF THE UNITED STATES OF AMERICA, 'THE FIRST NEW NATION'.

Left: The White House, the official presidential home, was completed in 1800.

THE PRESIDENTIAL ELECTION
1800

The presidential election of 1800 proved to be one of the most controversial in American history and was characterized by bitter personal attacks on members of both parties. It exposed a flaw in the Constitution's provisions for the election of the president and vice president, leading to the drafting of the Twelfth Amendment, which was ratified in 1804. It also marked the beginning of a period of Republican rule in government and the demise of the Federalist party.

There were four main candidates. John Adams, who was the incumbent president, and Charles Pinckney – the brother of Hamilton's favoured nominee four years earlier – represented the Federalists. The Republicans supported Thomas Jefferson and Aaron Burr.

The 16 states had 138 electors, so 70 votes were needed for a majority. The Philadelphia Convention had agreed that slaves should be counted as three-fifths of a free person in determining apportionment. This meant that in 1800, Jefferson had a potential advantage: Southern states had 12 more votes in the electoral college than they would have had if representation had been based on the free population alone. Jefferson, from Virginia, could expect to count on their support: indeed the South provided 53 of his electoral college votes. Nevertheless, the Republicans managed to make difficulties for themselves by failing to arrange for Jefferson to receive one more vote than Burr. This meant that there was no clear winner in the electoral college.

The Federalists were better organized. In the electoral college, they ensured that Pinckney was runner-up to Adams by allowing one elector to cast a solitary vote for someone else: John Jay, the governor of New York.

The dead heat between Jefferson and Burr meant that under the rules governing the electoral college, the contest would be decided by the House of Representatives. Before that happened, Jefferson made a crucial intervention that shaped the eventual outcome. It fell to him, as vice president and presiding officer of the Senate, to act as returning officer when the envelopes containing the electoral college votes were opened on 11 February 1801, and with this the problems began.

THE PROBLEM WITH GEORGIA

When Jefferson opened the envelopes it became apparent that Georgia had not complied with the statutory requirement to return two documents: one recording the names of the candidates for whom its four electoral votes had been cast and a second, signed by the governor, certifying the names of the electors selected by the state. Instead, there was a single piece of paper in Georgia's envelope. On one side it bore the governor's signed certificate and on the other the names of Jefferson and Burr with the signatures of the four electors underneath.

Had there been fraud? Had a second piece of paper been removed and the electors' votes scrawled on the back of the governor's document? Should the votes – four for the Republicans – be counted? Without Georgia, Jefferson and Burr (whose name on the ballot had guaranteed that the party won New York) had 69 votes each. Jefferson, as the Senate's returning officer, made a quick decision: Georgia's result was valid.

The acceptance of Georgia's votes meant that the Republicans had beaten

Left: Though Burr campaigned successfully for political positions he blamed his lack of prominence in that area on Hamilton.

Above: Charles Cotesworth Pinckney, from South Carolina, was the Federalist choice for vice president.

the Federalists. Their votes were still tied, however, and the winner from the Republican party still had to be decided. Had Georgia's votes been ruled out, no candidate would have achieved a majority in the electoral college, and the Federalist candidates, Adams, Pinckney and even John Jay would have remained in contention. As it was, the contest now was between Jefferson and Burr. The scene of political action moved from the Senate to the House of Representatives.

THE HOUSE DECIDES

In the House of Representatives, each of the 16 states had one vote, which was decided by ballot between the members for each state. The outcome would be decided on an absolute majority, so nine votes were needed to win. The Federalists had a majority in the House of Representatives, and they generally supported Burr in an attempt to prevent Jefferson becoming president. However, the Federalists' strength was concentrated heavily in the northern states of New England, enabling the

Right: After Jefferson and Burr received the same number of electoral college votes in the presidential election, the Twelfth Amendment (1804) separated the balloting for president and vice president.

Republicans to counteract it. They were able initially to influence six states' delegations in favour of Jefferson by a margin of a single vote. On the first ballot, therefore, the battle lines were drawn: Jefferson was preferred by eight states, Burr by six, and in two – Vermont and Maryland – the ballots were drawn and neither candidate was the winner.

Six days and 35 ballots later, after the votes had ebbed and flowed, and with supporters campaigning vigorously, Jefferson finally emerged victorious. James Bayard, a Federalist representative from Delaware, who in the final round of voting, along with his allies in Maryland and Vermont, cast blank ballots in order to break the impasse, wrote to Hamilton: "the means existed of electing Burr, but this required his co-operation. By deceiving one man (a great blockhead) and tempting two (not incorruptible) he might have secured a majority of the states." Hamilton's loathing for Burr had led him to work for Jefferson's election despite their mutual animosity.

To his critics, Burr was at fault for not indicating that he supported Jefferson's cause. It suggested that his personal ambition came before his loyalty to the Republican party. On the other hand, if he had aggressively pursued his self-interest, he might have split the Republicans and made the matter worse; instead his self-restraint helped towards the peaceful resolution of the election deadlock.

Before the crisis was over, it had threatened to escalate. A demonstration took place when a mob, suspicious that Federalists in the House were siding with Burr to prolong the constitutional confusion, gathered in the federal capital. The Republican governors of Virginia and Pennsylvania, James Monroe and Thomas McKean, called on their militias to prepare for action if it should prove necessary. The example of the French Revolution and its descent into violence and chaos was never far from their minds.

On 17 February 1801, the House decided. Through some political manoeuvring and a measure of luck, the American Republic had met and overcome a potentially disastrous challenge to its future. The author of its Declaration of Independence had triumphed in what he came to call "the Revolution of 1800": Thomas Jefferson was America's president elect.

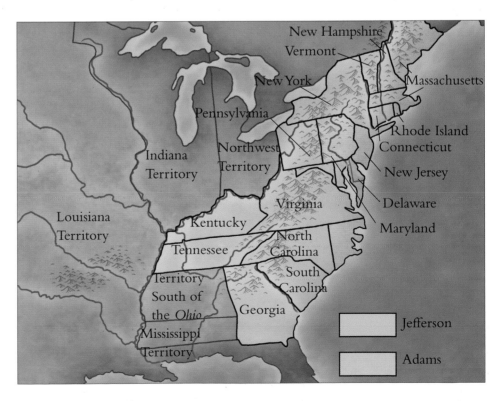

THE SUPREME COURT
THE HIGHEST COURT OF LAW

Convened for the first time in February 1790, the Supreme Court of the United States was the only court established by the Constitution. It was left to Congress to establish inferior courts, and to decide on the composition and procedures of all the courts.

The federal judiciary had been one of the most hotly debated issues during the framing of the Constitution, with Anti-Federalists seeing it as a means of tyrannizing the states, but for the first decade of its existence the judiciary was the weakest of the three branches of government: with no direction from the Constitution, the Supreme Court was unsure of its power over the laws passed by Congress. It had no permanent home and lacked prestige.

This situation changed at the beginning of the 19th century. In deciding a case that arose during the transition of power between retiring and incoming presidents, Chief Justice John Marshall, who had been appointed by John Adams, asserted the principle of judicial review, claiming for the Supreme Court the right to shape the law according to its interpretation of the Constitution. Its power to do so continues to rest on the precedent set by the case of Marbury v. Madison.

Above: John Marshall was instrumental in determining the judicial balance of power.

THE MARSHALL COURT

In January 1801, John Adams nominated John Marshall, then secretary of state, as the fourth chief justice of the Supreme Court. Marshall, born in 1755 in Virginia, was a contemporary of both Madison and Monroe, but he had gravitated to the Federalists rather than to the Republicans as those parties emerged in the early years of the republic. John Marshall and the future president Thomas Jefferson were distant cousins who disliked one another and who disagreed politically. The Senate confirmed Marshall's appointment just prior to its official count of the electoral college votes cast in the presidential election of the previous year.

In the febrile political atmosphere surrounding the outcome of the 1800 election, there was even a suggestion, possibly made by Marshall himself, that the chief justice should assume the presidency if there was no resolution to the political impasse that had resulted from the electoral college dead heat. In the end, however, he found ways of advancing his political views from his position on the Supreme Court. His tenure there of 34 years would far outlast the presidential administration of his cousin, to whom, in March 1801, he administered the oath of office.

MARBURY VERSUS MADISON

After the House of Representatives had finally voted Jefferson into the White House, and before he took office, President Adams made a concerted effort to appoint as many Federalist judges as possible – they became known as 'the midnight judges' – to ensure that the party would at least retain control of the courts under the administration of a Republican presidency.

Marshall combined his position as chief justice with his existing post as secretary of state and in that capacity he was responsible for ensuring that the newly appointed judges received the appropriate letters of commission. Those intended for 17 justices of the peace appointed by Adams remained undelivered by the time his administration ended, and at Jefferson's request Marshall's successor as secretary of state, James Madison, refused to send them on. The president's action was subject to

Left: The Supreme Court is the highest judicial body in the United States.

SUPREME COURT JUDGES

Originally there were six Supreme Court justices. In 1869 the number was fixed at nine. They are nominated by the president, and successive incumbents have tried to influence the Court's composition through their power of appointment, but their nominees must be confirmed by a majority vote in the Senate. They serve "during good behavior", in other words until they retire, die or are impeached, and the average tenure of Supreme Court justices is about 15 years. With its power of judicial review, the Court remains the heartbeat of American Constitutional government.

Below: The Supreme Court of 1911.

a legal challenge when one of the justices, William Marbury, petitioned the Supreme Court to force Madison to deliver the commissions, and the court was called upon to decide the case.

Marshall had set in motion events that would lead his court into a potential political minefield. If it insisted that Madison carry out his duty, which was seen to be its legal responsibility, then the administration would ignore it and its status within the framework of the federal government would be undermined. On the other hand, if the Supreme Court did not try to force the issue, it would look equally weak.

His solution to this dilemma was ingenious. Marshall reprimanded Jefferson for not ordering Madison to send William Marbury his commission. At the same time he argued that the provisions of the Judiciary Act of 1789, giving the Court the responsibility of judging the case, were unconstitutional. It was this aspect of Marbury v. Madison

(1803) that had the greatest constitutional reverberations. Marshall effectively asserted that the Court alone should interpret the original intent of the written Constitution agreed in Philadelphia in 1787.

Since "the Constitution is superior to any ordinary act of the legislature; the Constitution, and not such ordinary act, must govern the case to which they

both apply". Who makes that judgement? Marshall was in no doubt: "The judicial power of the United States is extended to all cases arising under the Constitution." In saying that the Supreme Court should interpret whether or not a law was constitutional, Marshall invested its justices with a political as well as a legal power to shape the contours of American politics.

As Jefferson pointed out, this principle of judicial review was potentially controversial: "The Constitution, on this hypothesis, is a mere thing of wax in the hands of the judiciary, which they may twist, and shape into any form they please." However, the full implications of Marshall's decision were not immediately felt. It was another 54 years before the Court again pronounced on a constitutional issue, and then, in the case of Dredd Scott v. Sandford (1857), it contributed to the deepening political crisis that was precipitating the nation towards the Civil War.

John Marshall remained chief justice until his death on 6 July 1835, having ensured that from Jefferson's time onwards no president could disregard either the constitutional force or the political impact of the decisions taken by the Supreme Court.

Below: The original meeting place of the Supreme Court in Old City Hall, Philadelphia, housed its six judges.

THOMAS JEFFERSON
1801–1809

Thomas Jefferson was 33 when he wrote the Declaration of Independence. He was born in 1743, in Shadwell, Virginia. His family, which on his father's side had Welsh ancestry, had settled in the state in the 17th century. He was a bright, committed student, graduating from William and Mary College, Virginia, in 1762.

Like John Adams, Jefferson practised law before becoming politically active. In 1768, he embarked on a lifetime project: building his mountain-top retreat at Monticello, Virginia. Four years later, Jefferson, like George Washington, married a wealthy widow: Martha Wayles Skelton. In 1782, following the birth of their sixth child, only three of whom survived beyond the age of two, Martha died. Jefferson remained a widower for the rest of his life.

Born: 13 April 1743, Shadwell, Virginia
Parents: Peter (1708–57) and Jane (1720–76)
Family background: Plantation owners, surveying
Education: William and Mary College (1762)
Religion: Not proclaimed
Occupation: Lawyer, planter
Slave owner: Yes
Political career: Virginia House of Burgesses, 1769–74
Continental Congress, 1775–6, 1783–5
Governor of Virginia, 1779–81
Minister to France, 1785–9
Secretary of state, 1790–3
Vice president, 1797–1801
Presidential annual salary: $25,000
Political party: Democrat-Republican
Died: 4 July 1826, Monticello, Virginia

A RISING POLITICAL STAR

In 1774 as a member of the Virginia House of Burgesses, Jefferson, overshadowed by the likes of George Washington and Patrick Henry, was not included in the state's delegation to the first Continental Congress. A year later he arrived in Philadelphia as the replacement for Peyton Randolph, his political mentor. His contemporaries saw his strength as lying not in his oratory but in the eloquence of his writing: when Adams left him to compose the Declaration of Independence, their judgement was vindicated.

Above: Thomas Jefferson's election represented the end of the Federalist party's influence in presidential politics.

As governor of Virginia during the War of Independence, Jefferson narrowly escaped capture by Cornwallis's cavalry. After his wife's death, he became ambassador to France, and was in Paris to witness the French Revolution. Following three years as Washington's secretary of state and four as Adams's vice president, as his party's acknowledged leader, and at the age of 57, he became president of the United States.

A POPULAR FIRST TERM

Jefferson's election was an important symbolic event: the Federalists abided by its controversial outcome and relinquished control of the executive. It also had another consequence.

In his inaugural address, Jefferson appeared to heed the advice that Washington had given when he warned of the threat that political parties posed to the republic. "But every difference of opinion is not a difference of principle. We have called by different names brethren of the same principle. We are all republicans – we are all federalists." This appeal to patriotic sentiment suggested that he would reach out across the partisan divide. That indeed was how relieved Federalists interpreted his words, giving them hope that there would be no political retribution following the increasingly acrimonious and polarizing debates that had taken place during the Adams administration. Jefferson's predecessor had left town rather than witness the inaugural ceremony of his successor.

However, the new president's strategy for ending party competition aimed to destroy the Federalists as a political force. Three weeks after his inaugural address he wrote: "Nothing shall be spared on my part to obliterate the traces of party and consolidate the nation." He hoped "to be able … to unite the names of federalists and republicans". In this he was largely successful. By the end of his first term, the Federalists were well on the way to becoming a spent political force.

The Republicans owed their continued electoral fortune in no small measure to the successes of Jefferson's first administration. In keeping with his philosophy of minimalist government, the president cut federal expenditure and the military budget, reduced the national debt, and abolished the tax on whiskey: all of which proved to be popular measures. At the same time, he pursued an aggressive policy towards the continuing harassment of American

Above: The Louisiana Purchase effectively doubled the territory held by the United States government.

merchant shipping in the Mediterranean. The US navy skirmished with Barbary pirates along the North African coast, winning enough of the time to fuel patriotic support for Jefferson's actions. However, the major political coup of his first term, which had enormous implications for the country's future, came in 1803.

THE LOUISIANA PURCHASE

When an impoverished Spain agreed that France could buy back Louisiana, giving Europe's great military power control of New Orleans (through which almost half of American exports then passed), and a base from which it might regain the American empire it had lost in the mid-18th century, Jefferson was naturally concerned. It was, he wrote, "the embryo of a tornado". He sent James Monroe to help Robert Livingston, America's representative in Paris, to negotiate the continued right to use New Orleans as a strategic port.

In April 1803, Napoleon Bonaparte, needing cash to finance his military campaigns in Europe, and stung by the loss of the force he had sent to the Caribbean to put down the slave revolt led by Toussaint L'Ouverture, decided

Below: In purchasing the Louisiana territory Jefferson acted independently of Congress, and set a precedent for increased presidential power.

to liquidate his American assets. He offered to sell not only New Orleans, but also the rest of the Louisiana territory. This would effectively double the size of the United States. Jefferson had given Monroe a budget of ten million dollars to secure New Orleans. The price for the whole territory was fifteen million.

The opportunity was too good to miss, and Jefferson grabbed it, even though he admitted that: "The Executive, in seizing the fugitive

Above: The land gained by the Louisiana Purchase was organized into territories which then achieved statehood on their admission to the Union.

occurrence which so much advances the good of their country, have done an act beyond the Constitution." The unique circumstances of the purchase, "a noble bargain" as the French foreign minister Talleyrand called it, allowed Jefferson to convince himself that in this instance pragmatic concerns about the

nation's security were more important than his constitutional principles. With a sense of the dramatic, he revealed that the purchase had been agreed on 4 July 1803. Five months later, Congress endorsed his action.

SECOND ADMINISTRATION

Jefferson won a convincing victory in the electoral college in 1804, beating Charles Pinckney by 162 votes to 14. There were now four times as many Republicans in the Senate as Federalists, and in the House of Representatives the margin was five to one. In his second inaugural address, the president congratulated the country on "the union of sentiment now manifested so generally" throughout the nation. Following the successes of his first four years, however, Jefferson's second term in the White House was something of an anti-climax.

The problem, once more, was Europe, and the effect upon the United States of the Napoleonic Wars. In his first inaugural address Jefferson had

SALLY HEMINGS

After Jefferson became president, his political opponents in the Federalist party circulated rumours that he was the father of several children by Sally Hemings, one of his slaves at Monticello (and the half sister of his wife). Historians speculated whether there was any truth in the accusation, and in 1998 scientists published DNA test results indicating that there was. The complexities of Southern attitudes to race and slavery were revealed in the character of one of the most eminent among the generation of Virginians who contributed to the founding and development of the United States.

Above: Julia Jefferson Westerinen, a descendant of Thomas Jefferson and his slave Sally Hemings.

STATES ENTERING THE UNION DURING JEFFERSON'S PRESIDENCY: OHIO

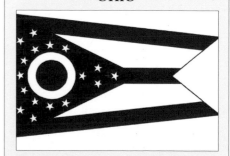

Entered the Union: 1 March 1803
Pre-state history: Acquired by British (1763); ceded to US (1783); part of Northwest Territory (1787); first part of Territory to be organized for statehood
Total population in 1810 census: 230,760
Total number of slaves in 1810 census: 0
Electoral College votes in 1804: 3

MARTHA JEFFERSON

"My dear wife died this day at 11:45 A.M.," wrote Thomas Jefferson on 6 September 1782. Born in October 1748, Martha Wayles Skelton Jefferson was not quite 34 when she died. She had been a widow for four years when she married Jefferson on New Year's Day 1772, and her son by Bathurst Skelton, her first husband, had died, aged four, the previous year. She survived the birth of her sixth child by Jefferson by only a few months. Jefferson never remarried. He hosted White House events alone, occasionally calling upon Dolley Madison for help. His eldest daughter Martha 'Patsy' Randolph was his hostess in 1802 and again in 1806, when she gave birth to a son, named for James Madison, and the first child to be born in the White House.

Above: Martha Jefferson

Above: Dolley Madison

proclaimed that the United States would not involve itself in "entangling alliances" with other nations. Yet this did not mean that it could remain untroubled by events elsewhere. War between France and Britain in 1803 brought with it not only the opportunity of the Louisiana Purchase but also the huge costs associated with European naval blockades, which had a detrimental impact on America's transatlantic and Caribbean trade.

MISJUDGED MEASURES

Jefferson and James Madison, his secretary of state throughout his time in the White House, decided on measures that were politically inept and economically disastrous. Congress prohibited imports from Britain with the Non-Importation Act (1806) and followed it with the Embargo Act (1807), preventing US ships from leaving port. This proved so counter-productive that it was repealed in the year Jefferson left office. On his final day, he looked forward to retiring from public life: "Never did a prisoner, released from his chains, feel such relief as I shall on shaking off the shackles of power."

RETIREMENT

Jefferson lived out his remaining 17 years at Monticello, where the spiralling costs of his architectural project and his expensive tastes, including a liking for fine French wine, left him hopelessly in debt. He also supervised the construction of the University of Virginia in nearby Charlottesville.

Following Washington's example, and like John Adams, he was concerned with how history would judge him: his correspondence and renewed friendship with his predecessor allowed both to explain to each other and to posterity their political beliefs and principles.

With an immaculate sense of timing he died on 4 July 1826, aged 83. In his will he freed five members of the Hemings family, but not their mother, Sally. He gave instructions that his principal achievements should be engraved on his tombstone: "Author of the Declaration of Independence of the Statute of Virginia for Religious Freedom and Father of the University of Virginia". That he had been president was left unmentioned.

Below: Monticello, the mountain-top home that Jefferson spent his life building.

THE LEWIS–CLARK EXPEDITION
1803–1808

Even before negotiations had been concluded with Napoleon over the Louisiana Purchase, President Jefferson had proposed to investigate whether, by following the route of the Missouri and Columbia Rivers that flowed east and west of the Rocky Mountains, it was possible to journey across America to the Pacific Ocean. He was also motivated by scientific curiosity about the Pacific Northwest. On 28 February 1803, Congress approved the funds for an expedition. Jefferson selected Meriwether Lewis, a former army captain and neighbour from Virginia, whom he had taken to Washington as his private secretary, to lead the expedition. In turn, Lewis asked an old army friend, William Clark, to go with him as co-leader.

Jefferson took a personal interest in the preparations, sending Lewis to meet members of the American Philosophical Society, of which he was an active member (and its president from 1797 to 1815). At the Society's headquarters in Philadelphia, Lewis consulted with, among others, botanists, mathematicians and surveyors, receiving advice on the scientific instruments he should take with him to explore the West.

THE EXPEDITION

By the time Lewis and Clark reached their starting point near St Louis, in December 1803, the Louisiana Purchase had been made. They set out on 14 May 1804, making their way west up the Missouri River. Despite bad weather, navigational hazards, disciplinary problems and occasional harassment from Native Americans, by November they had reached what would later become the state of North Dakota. They stayed there for five months, in Fort Mandan, which they built and

Above: Meriwether Lewis and William Clark prepared for their expedition with the help of Native Americans.

named after a local Native American tribe. During that time they were joined by Toussaint Charbonneau, a French fur trader, and his wife Sacagawea, a Shoshone Indian. She would act as an interpreter, accompanying the expedition along with her newborn child, Jean-Baptiste. While they were at Fort Mandan, Lewis and Clark also sent back a number of items that they had collected to the president in Washington. Beside Native American artefacts, these included animal skins, examples of plants, soil and rocks, and even a live prairie dog.

In April 1805 the expedition moved on. Two months later, where the Missouri branched, they travelled south along the river until they came to a succession of waterfalls in what is now

Above: The white line indicates the outward journey. For the return journey the leaders followed different paths.

Montana. They were forced overland. Rejoining the river, by July they had reached the point where it again divides: they called two of the branches Gallatin and Madison, after Jefferson's secretaries of the treasury and state, and followed the third, which they named in honour of the president himself.

The following month the expedition crossed the continental divide and travelled through the mountains in what are now the states of Montana and Idaho. The arduous 11-day journey was a formidable challenge: members of the expedition almost starved, surviving only with help given to them by friendly Native Americans.

On 16 October 1805 they reached the Columbia River, and the following month ended their 6,500km (4,000-mile) journey at the Pacific Ocean. It had taken 554 days. One member had died on the expedition: Charles Floyd had suffered what was probably a ruptured appendix, soon after they had left St Louis. The expedition spent the winter in what is now Oregon, preparing for the journey back across the continent.

RETURN AND AFTERMATH

Lewis and Clark set out on their return journey in March 1806, and it took them another two and a half years to reach home. They had established that Jefferson's idea for a continental route from east to west via the two rivers was not feasible: the Rocky Mountains obstructed the way. Later travellers would go south through Wyoming. The expedition was nevertheless significant in fulfilling Jefferson's other purpose: it had gathered information about the American interior and the West, its native peoples, the topography, fauna and flora. In addition to detailed observations written by both Clark and Lewis, Clark produced maps of the route that became the basis for a more accurate cartography of the West.

Jefferson appointed Meriwether Lewis governor of the Upper Louisiana Territory. William Clark joined him as brigadier general of its militia and Indian agent, and subsequently became governor of the Missouri Territory.

Lewis died in mysterious circumstances in 1809; it is unclear whether he was murdered or took his own life. Clark lived for another 30 years, until his death in St Louis in 1838. The achievements of the expedition were written into American history, demonstrating the pioneer spirit that would infuse a generation of those who followed Lewis and Clark across the continent of the United States.

Below: The expedition survived the harsh conditions because of the help given by friendly native tribes.

JAMES MADISON
1809–1817

If anyone was qualified to be president, James Madison assuredly was. Born in 1751 into a family of well-to-do Virginia planters, he was a graduate of Princeton College in New Jersey. In 1776, aged 25, he first met Thomas Jefferson, and in that year he helped to draft the Virginia Constitution. He was the youngest delegate at the Continental Congress, and after the War of Independence ended he returned to Virginia as a member of its legislature. Formidable in political debate, Madison was personally reticent, the opposite to his extrovert wife, Dolley, whom he married in 1794. Like Washington, Madison had no children.

Madison was the guiding spirit of the Philadelphia Convention, proposing the plan of union, participating in the deliberations over its final form, and even recording the most complete account

Born: 16 March 1751, Port Conway, Virginia
Parents: James (1723–1801) and Eleanor (1731–1829)
Family background: Farming
Education: College of New Jersey (Princeton) (1771)
Religion: Episcopalian
Occupation: Lawyer
Slave owner: Yes
Political career: Virginia Constitutional Convention, 1776
Continental Congress, 1780–3
Virginia State Legislature, 1784–6
Constitutional Convention, 1787
US House of Representatives, 1789–97
Secretary of state, 1801–9
Presidential annual salary: $25,000
Political party: Democrat-Republican
Died: 28 June 1836, Montpelier, Virginia

of its secret deliberations. He helped in the ratification process, contributing to the Federalist Papers and fulfilling the commitment to frame a Bill of Rights, a task that President Washington left to him as a member of the first Federal House of Representatives. After promoting the Republican party's cause in Congress, in 1801 he became Jefferson's secretary of state.

Madison supported the introduction of the Embargo Act, the measure by which Jefferson hoped to curtail the warring British and French blockades of American trade by stopping foreign trade altogether. By 1808 its disastrous economic repercussions were causing widespread discontent in New England, where the act was so unpopular that there was talk of secession, and the

Above: Known as the Father of the Constitution, Madison designed the blue-print for America's republican democracy.

Federalist party, which Jefferson and Madison had worked so hard to destroy, was optimistic about a comeback. But Republicans still managed to dominate the electoral college. Madison, now the leading figure in the Republican party that he had helped to create, defeated Charles Pinckney to become the fourth president of the United States.

EUROPEAN PROBLEMS
The turbulent world of European rivalries shaped the politics of Madison's presidency, as it had shaped those of his predecessors. Madison continued the policy that he and Jefferson had started:

attempting economic warfare against France and Britain so that both might be persuaded to respect the United States' maritime rights. The actions were self-defeating. Congress had repealed the Embargo Act in 1809, but in March that year, just before Madison took office, it again banned trade with the European powers. The following year, it authorized Madison to resume transatlantic commerce on the understanding that if either the French or the British stopped their illegal searches of American merchant ships, trade with the other would cease. Napoleon announced his intention to comply. On 2 November 1810, Madison issued a proclamation resuming trade with France and at the same time stopping American trade with Britain.

In 1811, the threat of war became more of a reality as the continuing conflict with Native American tribes in the Ohio Valley, who had formed an alliance led by the Shawnee chief Tecumseh, escalated. Meanwhile the British continued to ignore the United States' maritime rights as a neutral nation.

In Congress, 'War Hawks' – those from the South and West advocating war with Britain – argued for a more aggressive approach. The president was persuaded, not least because his electoral base was in those two regions. On 1 June 1812, 15 days after he had been nominated for a second term, he sent a message to Congress. The British had committed a "series of acts hostile to the United States as an independent and neutral nation". Just over two weeks later Congress declared war.

CONFLICT AT HOME

Madison's re-election showed that the conflict had increased sectional tensions: New England's transatlantic trade remained disrupted and the war was unpopular there. Madison won by 37 electoral college votes over his opponent, Dewitt Clinton from New York, whose support was concentrated in the New England states bordering the Atlantic.

The conflict with Britain preoccupied the nation until its end in 1814, but a political controversy that

DOLLEY MADISON

Born in May 1768, Dorothea Dandridge Payne Todd was a widow with a two-year-old son when she married James Madison in 1794. She was a vivacious hostess, and began to define the public role of first ladies by associating herself with charitable causes.

Below: Dolley Madison saved Washington's portrait when British troops set fire to the White House during the War of 1812.

stretched back to the first years of the federal republic continued throughout Madison's second term. The charter of the Bank of the United States, which Madison had opposed in 1791, had expired in 1811 and the bank had closed. In 1815, the president vetoed a compromise measure agreed between Republicans and Federalists in Congress that would have allowed it to reopen. However, following the difficulties of financing the War of 1812, the Second National Bank was finally given a 21-year charter in 1816 and opened for business in Philadelphia.

RETIREMENT

Madison retired to Montpelier, his Virginia plantation, succeeding Jefferson as the second rector of the University of Virginia. He died in 1836. His enduring legacies remain the American Constitution and the Bill of Rights.

STATES ENTERING THE UNION DURING MADISON'S PRESIDENCY:

LOUISIANA

Entered the Union: 30 April 1812
Pre-state history: Orleans Territory organized from Louisiana Purchase (1804)
Total population in 1820 census: 153,407
Total number of slaves in 1820 census: 69,064
Electoral College votes in 1812: 3

INDIANA

Entered the Union: 11 December 1816
Pre-state history: Acquired by British (1763); ceded to US (1783); part of Northwest Territory (1787); organized as Indiana Territory (1800)
Total population in 1820 census: 147,178
Total number of slaves in 1820 census: 190
Electoral College votes in 1816: 3

TECUMSEH
SHAWNEE LEADER

Native Americans were generally the losers in the military confrontations that took place in North America in the late 18th and early 19th centuries. Nevertheless, the tactical alliances that different tribes made with the European powers competing for control of the continent made sense, given that expanding settlement in America encroached upon territory they regarded as theirs by right of prior occupation. Having sided with the French during the Seven Years War, and with the British during the War of Independence, Native Americans rejected the new United States government's claims on land to the west of the original colonies and resisted the effort to organize it into new states.

As Lewis and Clark discovered on their journey through the Louisiana Territory, the American continent was

Below: Native Americans fought to prevent the United States taking over their land. In 1794 they were defeated at the Battle of Fallen Timbers.

peopled with many different tribes, or nations, of Native Americans, which like the newly independent states could squabble among themselves as well as unite for the common good. In 1787, the shifting network of alliances among the native peoples of the Ohio Valley consolidated in opposition to US settlement there. When conflict erupted, the regular troops in the United States army, few in number, faced a formidable opposition. In 1791, at Fort Wayne in what is now Indiana, they suffered their heaviest defeat ever at the hands of Native Americans.

The alliance of tribes opposing the United States was weakened when the British, who had supported their cause, withdrew, unannounced, from the Northwest Territory following the signing of the Jay Treaty. In 1794, American troops (including the future president, then Lieutenant William Henry Harrison) prevailed at the Battle of Fallen Timbers, and the following year the Treaty of Greenville forced the tribes to give up their claims to most of

Above: A natural leader, Tecumseh spent his life trying to unite the differing Native American tribes.

what would become the state of Ohio. It was not the end of the matter. In the early 19th century, a Shawnee chief revived the spirit of co-operation between the native tribes and again confronted the Federal government. His name was Tecumseh.

TECUMSEH'S WAR
Born in 1768, Tecumseh had fought at the Battle of Fallen Timbers. Refusing to accept the terms of the Treaty of Greenville, he started to rebuild the confederation of tribes, broadening its support, and by 1808, the year Madison was elected to the White House, he had established a base at Tippecanoe, near Lafayette in the Indiana Territory. His brother, Tenskwatawa, 'The Prophet', was the spiritual leader of the movement. As war fever grew, this revitalized alliance was able to gain the support of the British in Canada.

William Henry Harrison was now governor of the Indiana Territory, and in command of a unit of the US army. He decided to take action. In

November 1811, with Tecumseh absent on one of his many trips to rally support, he and his forces approached Tippecanoe and were confronted by Tenskwatawa. The battle was inconclusive, but Tenskwatawa was disgraced by his lack of success and fled to Canada. The Native Americans subsequently abandoned their headquarters and the alliance broke up.

Tecumseh remained defiant. In the War of 1812 between the United States and Britain, his followers were involved on the British side when the American attempt to invade Canada came to a disastrous end. In October of the following year, however, Tecumseh was killed at the Battle of the Thames, which took place as American forces, once again commanded by William Henry Harrison, pursued the British and their Native American allies during their retreat from Detroit.

AMERICAN EXPANSION

The expansion of the United States westwards across the continent is a defining theme in the nation's history. It is superimposed on an earlier migration that took place from north to south as, during the Ice Age, those who would become Native Americans walked across a land bridge over the

Bering Strait from Asia. Later arrivals, from the 15th century onwards, brought with them different cultures and traditions, which ultimately proved incompatible with Native American life.

Colonial America was organized into settlements, towns, cities and eventually the United States. Native American tribes had an alternative sense of the land, which was nomadic and recognized only natural borders. Moreover, the sheer numbers who came from Europe to America meant that the population expanded rapidly. By 1810

Above: Tecumseh was fatally shot in the War of 1812 at the Battle of the Thames in Canada. With his death, the union of Native American tribes disintegrated.

more than a million people lived west of the Appalachian Mountains. Native Americans, diminished through disease and war, tried to resist the settlement of the West. Like Tecumseh, however, they fought a losing battle.

Below: American settlers claimed the land once occupied by Native Americans.

THE WAR WITH BRITAIN
1812

As his term of office came to an end in 1797 George Washington knew that the United States was neither economically nor militarily strong enough to fight a war with Britain. He thought that conflict should be avoided "for about 20 years". The War of 1812 arrived more or less on cue, but for the United States, a politically divided nation, it was still a risky undertaking.

There were a number of reasons for the conflict. Britain's press-ganging of American sailors to fight against the French, as well as the imposition of trade restrictions across the Atlantic, had caused outrage in the United States. British attempts to stir up unrest among Native American tribes in the Midwest added fuel to such resentment, and some Americans saw an opportunity to expel the British governors from Canada: the pro-war 'hawks' in Congress argued that this would be another war for American independence.

The war was fought on three fronts: in Canada and the Great Lakes, at sea in the Atlantic Ocean, and in the South and West of America where American forces confronted hostile tribes of Native Americans.

WAR IN CANADA
Early American hopes of annexing Canada from Britain proved misplaced. The United States attempted to invade from three different directions: from Detroit into Upper Canada, where the absence of British troops and the presence of US settlers was thought to guarantee success; across the border at Niagara; and from Lake Champlain towards Montreal. One after another these attacks failed.

In August 1812, the British forced an American retreat and captured Detroit. In October the United States lost the Battle of Queenstown Heights on the Niagara River, and the following month

they withdrew from Lake Champlain without confronting the British. US fortunes turned when, on the Great Lakes, Captain Oliver Perry's victory in the Battle of Lake Erie in September 1813 forced the British to abandon Detroit. A second invasion of Canada culminated in the Battle of the Thames on 5 October, in which the US forces were victorious.

WAR IN THE ATLANTIC
In January 1814, Madison asked a visitor from Britain to sum up British public opinion on the war. The reply was revealing: "Half the people … do not know there is a war with America, and those who did have forgotten it." From a British perspective, the pre-eminent concern remained its military struggle with France in Europe rather than the conflict in America. In April 1814, Napoleon abdicated and the following month another Treaty of Paris temporarily ended the fighting in Europe. Britain refocused its energies across the Atlantic in America.

The US navy, whose exploits were symbolized by the USS *Constitution*, proved better equipped and better led than its British counterpart, while American privateers successfully harassed British merchant ships, but the first attack in the war in the Atlantic surprised the United States. It came in

Left: The burning of Washington had a significant effect in curbing the public's enthusiasm for war.

August 1814 via Chesapeake Bay, where British forces met with little opposition and advanced on Washington DC. The president was among those forced hurriedly to leave town, and the Capitol building and the White House were set ablaze. The British continued to Baltimore, but failed to take the city and withdrew. The United States' humiliation was partially redeemed, and it was

'OLD IRONSIDES'
USS *Constitution*, the American navy's oldest commissioned ship, was made of oak, but received its nickname, 'Old Ironsides', because its sides were proof against enemy cannonballs. One of six frigates that made up the original navy, it was built in Boston in 1797, equipped with 44 guns and carried a crew of over 450. During the War of 1812, it defeated British ships in battles off the coasts of the United States and Brazil. It last saw combat in 1815. Fifteen years later it was scheduled for the scrap yard, but a celebratory poem by Oliver Wendell Holmes led to a successful public campaign to preserve it as part of the nation's naval heritage.

Below: The USS Constitution.

Above: Oliver H. Perry, officer of the United States navy, led a decisive victory at the Battle of Lake Erie.

the fight to defend Baltimore that inspired Francis Scott Key to compose what became America's anthem, "The Star Spangled Banner".

DISSENSION IN THE STATES
In New York, from Lake Champlain and down the Hudson River, war also raged. The British aimed to isolate New England from the rest of the United States. New Hampshire, Connecticut and Massachusetts had already refused to support the American war effort and among those states where its economic impact was most acutely felt there was growing opposition to the war. In September 1814, at the Battle of Plattsburgh on Lake Champlain, the British were defeated and retreated to Canada, but at the Hartford Convention in December, New Englanders talked of secession if the war continued.

However, both sides had wearied of the fight. The Treaty of Ghent, which ended hostilities, was negotiated by, among others, a future president, John Quincy Adams, and was signed on

Right: Andrew Jackson's military exploits during the War of 1812 made him a national hero.

Christmas Eve, 1814. Before it was ratified by the Senate the following month, a final act of war was played out by another future chief executive: Andrew Jackson.

ANDREW JACKSON'S WAR
The third element of the British strategy involved a blockade of the Mississippi at New Orleans. Here they encountered Andrew Jackson, who during the war had spent his time in the South leading an army that fought brutal campaigns and seized land from Native Americans, the Spanish and the British. By December 1814, he had occupied New Orleans. On 8 January 1815, unaware that the peace treaty had been signed, the British tried to capture

THE HARTFORD CONVENTION
The trading economies of the New England states had been badly affected before hostilities broke out in 1812 by British harassment of US merchant ships and the backfiring of the Embargo Act. The Federalist party, which opposed 'Mr Madison's War', exploited this sectional discontent. In October 1814, representatives from Massachusetts, Connecticut, Rhode Island, New Hampshire and Vermont met in Hartford, Connecticut. They considered, but rejected, the idea of secession. Suggested Constitutional amendments were agreed and a delegation sent to Washington to present them to the federal government. It arrived after the war had been won, fatally undermining its protest. The Federalist party never recovered and within four years had been destroyed as a political and electoral force.

the city, but Jackson fought a swift and decisive battle, with few American casualties, and emerged victorious.

If the War of Independence made Washington an inevitable choice for president, Andrew Jackson, the hero of New Orleans, similarly used his military reputation to advance a political career that would lead him to the White House.

JAMES MONROE
1817–1825

Born in 1758, James Monroe was the last president to be elected who, as a young man, had been directly involved in the struggle for American independence. While at William and Mary College, he had helped to steal British weapons, giving them to the Virginia militia. In 1776, aged 18, as an officer in the Continental Army, he was severely wounded at the Battle of Trenton.

After the war Monroe studied law under Jefferson's guidance, then entered politics in 1783, as a representative in the Continental Congress. He married Elizabeth Kortright in 1785. Two daughters survived to adulthood, and a son died before the age of two.

Losing out to Madison in elections to the new federal House of Representatives, Monroe was appointed instead to the Senate. After serving as America's representative in Paris he became

Born: 28 April 1758, Westmoreland County, Virginia

Parents: Spence (? –1774) and Elizabeth (?)

Family background: Farming

Education: William and Mary College (1776)

Religion: Episcopalian

Occupation: Lawyer

Slave owner: Yes

Political career: Continental Congress, 1783–6

United States Senate, 1790–4

Minister to France, 1794–6

Governor of Virginia, 1799–1802

Minister to France and England, 1803–7

Secretary of state, 1811–17

Secretary of war, 1814–15

Presidential annual salary: $25,000

Political party: Democrat-Republican

Died: 4 July 1831, New York

governor of Virginia in 1799. He returned to France to negotiate the Louisiana Purchase and remained in Europe as a diplomat for four years, serving in Britain and Spain. He was again briefly Virginia's governor before joining Madison's administration as secretary of state and also as secretary of war. By 1816, Monroe was Madison's obvious successor, winning a convincing victory over Rufus King, from New York, in the electoral college.

GOODWILL ERA BEGINS

Monroe worked hard to overcome sectional and party tensions. His cabinet included John Calhoun from South Carolina and John Quincy Adams from Massachusetts. Henry Clay from

Above: James Monroe presided in a period of relative political calm. His presidency embraced the "Era of Good Feelings".

Kentucky might also have joined the administration but preferred to remain in Congress. The inclusion of Adams who, like his father, was a Federalist, as secretary of state demonstrated that its leading members no longer considered the party a vehicle for their political ambitions: indeed, even its name was no longer much used.

The new president imitated Washington, embarking on a national goodwill tour. A Boston newspaper described his presence in the city as marking the start of an "Era of Good Feelings" for the whole United States.

Born in the same year as her predecessor in the White House and married in 1786, Elizabeth Monroe was in her early twenties when in 1794 she accompanied her husband to Paris, which was then in the throes of revolution. Her intervention helped to obtain the release from prison of the wife of George Washington's close friend, the Marquis of Lafayette. As first lady, health problems meant that she was both less active and less accessible than her popular predecessor. She died in 1830, survived by her two daughters and her husband. When he died ten months later their correspondence had been destroyed.

In 1818, General Andrew Jackson, combating raids into Georgia by Native American tribes from Spanish Florida, invaded that territory and in so doing demonstrated the weakness of Spain's control over its North American possessions. Spain protested, but did not have the means to retaliate, or retake the territory by force. Adams was able to negotiate a treaty with Spain by which the United States acquired Florida in return for payment of five million dollars, and the Mexican border was extended to the Pacific Ocean.

In February 1819, as an economic downturn started to sour the political atmosphere, slavery again caused controversy. The border between slave and non-slave states was defined by the Mason–Dixon line. Missouri, which like other slave states lay to its south, had applied to join the Union. An amendment prohibiting slavery was added to the bill giving it statehood, even though there were already slaves there. As Congress wrestled with this problem, mindful that if Missouri entered the Union the balance between slave and non-slave states – at that time there were 11 of each – would be upset, Monroe gave his support to the creation

STATES JOINING THE UNION DURING MONROE'S PRESIDENCY:

MISSISSIPPI

Entered the Union: 10 December 1817

Pre-state history: Organized as American territory (1798) and expanded (1804 and 1812)

Total population in 1820 census: 75,440

Total number of slaves in 1820 census: 32,814

Electoral College votes in 1820: 2

ILLINOIS

ILLINOIS

Entered the Union: 3 December 1818

Pre-state history: Acquired by British (1763); ceded to US (1783); part of Northwest Territory (1787); organized as Illinois Territory (1809)

Total population in 1820 census: 55,211

Total number of slaves in 1820 census: 917

Electoral College votes in 1820: 3

ALABAMA

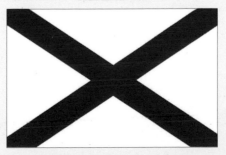

Entered the Union: 14 December 1819

Pre-state history: Part of Mississippi Territory (1798); western portion became Mississippi, eastern portion organized as Alabama Territory (1817)

Total population in 1820 census: 144,317

Total number of slaves in 1820 census: 47,449

Electoral College votes in 1820: 3

MAINE

Entered the Union: 15 March 1820

Pre-state history: Part of Massachusetts; became independent state through Missouri Compromise

Total population in 1820 census: 298,335

Total number of slaves in 1820 census: 0

Electoral College votes in 1820: 9

MISSOURI

Entered the Union: 10 August 1821

Pre-state history: Part of Louisiana Territory, renamed Missouri Territory following Louisiana's admission to the union (1812)

Total population in 1820 census: 66,586

Total number of slaves in 1820 census: 10,222

Electoral College votes in 1820: 3

of a West African colony where freed slaves could be repatriated. In 1824, when Liberia was established, its capital was named Monrovia.

Meanwhile, Henry Clay emerged as the political fixer, engineering the Missouri Compromise (1820). Under its terms Maine was created from the northernmost parts of Massachusetts and admitted as a free state, while Missouri became the twelfth slave-holding state in the union. No further extension of slavery was permitted to its north and west.

In the 1820 election, Monroe was unopposed. However, one member of the electoral college with a sense of history voted instead for John Quincy Adams, so that George Washington would remain the only president to be elected unanimously.

SECOND TERM

At the beginning of the 19th century the Spanish Empire was in decline, not only in North but also in South America. In 1822, following the acquisition of Florida, Monroe extended diplomatic recognition to Argentina, Chile, Colombia and Mexico, which had all freed themselves of Spanish imperial rule. In 1823, when it appeared that Spain might attempt to rebuild its empire to the south, the president set out what subsequently became known as the Monroe Doctrine (see opposite). As his second term came to an end, the "Era of Good Feelings" disintegrated, and Monroe's colleagues jockeyed to succeed him. The president refused to name his preferred candidate. The result was an acrimonious and disputed election in 1824.

RETIREMENT

Monroe lived for only six years after he left office. Like John Adams and Thomas Jefferson, he died as the nation celebrated the day that marked its Declaration of Independence. The 'Virginia Dynasty' was at an end.

THE MASON–DIXON LINE

Above: The boundary lines established by Mason and Dixon remain legal boundaries today.

The original boundary line was drawn by Charles Mason and Jeremiah Dixon, two British surveyors called in after a legal ruling had settled the disputed boundary between two British colonies. They established the east–west border between Pennsylvania and Maryland, beginning their work in 1763 and completing it four years and 375km (233 miles) later. As a result of the Missouri Compromise in 1820, the Mason–Dixon line was

extended west to the Ohio river, then to the Mississippi, and finally along a latitude 36 degrees west and 30 minutes north. It became the popular description of the boundary between Northern free states and those in the South where slavery was permitted.

Above: The Mason–Dixon line resolved the boundary dispute between Maryland and Pennsylvania over ownership of land between the 39th and 40th parallels. Both states claimed it for their own. The new boundary was marked every mile with stones.

THE MONROE DOCTRINE
1823

Left: Monroe with his Cabinet: the Monroe Doctrine became one of the foundation stones of American foreign policy.

The Monroe Doctrine, which outlined the foreign policy of the United States in the hemisphere of the Americas, was outlined in the president's annual message to Congress on 2 December 1823. There had been widespread concern that an alliance of European powers including France and Spain once more had designs on America. The British foreign minister, George Canning, had suggested that the United States join Britain in a declaration that would make clear their opposition to any such intervention.

Monroe's two predecessors advised him that this was a good idea. Jefferson wrote to him in October that the issue was: "the most momentous … since that of Independence. That made us a nation, this sets our compass and points the course which we are to steer thro' the ocean of time opening on us."

John Quincy Adams thought differently. He persuaded Monroe that the United States should act alone, and helped to draft the message to Congress in which the president made clear that the Americas – North and South – were not there to be colonized by Europe. "We should consider any attempt on their part to extend their system to any portion of this hemisphere as dangerous to our peace and safety." Europe should not meddle in the Americas' business and neither would the United States be concerned with Europe's internal rivalries.

The Monroe Doctrine had no real force: the United States was not yet strong enough to resist European military power. For the next century, it would rely upon British sea power to help deter other European nations that might have imperial ambitions across the Atlantic. American and British interests coincided, not for the last time. The Americans wanted to preserve their independence and the British, having accepted the loss of their colonies in the New World, did not want rival powers to supplant them.

NEIGHBOURS TO THE SOUTH

Initially, Monroe's statement suggested that the United States had much in common with the republics that had fought for their independence from Spain, just as the Americans had successfully resisted the British. But in time, as the United States became more powerful, it ignored the principle of non-interference outlined in the doctrine as it sought to influence the politics of its neighbours to the south.

Below: "That's a live wire, gentlemen." Uncle Sam warns John Bull and Kaiser Wilhelm not to transgress US territory.

CHAPTER THREE

JOHN QUINCY ADAMS TO JAMES POLK

1824–1848

It was 'the Age of Jackson'. The military hero lost to John Quincy Adams in 1824, but became the figurehead of a new party, the Democrats, which swept him into office four years later. 'Old Hickory', as he was known, was the only president during this time to be re-elected. The Whig party, named after its British anti-monarchical counterpart, confronted 'King Andrew' and in 1840 defeated his Democrat successor, Martin Van Buren. Whigs occupied the White House for just four years: William Henry Harrison became the first president to die in office, and John Tyler lost in 1844 to James Polk, whose ties to Jackson earned him the nickname 'Young Hickory'. The era ended with the nation still adding to its territory, but with the problem of slavery unresolved.

Left: Andrew Jackson at the Battle of New Orleans, the last major battle of the War of 1812.

THE PRESIDENTIAL ELECTION
1824

Four years after the Federalist party had been unable to offer even token opposition to the re-election of President Monroe, the political momentum of Democratic-Republicanism, first represented by Thomas Jefferson, and which had carried all before it during the 'Era of Good Feelings' stalled under the leadership of James Monroe. So one era ended and another began. Once more the outcome of a presidential election was to be decided in the House of Representatives. This time, it was John Quincy Adams, the son of Jefferson's defeated opponent in 1800, who would emerge victorious.

Initially there were five candidates, one from the North (Adams), two from the South (Crawford and Calhoun) and two from the West (Clay and Jackson).

Adams, the New Englander, was then secretary of state and the leading contender. His politics agreed with those of Henry Clay, the congressman from Kentucky and the broker of the Missouri Compromise, but Clay harboured presidential ambitions of his own. William Crawford, from Georgia, was Monroe's secretary of the treasury, and John Calhoun, from South Carolina, was his secretary for war. Then there was Andrew Jackson.

Underestimated by all his rivals, who viewed him as an irascible rabble-rouser, Jackson, then a senator from Tennessee, managed to win outright in eight states and gained a majority of the electoral college in three others. With the support of one representative from New York, he eventually won 99 electoral college

votes in 12 states. Not all states elected representatives to the electoral college – some still used their legislatures to nominate them – but Jackson also won the greatest number of the popular votes cast.

Adams came second. He won the entire support of six states and additional electoral college votes in five others, including a majority in New York, to reach a total of 84. Crawford had the support of only his home state and Virginia, but his 41 electoral college votes meant that he still beat Henry

Below: The presidential candidates in the 1824 election were favoured in different parts of the country. The race for the presidency was based on personality rather than policy.

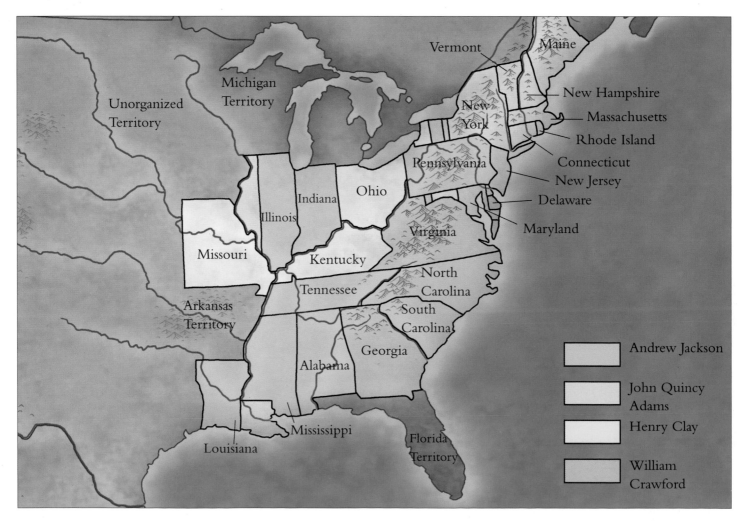

Above: John Quincy Adams.

Above: William Crawford.

Above: John Calhoun.

Clay, with 37, into last place. Calhoun had withdrawn his candidacy and won the vice-presidential contest convincingly instead.

THE 'CORRUPT BARGAIN'

No candidate had the required electoral college majority of 131 votes. The next step was clear. The revised rules for electing the president, agreed in the Twelfth Amendment to the Constitution, meant that the final choice was between the top three candidates: Jackson, Adams and Crawford. The 24 states in which the election had been fought now had just one vote each in the House of Representatives to determine the outcome. Henry Clay, whose name did not go forward, still had a role to play in his capacity as Speaker of the House and gave his support to Adams.

On 9 February 1825, the House of Representatives chose John Adams on the first ballot. He won the support of 13 states, to Jackson's seven and Crawford's four. Adams had retained the support of the six states in which he had won outright in the electoral college, as well as New York, where he had been the overwhelming favourite. He gained the votes of Illinois and Louisiana, where in the election he had run a close second to Jackson. Maryland, which on the basis of its votes in the first stage of the election might have

supported Jackson, now switched to Adams. The three states making up the rest of his majority, Kentucky, Ohio and Missouri, were all in the gift of the candidate who had won them in the electoral college: Henry Clay.

The journal of the House of Representatives records that, when the outcome of the election was announced, "some clapping and exultation took place in the galleries, and some slight hissing followed. The House suspended its proceedings until the galleries were cleared."

Rumours circulated that Clay and Adams had made a 'corrupt bargain', and that in return for his support Adams would offer Clay his choice of

Below: Henry Clay.

position in the new administration. The suspicion was apparently confirmed when soon afterwards Clay, the Speaker of the House, became secretary of state. Jackson resigned from the Senate in protest at the result.

The election, in which 18 of the 24 states had allowed popular participation in the selection of representatives to the electoral college, had ended amid accusations that this more open and democratic process had been hijacked by establishment politicians, deciding matters behind closed doors. Jackson exploited this sentiment, and four years later, like many future candidates, ran 'against Washington' in his successful campaign for the White House.

Below: Andrew Jackson.

JOHN QUINCY ADAMS
1825–1829

John Quincy Adams grew up during the era of independence and revolution, witnessing the Battle of Bunker Hill three months before his eighth birthday. He followed, literally, in his father's footsteps, accompanying John Adams on diplomatic trips abroad, graduating at the same age from Harvard, and also initially pursuing a career as a lawyer.

George Washington started Adams's career in public service, sending him to represent the United States in Holland, and his diplomatic career in Europe continued during his father's presidency. While in London, in 1797, he married Louisa Johnson, the daughter of the American consul there. Shortly afterwards, he was posted to Prussia, returning to the United States after Thomas Jefferson won the 1800 election. In 1801 the first of his four

Born: 11 July 1767, Braintree (now Quincy), Massachusetts
Parents: John (1735–1826) and Abigail (1744–1818)
Family background: Law, politics
Education: Harvard College (1787)
Religion: Episcopalian
Occupation: Lawyer
Slave owner: No
Political career: Minister to the Netherlands, 1794
Minister to Prussia, 1797–1801
United States Senate, 1803–8
Minister to Russia, 1809–11
Peace commissioner: Treaty of Ghent, 1814
Secretary of state, 1817–25
House of Representatives, 1831–48
Presidential annual salary: $25,000
Political party: Democrat-Republican
Died: 23 February 1848, Washington DC

children, named for George Washington, was born and in the same year he entered the federal Senate.

In the shifting party politics of the time, Adams gravitated from his father's party towards the Jeffersonian Republicans. In 1807 he supported the Embargo Act, alienating both the Federalists and his Massachusetts constituency. Having resigned from the Senate when Madison came to the White House, Adams took up a succession of diplomatic posts in Europe, witnessing Napoleon's invasion of Russia in 1812 and helping to negotiate the peace treaty between America and Britain. He won the election of 1824 at 57, four years younger than his father had been when he became president.

Above: The election debacle created mistrust of John Quincy Adams, who suffered from a lack of support for his domestic reforms.

TAINTED ADMINISTRATION

"The spirit of improvement is abroad upon the earth" was the message of Adams's first annual message to Congress. Despite the circumstances surrounding his election, he assumed a mandate to propose an ambitious programme of public works aimed at improving the transport infrastructure of the United States. Roads and canals were the nation's arteries of trade, and better communications encouraged Americans to travel and settle across the continent. He also suggested that a national university should be established

LOUISA ADAMS

Louisa Johnson was born in 1775 in London, and married Adams in 1797. She was profoundly depressed by the political controversy surrounding her husband's election. She shunned Washington while he was president but defended his reputation after his death. When she died in 1852, Congress adjourned as a mark of respect. Of her four children, only her youngest son survived her.

as part of his ambition to promote the arts and scientific knowledge. In many ways he appeared to be returning to his Federalist roots, believing that it was the role of the national government to take the lead in developing the nation's resources, economy and wealth.

Adams's independence of thought and aloofness of manner did not win him political friends, and the 'corrupt bargain' accusation tainted his administration from the start. John Calhoun, his vice president, was among those who were convinced that Adams and Clay had connived to deny the popular choice, Andrew Jackson, the presidency. In Calhoun's opinion it was "the most dangerous stab which the liberty of this country has ever received". As Adams's popularity declined, he could no longer rely on the support of Congress, which

in 1828 passed a new Tariff Act, aimed at protecting northern manufacturers and western agricultural products through setting high rates of duty on imports. In the South this 'Tariff of Abominations' was condemned as unjust and unconstitutional, and Adams, who had signed it into law reluctantly, was blamed.

Later that year he stood for re-election. Calhoun, who throughout the administration had conspired with Adams's political adversaries, openly supported Jackson, while continuing in office as vice president. Adams received only one less electoral college vote than he had four years previously, but this time, with Jackson as his only opponent, the incumbent president suffered a comprehensive defeat.

AFTER THE PRESIDENCY

On leaving the White House, Adams enhanced his reputation among those arguing for the abolition of slavery through his implacable opposition to the South's 'peculiar institution'. Two years after his retirement he returned to Washington as a member of the House of Representatives, the only ex-president to be elected to Congress. He famously argued the '*Amistad* Case' before the Supreme Court.

Adams spent the remaining 18 years of his life as a congressman. He campaigned relentlessly and ultimately

TARIFF ACTS

Following the War of 1812, Congress passed a number of Tariff Acts. These placed import duties on cheaper foreign goods, protecting northern manufacturing industry and the domestic prices of western raw materials. The South's market for its primary export crop, cotton, was vulnerable to retaliation from abroad, and it increasingly opposed the Tariffs. South Carolina argued for its right to disregard them, sparking the 'Nullification Crisis'. It was a graphic warning of what was to come: the South's secession and Civil War.

successfully for the repeal of the 'gag rules', passed by Southerners in the years before the Civil War to prevent the discussion of anti-slavery petitions. In 1846 he was a leading opponent of the war with Mexico.

Following a lifetime of public service, it was fitting that, on 23 February 1848, Adams died, aged 80, in the Speaker's Room, after suffering a stroke in the chamber of the House itself. He was the last survivor of that generation of prominent politicians whose lives encompassed the fight for independence, the creation of the United States, and the challenges it faced during its first 60 years as a democratic republic.

THE *AMISTAD* CASE

In 1839 the Spanish ship *Amistad* anchored in US territorial waters off New York. On board were 49 adult Africans, who had managed to take control of the ship near Cuba. Spain argued that America should return the vessel and its human cargo. Eventually the Supreme Court decided that since a treaty signed by Spain and Britain in 1817 prohibited the slave trade to the Spanish colonies, the *Amistad* had carried "kidnapped Africans, who by

the laws of Spain itself were entitled to their freedom". In 1841, they were repatriated.

Below: A contemporary engraving depicting the African slaves killing the captain of the Amistad.

POLITICAL PARTIES
AND THEIR APPEAL TO THE ELECTORATE

By the early years of the 19th century the Federalists had disappeared. The Republicans, led by Jefferson, Madison and Monroe, who had renamed themselves Democrat-Republicans, became the all-inclusive political vehicle that drove Jefferson and his compatriots in the 'Virginia Dynasty' to the White House. The Democrat-Republicans were the only party capable of nominating candidates for office by 1820, but four years later they had fragmented. By 1828 the party was irretrievably divided.

During Andrew Jackson's presidency, a more durable party system began to emerge. Andrew Jackson's Democrat

Below: The view of the Capitol from the White House, 1840.

party, egalitarian, expansionist and populist in its appeal to small landowners and working-class labourers, was opposed from the 1830s onwards by the Whigs, the party of commercial and manufacturing interests. Within 20 years, however, the Whigs too would be swept away by a political wave identifying itself with America's past and adopting a very familiar name: the Republican party.

Party competition in the United States re-emerged through a complex alchemy of personalities, competing sectional priorities and two continuing political arguments: what should be the extent of the federal government's powers and how could the issue of slavery be resolved?

THE IMPORTANCE OF ANDREW JACKSON

The catalyst for the development of the Democrat party was Andrew Jackson. Following his defeat in 1824, his supporters built a grass-roots coalition that enabled him to win the presidency four years later. The organizational genius behind it was Senator Martin Van Buren from New York, but it was Jackson's status as a national military hero, coupled with the widespread sentiment that he had been cheated by the 'corrupt bargain' between Adams and Clay in 1824, that made him an irresistible candidate.

Other developments helped Jackson. By 1828, congressional representatives in Washington no longer chose

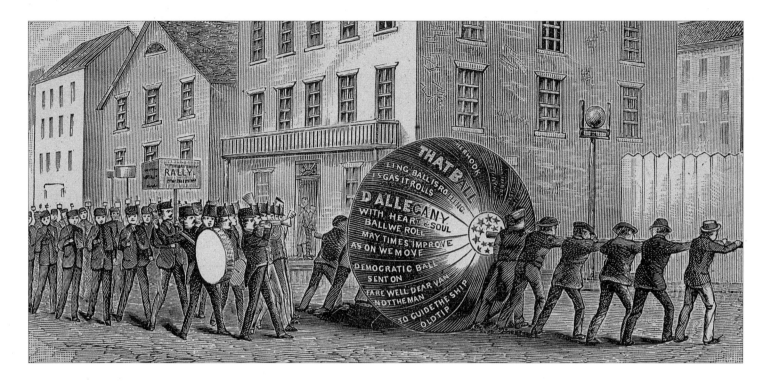

presidential candidates: instead the candidates were nominated by state conventions or in state legislatures. Although the suffrage was still restricted to white men, the right to vote had been extended through the abolition of property qualifications. The new voters had greater opportunities for democratic participation as most states moved towards popular elections for state offices and the electoral college. For Jackson, the symbolism of running as an outsider 'against Washington' had an enormous electoral appeal.

Political labels were still confusing: in 1828 Jacksonians co-opted the old party name, calling themselves Democratic-Republican. Adams reinvented himself as the candidate of the National Republicans. Whatever they were called, the core constituencies of both political groupings were still based in different geographical sections of the nation. Adams's support was in the old Federalist stronghold of New England. Jackson's was overwhelmingly in the South and West, although with Van Buren on the ticket, the Democratic-Republicans won New York. They were also victorious in Pennsylvania.

The 1828 election was the second round in the fight that had broken out within Jefferson's Democrat-Republican party, which had held on to power so tenaciously since 1800. The contest continued as the 'Age of Jackson' took shape, but by 1836 the party that had fragmented from the Republicans, and was now known simply as the Democrats, faced a more organized challenge to its political supremacy.

THE WHIGS

By the end of Jackson's administration, the personal rivalries that had characterized presidential politics for the previous 12 years had played out. John Quincy Adams was in the House of Representatives. Henry Clay, defeated by Jackson in 1832, was in the Senate, and so too was John Calhoun after his resignation as vice president at the end of that year. The 1836 presidential election pitted Calhoun's successor, Van Buren, against opposition from a newly formed party. The Whigs were a disparate coalition, united in their dislike of everything Jacksonian. The first time they challenged the Democrats, they fielded three candidates: two from the South and one from the North. By 1840, however, they had learnt the new realities of presidential politics, nominating William Henry Harrison, a

Above: Harrison was the hero of the Battle of Tippecanoe. His procession marched in triumph to Washington.

Virginia-born patrician whose father had signed the Declaration of Independence, and presenting him as another Jackson: a former general, war hero and rough-hewn frontiersman. This strategy worked and in 1836 the Whigs won the White House.

THE POLITICS OF SLAVERY

As the Democrats became increasingly identified with the slave-owning South, the anti-slavery and abolitionist movement organized politically: after 1854 many Whigs, including Abraham Lincoln, joined the new Republican party. The American party system, emerging from the clash of personalities and competing visions of the powers that should be exercised by federal and state governments, now coalesced around the fundamental faultline of slavery. By the 1860s, the compromises that had been managed in earlier times were no longer possible, as the political parties became increasingly identified with pro-slavery or abolitionist sentiment and war loomed between the states.

ANDREW JACKSON
1829–1837

In 1767, a few weeks after his father's death, Andrew Jackson, the son of first-generation Irish immigrants, was born in a small settlement on the border between North and South Carolina. He was four months older than his predecessor as president, but their early lives could not have been more different. While the teenage John Quincy Adams accompanied his father on diplomatic missions in Europe, Andrew Jackson was acquiring a taste for war in America's fight for independence. He was captured by the British in 1781, and later released in a prisoner exchange. Before the war ended his two elder brothers and his mother had all died. Jackson was 15.

Jackson's education was rudimentary, but he qualified as a frontier lawyer, practising in Nashville, in territory that would later become the state of Tennessee. He embarked on a successful career acquiring land and slaves. In 1791 he married Rachel Donelson Robards, whose father had been one of Nashville's founders.

Born: 15 March 1767, Waxhaw, South Carolina
Parents: Andrew (1730?–67) and Elizabeth (1740?–81)
Family background: Farming
Education: Not formally educated
Religion: Presbyterian
Occupation: Lawyer, soldier
Slave owner: Yes
Political career: US House of Representatives, 1796–7
US Senate, 1797–8, 1823–5
Tennessee Supreme Court judge, 1798–1804
Governor of Florida Territory, 1821
Presidential annual salary: $25,000
Political party: Democrat
Died: 8 June 1845, The Hermitage, Nashville, Tennessee

THE PATH TO THE PRESIDENCY
Jackson's career was spent aggressively adding to US territory, whether invading and occupying Florida to the south, or forcing Native American removal along the 'Trail of Tears' from Georgia to the west. He represented the traditions of the slave-holding South and the opportunism of the expanding West. He settled in Tennessee, which, when it was admitted to the Union in 1796, joined those states south of the Mason–Dixon line while remaining part of the US frontier. He himself owned and traded slaves: in the 1820s he had more than 100 of them.

When Tennessee achieved statehood, Jackson served in both the federal House of Representatives and the

Above: Andrew Jackson, the military hero, swept to victory in the 1828 election, such was the popular sense of injustice at his losing that of 1824.

Senate, before returning to a position on the state's Supreme Court. In 1802, he beat Tennessee's first governor, John Sevier, to become commander of the state militia; it was an acrimonious election, which led to Jackson challenging his opponent to a duel. Two years later, having resigned from the Court, he bought the Hermitage, his plantation near Nashville. He lived privately for eight years, during and after the War of 1812, before using his military successes to relaunch his career on a national platform.

RACHEL JACKSON

Rachel Donelson was born in 1767. Her marriage to Jackson in 1791 was the subject of vitriolic attacks during his 1828 presidential campaign, when rumours about her first marriage and the timing of her divorce were reported in the press. Her husband blamed his enemies for her death two months before he took office. The Jacksons had no children. Emily Donelson, Jackson's niece, was his official hostess until her early death in 1836, the year before he left the White House.

Jackson led the Tennessee Militia in campaigns against Native American tribes to acquire their land, and his victory over the British at the Battle of New Orleans gave him a hero's reputation, but he remained a military maverick. Later on, more ruthless and effective campaigns against native tribes culminated in his effective annexation of Florida from Spanish control, and he became military governor of the Florida Territory in 1821.

On his resignation from the army he returned to Tennessee, and had his political plans turned out as expected, becoming a senator for the second time in 1823 would have been merely a prelude to his election to the presidency a year later. But John Quincy Adams and Henry Clay had other ideas and Jackson resigned once more, returning home to wait. His revenge in 1828 was comprehensive: he received more than twice as many electoral college votes as the incumbent president.

Jackson's wife died three weeks after the results were declared. Like Thomas Jefferson, he was a widower when he entered the White House. Older than any of his predecessors, he took office 11 days before his 62nd birthday.

Right: Americans rushed to the White House to witness the inauguration of their popular hero Andrew Jackson.

SCANDAL AND CONSPIRACY

Throughout his life, Jackson squabbled, fought and occasionally duelled with his political enemies. On becoming president he rewarded his friends, effectively introducing an aspect of United States government that became known as the 'Spoils System': appointees of the former administration lost their positions and Jackson's supporters were given jobs. He also relied on his 'Kitchen Cabinet' – his close friends

Left: Jackson being abandoned by the Cabinet after the 'Peggy Eaton Affair'.

and cronies – for political advice. Early in his administration, his loyalty to one of them, John Eaton, whom he appointed war secretary, caused a scandal in Washington. Eaton's wife Peggy, with whom he had lived before they were married and who was rumoured to have had a colourful private life, was shunned by polite Washington society, notably the wives of the other members of his Cabinet. The vice president's wife, Floride Calhoun, stayed away from the federal capital in case she and Peggy might meet. Jackson convinced himself that what might have begun as moral condemnation was a political conspiracy. In 1831, the ramifications of the 'Peggy Eaton Affair' culminated in Jackson sacking most of his Cabinet. The rift between president and vice president widened. Calhoun did not run for re-election with Jackson in 1832 and resigned in December that year, the month after the election took place.

There was some substance to the president's suspicions. In 1830, Jackson learnt that 12 years previously Calhoun

Above: The first ever assassination attempt on a president was in 1830, while Jackson was attending a funeral.

had been among those in favour of pursuing disciplinary action against him for exceeding his military authority in invading Florida. Earlier that same year the two had clashed when the vice president suggested that his home state of South Carolina could unilaterally ignore a federal tariff on cotton. The doctrine of nullification, which Calhoun had first advanced in protest against the 'Tariff of Abominations' in South Carolina, implied that a state could defy the federal government. For Jackson, nullification meant the potential break-up of the Union, which he was adamant had to be preserved.

DISSENSION IN THE SOUTH

In December 1832, Jackson issued a 'Proclamation to the People of South Carolina', challenging that state's rejection of the 1828 and 1832 Tariff Acts. Persistent clashes between states' rights and federal authority could only have one outcome: "If this doctrine had been established at an earlier day, the Union would have been dissolved in its infancy … You must perceive that the crisis your conduct presents at this day would recur whenever any law of the United States displeased any of the

Right: A political cartoon of Jackson demanding public money be reclaimed from the National Bank.

States, and that we should soon cease to be a nation." His proclamation came a month after he had been re-elected. South Carolina's support had proved unnecessary as Jackson comprehensively defeated another of those whom he thought had conspired to deprive him of the presidency eight years previously: Henry Clay.

Following his victory, the president threatened to use force to collect the duties that Calhoun's home state had refused to pay and to arrest and hang the leaders of the nullification movement. Congress supported him,

passing the so-called 'Force Act'. It was his defeated opponent who defused the nullification crisis by negotiating a new compromise tariff, just before Jackson was re-inaugurated in March 1833.

Native Americans and the National Bank were not so sacrosanct. In May 1830, the Indian Removal Act cleared the way for the resettlement of tribes to reservations on land to the west of the Mississippi River. Jackson ignored the Supreme Court's ruling that Cherokee Indian land in Georgia was sovereign territory where state laws did not apply, allegedly declaring: "John Marshall [chief justice of the Supreme Court] has made his decision, now let him enforce it!" The Cherokees were forced to migrate from Georgia along the 'Trail of Tears' to Oklahoma.

In the same year, Jackson also vented his longstanding opposition to the National Bank, by vetoing the Act of Congress re-chartering it. "We can at least take a stand", he argued, "against all new grants of monopolies and exclusive privileges". The director of the Bank, Nicholas Biddle, denounced the President's veto message as "a manifesto of anarchy" reminiscent of the declarations that incited mob rule in the aftermath of the French Revolution. Nevertheless, it was Jackson who proved politically astute, even if his grasp of the economics of banking was somewhat shaky. The Bank became an important

issue in his 1832 campaign and his action gained him widespread support.

On 28 February 1827, the Baltimore and Ohio Railroad, running from Maryland across Virginia to the Ohio River, received its charter. The first US railroad had opened the previous year in John Adams's home town of Quincy, but the Baltimore and Ohio would enable passengers to travel from east to west. In 1833, Andrew Jackson became the first president to travel on one of its steam trains.

BATTLE WITH THE BANK

Jackson's battle with the National Bank continued. When his treasury secretary refused to switch federal government deposits to state banks, the president sacked him. His replacement, the attorney general Roger B. Taney, was not confirmed by the Senate, which, led by Calhoun and Clay, passed a motion of censure against Jackson. The president was not deterred.

In 1835, on the death of John Marshall, Jackson became the first president since John Adams in 1801 to appoint a chief justice of the Supreme Court. His choice was Taney, whose nomination again caused controversy, but who was eventually confirmed by the Senate. Taney, from Maryland, south

of the Mason–Dixon line, would have a major influence in shaping the Court's decisions during the next 30 years.

RETIREMENT

Jackson lived at the Hermitage for his last eight years, remaining involved in Democrat party politics. In 1844 he was instrumental in its nomination of James

Above: Jackson's meeting with the Native American leader Red Eagle.

Polk, known as 'Young Hickory', as its presidential candidate. Andrew Jackson, a leading actor in the developing drama of presidential politics during his lifetime, died peacefully, aged 78, on 8 June 1845.

STATES ENTERING THE UNION DURING JACKSON'S PRESIDENCY:

ARKANSAS	MICHIGAN

Entered the Union: 15 June 1836
Pre-state history: Part of Missouri Territory, organized as Arkansas Territory (1819)
Total population in 1840 census: 97,574
Total number of slaves in 1840 census: 19,935
Electoral College votes in 1836: 3

Entered the Union: 26 January 1837
Pre-state history: Acquired by British (1763); ceded to US (1783); part of Northwest Territory (1787); organized as Michigan Territory (1805)
Total population in 1840 census: 212,267
Total number of slaves in 1840 census: 0
Electoral College votes in 1836: 3 (Michigan entered the union nine days before the electoral college met.)

THE REVOLT AGAINST SLAVERY
1831

In his farewell address in 1837, Andrew Jackson drew attention to what he called "systematic efforts publicly made to sow the seeds of discord between different parts of the United States, and to place party divisions directly upon geographical distinctions; to excite the South against the North, and the North against the South, and to force into the controversy the most delicate and exciting topics upon which it is impossible that a large portion of the Union can ever speak without strong emotions". He was referring to slavery and abolitionism, which, during his presidency, had become the two

Below: Turner's rebellion, which he believed was directed by God, was one of the bloodiest in history.

political poles that increasingly threatened to tear the United States apart.

Unlike his predecessors, Jackson did not agonize over the morality of slavery but he did appreciate clearly its destructive potential. He had seen in the

Left: The Liberator *advocated an immediate end to slavery.*

nullification crisis in South Carolina an example of the serious consequences of a slave-holding state's refusal to accept the legitimacy of the federal government's laws. He had also witnessed the growth of the abolitionist movement in the North.

In the year Jackson left office, the federal Constitution was 50 years old but the problem that had been present from the beginnings of the American republic had still not been resolved. It had been dramatized during his presidency by the agitations of an abolitionist, William Lloyd Garrison, and the actions of a slave, Nat Turner, who led a rebellion in Virginia.

WILLIAM LLOYD GARRISON

In January 1831, in the inaugural editorial of *The Liberator*, William Lloyd Garrison, the newspaper's editor, announced that during a tour of New England, speaking out against slavery, he had: "determined, at every hazard, to lift up the standard of emancipation in the eyes of the nation, within sight of Bunker Hill and in the birthplace of liberty". The weekly newspaper he was driven to publish would appear continuously for the next 35 years.

Garrison was born in Massachusetts in 1805. In the 1820s he joined the American Colonization Society, which, with the support of President Monroe, worked to establish Liberia on the coast of West Africa as a place of repatriation for former slaves. However, Garrison became disillusioned with the society's policy of helping those already free rather than attacking the institution of slavery itself. After he had founded *The Liberator* he joined other abolitionists in establishing pressure groups dedicated to the cause, including, in 1833, the American Anti-Slavery Society.

NAT TURNER'S REBELLION

While Garrison was becoming an increasingly vociferous advocate for abolitionism, Nat Turner, an intelligent and deeply religious slave in Virginia, took matters into his own hands. In August 1831, Turner's spontaneous uprising began with a handful of his followers and turned into the South's nightmare: a rebellion in which more than 80 slaves joined in a killing spree, indiscriminately attacking white families until the state militia regained control of the situation. For Garrison, writing in *The Liberator* the following month: "What was poetry, imagination, in January, is now a bloody reality."

Right: The American Anti-Slavery Society had become a national organization by 1840. It was supported by religious groups and free black people, and soon became a platform for women to speak in public.

After a perfunctory trial, Turner was found guilty of murdering 55 white men, women and children. He had, he confessed, been motivated by mystical visions and had seen "white spirits and black spirits in battle, and the sun was darkened, the thunder rolled in the heavens, and blood flowed in streams".

Abolitionists and slave owners reacted to the revolt in predictable ways. For Garrison it was a vindication of his argument that the continuation of slavery would lead inevitably to violence. The South's only hope was the immediate emancipation of its slaves. On the other hand, John Floyd, then governor of Virginia, had no doubt what had caused the uprising: "The spirit of insubordination … had its origin among, and emanated from, the Yankee population." Floyd blamed the abolitionists for their "incendiary publications" – such as *The Liberator* – which were encouraging the slaves to rebel, and he proposed stringent measures in an attempt to prevent any further such incidents.

Turner's revolt occurred while Alexis de Tocqueville, one of the most famous commentators on 19th-century American politics, society and culture,

ALEXIS DE TOCQUEVILLE

French aristocrat, Alexis de Tocqueville (1805–59), embarked on an 18-month tour of the United States in 1831. His analysis of its class structure and the importance of the work ethic, with other perceptive observations on US politics, society and culture, were published in two volumes under the title *Democracy in America* (1835 and 1840). His work soon became established as the most famous and influential 19th-century study of the United States.

was visiting the United States from France. After touring the South, he had been left in no doubt about the future of its 'peculiar institution', predicting that, "If liberty be refused to the Negroes of the South, they will in the end forcibly seize it for themselves."

De Tocqueville was wrong in one vital respect. It would take a civil war between the white populations of the North and the South, and a proclamation by one of America's greatest presidents, Abraham Lincoln, to bring the slaves their freedom.

INDIAN REMOVAL
THE 'TRAIL OF TEARS'

In his first inaugural address, Andrew Jackson proclaimed: "It will be my sincere and constant desire to observe toward the Indian tribes within our limits a just and liberal policy, and to give that humane and considerate attention to their rights and their wants which is consistent with the habits of our Government and the feelings of our people." His rhetoric did not match reality. He had fought against Native Americans as a military commander. As president he displaced them from their ancestral lands.

NATIVE DISPLACEMENT

Following the Indian Removal Act of 1830, some tribes, the Choctaws and the Chickasaws among them, signed treaties with the federal government and moved west, reluctantly and only after white settlers had occupied their lands.

At the end of Jackson's administration, in 1837, the Seminole Indians went to war rather than leave. Their struggle lasted seven costly years.

No treaty was signed with the Creeks living in Alabama. The secretary of war, Lewis Cass, sent General Winfield Scott to force them off their land. After the Senate ratified the Treaty of New Echota, which agreed terms for American Indian removal in 1836, the Cherokee had two years to move west voluntarily, but only 2,000 members of the tribe complied. In 1838, Winfield Scott arrived in Georgia. Sixteen thousand Cherokee were rounded up by his troops, and forced to move west from their homelands there as well as from Tennessee, Alabama and North Carolina. Four thousand died on the 'Trail of Tears', the most visible symbol of the impact of this forced migration of Native American tribes westwards to land that later became part of Oklahoma. By the time he left office, Jackson's policy had resulted in the removal of most members of the five major tribes inhabiting the south-east of the United States to territory beyond the Mississippi River.

Alexis de Tocqueville observed that the United States was able "to exterminate the Indian race ... without violating a single great principle of morality in the eyes of the world". Whereas the reaction against slavery inspired the abolitionist movement, action against Native Americans proceeded with only the occasional objection to its legality, and no sustained condemnation of its immorality.

Below: With the settler population burgeoning, native tribes were stripped of their land.

MARTIN VAN BUREN

1837–1841

It should have been the crowning achievement of a long political career, but as president, Martin Van Buren found difficulty in escaping from Andrew Jackson's long shadow. At his inauguration, as Thomas Hart Benton put it, "For once, the rising was eclipsed by the setting sun."

Van Buren was born in New York in 1782 and was the son of immigrants from Holland. In 1803, he qualified as a lawyer and four years later he married Hannah Hoes, who was also of Dutch descent. They had four children.

In 1812 Van Buren became a state senator and by 1820 he was leader of the 'Albany Regency', the power-brokers in New York's capital city who controlled state politics. The following year he entered the Senate in Washington. After 1824, as a leading opponent of John Quincy Adams, Van Buren organized the Democrats behind Jackson's candidacy. He served as secretary of state and vice president.

To gain Southern support during the 1836 election campaign, Van Buren made it clear that he tolerated slavery where it existed, and was against the abolitionists' campaign to prohibit it in Washington DC. On the other hand, he was opposed to the annexation of Texas if it was to bring with it a further extension of slavery. Successive presidential candidates had to walk a political tightrope between the pressures of expansion and the mounting opposition to slavery, and Van Buren was no exception. Winning the 1836 election as Jackson's chosen successor, he was the third widower to enter the White House: in 1819 his wife had died from tuberculosis at the age of 35.

Above: Van Buren's presidency was defined by the poverty of the era in which he occupied the White House.

ADMINISTRATION

In his inaugural address Van Buren graciously praised his "illustrious predecessor", but the economic problems that Van Buren faced in his own presidential term were in part of Jackson's making. Jackson had encouraged demand for hard currency, gold and silver. In 1837 America's banks could no longer exchange paper money for the precious metals. The resulting financial panic soon became a full-blown economic depression, with a predictable impact on Van Buren's political popularity.

Conscious of potential divisions among Democrats and between North and South, Van Buren did his best not to inflame the increasingly bitter argument over slavery. His level-headed refusal to bow to agitation for the annexation of Texas by the United States avoided war with Mexico but also lost him popular support. In 1840, he failed to gain re-election.

RETIREMENT

Van Buren professed that the two happiest days of his life were the one on which he became president and the one on which he left the White House. This did not stop him trying to regain the presidency in 1844 and in 1848. For the remainder of his life he lived near Kinderhook, the village in which he had been born. He died in 1862, having seen his greatest fear, civil war, become a catastrophic reality.

Born: 5 December 1782, Kinderhook, New York
Parents: Abraham (1737–1817) and Maria (1748–1817)
Family background: Farming and tavern keeping
Education: Kinderhook Academy (1796)
Religion: Dutch Reformed
Occupation: Lawyer
Slave owner: Yes – but not while president
Political career: New York State senator, 1813–15
New York attorney general, 1815–19
United States Senate, 1821–9
Governor of New York, 1829
Secretary of state, 1829–31
Minister to England, 1831
Vice president, 1833–7
Presidential annual salary: $25,000
Political party: Democrat
Died: 24 July 1862, Kinderhook

HANNAH VAN BUREN

Hannah Hoes was born in 1783 in the same town as her cousin, Martin Van Buren, and her first language, like his, was Dutch. They married in 1807 and had four sons who survived to adulthood. Hannah died in 1817 and Van Buren did not re-marry. While president, he invited his daughter-in-law, Angelica Singleton, to act as his official White House hostess.

WILLIAM HENRY HARRISON

1841

The third former general to become commander-in-chief, following his second campaign for the White House, William Henry Harrison was the first president to die in office. He was born in Virginia in 1773 into a well-off family: his parents were friends of George and Martha Washington, and his father served three times as state governor. He entered the military in 1791, spending four years battling Native Americans in the Ohio Territory and taking command of Fort Washington near Cincinnati, which was founded by his future father-in-law.

In 1800, President John Adams appointed William Harrison to be governor of the Indiana Territory, a post in which he remained for 12 years. In 1811, he led the military expedition against Tecumseh's Native American

Born: 9 February 1773, Berkeley, Virginia

Parents: Benjamin (1726–91) and Elizabeth (1730–92)

Family background: Plantation owners, politics

Education: Hampden-Sydney College, near Richmond, Virginia

Religion: Episcopalian

Occupation: Soldier

Slave owner: Yes – but not while president

Political career: Secretary of Northwest Territory, 1798
Territorial delegate to Congress, 1799–1801
Territorial governor of Indiana, 1801–13
US Congressman from Ohio, 1816–19
United States senator, 1825–8
Minister to Colombia, 1828–9

Presidential annual salary: $25,000

Political party: Whig

Died: 4 April 1841, Washington DC

confederation and emerged victorious from the battle that would earn him his nickname: 'Old Tippecanoe'. Further success in the War of 1812 enhanced his military reputation, but his political career spluttered along.

THE FIRST WHIG PRESIDENT

Although John Quincy Adams objected to Harrison's "rabid taste for lucrative public office", he appointed him ambassador to Colombia, where he remained for a year. In 1829 Andrew Jackson, an old political enemy, recalled him. Harrison retired to Ohio, where he became involved with the Whig opposition, and in 1836 campaigned unsuccessfully for the White House as one of three Whig candidates. Four years later, he defeated Van Buren to become the Whigs' first president.

Harrison had just celebrated his 68th birthday when he made his fatal mistake. On 4 March 1841, he delivered

Above: Harrison gave the longest inaugural address on record, but his presidency was the shortest in American history.

the longest inaugural speech in presidential history. He spoke for almost two hours, coatless and hatless on a cold wet Washington day. He pledged not to serve a second term and ended by taking "an affectionate leave" of his audience. He did just that: a month later he died from pneumonia.

ANNE HARRISON

Anne Symmes was born in 1775 and married Harrison in 1795. They had ten children, of whom four survived to see him become president. Anne did not accompany her husband to his inauguration, and was about to join him when he died. She lived on for 23 more years, dying in 1864 aged 88.

JOHN TYLER
1841–1845

The first president to inherit the office rather than be elected to it, John Tyler asserted what he claimed was his constitutional right of succession and took the oath of office two days after William Henry Harrison's death. He was a lawyer and an experienced politician, and knew the value of establishing a precedent. His action stopped speculation that he would be a caretaker chief executive but he was still regarded as the 'Accidental President'.

Born in 1790, he came, like his predecessor, from an affluent Virginia family: Tyler graduated from William and Mary College and embarked on a legal career. In 1811 he took his seat in Virginia's House of Delegates. For the following quarter of a century, with the exception of one year – 1822 – he served variously in the federal House of Representatives, the State Legislature,

Above: Tyler's father was a governor of the state and a friend of Thomas Jefferson.

like his father as governor, and in the federal Senate. A slave-owner and ardent supporter of states' rights, Tyler was fiercely critical of Andrew Jackson. In both 1836 and 1840 he was a Whig candidate for the vice presidency, campaigning as William Henry Harrison's running mate under the slogan 'Tippecanoe and Tyler Too'.

PRESIDENT WITHOUT SUPPORT

When he became president on Harrison's death he lacked an electoral mandate and his political relationships were turbulent. His opponents consistently referred to him as 'the acting president' and he was not taken seriously. When, for the second time, he vetoed a congressional bill re-establishing a National Bank, all but one of his Cabinet, which he had kept intact after Harrison's death, resigned.

His party rejected him. Seeking a populist issue to rally support, Tyler seized on Texas. He advocated its annexation but it did not save his political career. In 1844 Henry Clay became the Whigs' presidential candidate, and Tyler,

Born: 29 March 1790, Greenway, Virginia
Parents: John (1747–1813) and Mary (1761–97)
Family background: Law, politics
Education: William and Mary College (1807)
Religion: Episcopalian
Occupation: Lawyer
Slave owner: Yes
Political career: Virginia House of Delegates, 1811–16
US House of Representatives, 1816–21
Virginia State Legislature, 1823–5
Governor of Virginia, 1825–6
US Senate, 1827–36
Vice president, 1841
Confederate States Congress, 1861–2
Presidential annual salary: $25,000
Political party: Whig
Died: 18 January 1862, Richmond, Virginia

bowing to pressure – ironically from, among others, Andrew Jackson – withdrew from the contest.

He retired to Virginia. In 1861, following the South's secession, he was elected to the Confederate States Congress, but died the following year just prior to its first meeting.

STATES ENTERING THE UNION DURING TYLER'S PRESIDENCY: FLORIDA

Entered the Union: 3 March 1845
Pre-state history: Alternating Spanish and British control until acquired for US by Andrew Jackson (1821) and organized as Florida Territory (1822)
Total population in 1840 census: 54,477
Total number of slaves in 1840 census: 25,717
Electoral College votes in 1848: 3

LETITIA AND JULIA TYLER

Born in 1790, Letitia Christian married John Tyler in 1813. In 1842, she was the first president's wife to die in the White House, six months after she moved in. Two years later Tyler married Julia Gardiner, who was born in 1830. She died in 1889. Tyler had a total of 15 children, eight by Letitia and seven by Julia.

JAMES POLK
1845–1849

James Polk became president with the support of those Americans who were anxious to incorporate Texas into the United States. By the time he left office in 1849 he had acquired Oregon from the British and fought a war with Mexico that resulted in the United States gaining territories that would become seven new states in the West. Although it appeared to be the fulfilment of the United States' 'Manifest Destiny' to expand across the North American continent, these new lands once again focused attention on the fundamental fault line of slavery: the issue that, 12 years later, would plunge the nation into civil war.

Polk was born in North Carolina in 1795, but, like Andrew Jackson, his political life began in Tennessee. When he was 10, Polk's family moved there and prospered, building a plantation and owning slaves. He returned to North

Above: During Polk's presidency, the United States expanded westwards. The prospect of the extension of slavery into this new territory by including new states in the union agitated abolitionists.

Born: 2 November 1795, Mecklenburg County, North Carolina
Parents: Samuel (1772–1827) and Jane (1776–1852)
Family background: Farming
Education: University of North Carolina (1818)
Religion: Presbyterian
Occupation: Lawyer
Slave owner: Yes
Political career: Tennessee House of Representatives, 1823–5
US House of Representatives, 1825–39
Speaker of the House, 1835–9
Governor of Tennessee, 1839–41
Presidential annual salary: $25,000
Political party: Democrat
Died: 15 June 1849, Nashville, Tennessee

STATES ENTERING THE UNION DURING POLK'S PRESIDENCY:

TEXAS	IOWA	WISCONSIN

Entered the Union: 29 December 1845
Pre-state history: Claimed by Mexico following War of Independence against Spain (1821); proclaimed Independent Republic (1836); annexed by US (1845)
Total population in 1850 census: 212,592
Total number of slaves in 1850 census: 58,161
Electoral College votes in 1848: 4

Entered the Union: 28 December 1846
Pre-state history: Part of Louisiana Purchase (1803); organized as Iowa Territory (1838)
Total population in 1850 census: 192,214
Total number of slaves in 1850 census: 0
Electoral College votes in 1848: 4

Entered the Union: 29 May 1848
Pre-state history: Acquired by British (1763); ceded to US (1783); part of Northwest Territory (1787); organized as Wisconsin Territory (1836)
Total population in 1850 census: 305,391
Total number of slaves in 1850 census: 0
Electoral College votes in 1848: 4

MANIFEST DESTINY

In July 1845, the journalist John L. O'Sullivan wrote an article in the *United States Magazine and Democratic Review* supporting the annexation of Texas. He argued that it was the United States' "manifest destiny to overspread the continent allotted by providence for the free development of our yearly multi-plying millions". His phrase – "manifest destiny" – was subsequently widely used as a justification of the continued expansion of the United States across the North American continent.

Left: Columbia, the personification of the United States, is seen leading settlers in a westward expansion, while the native people flee.

Carolina to attend university, graduating in 1818. After studying law in Nashville, in 1823 he entered the Tennessee House of Representatives.

Polk was first elected to the federal House of Representatives in 1825, and served there for 14 years. With Jackson's support, in 1835 he became its Speaker. His endorsement of President Jackson's policies earned him his nickname, 'Young Hickory'. In 1839 he returned to Tennessee and served one term as state governor.

THE 1844 ELECTION

The major issue in the 1844 election was whether the independent republic of Texas, a slave-owning region, should be annexed – in other words added – to the Union as a slave state. Polk, again helped by Jackson's endorsement, became the party's compromise candidate. The Whigs chose Henry Clay, who, like Van Buren, was against annexation. Initially Tyler, who had been denied the Whig nomination, was

Right: Canada and the United States both claimed the right to Oregon in the north-west of America.

convinced that by incorporating Texas in the Union he could win the election in his own right, without needing the support of a party organization. Instead he was persuaded that his candidacy would split the pro-Texas vote and benefit Clay. He stepped aside, allowing a straight fight between the two major parties. Polk won by a narrow margin. Just before he left the White House,

Tyler, acting on a joint congressional resolution, offered Texas the prospect of admission to the Union before 1 January 1846.

TEXAS

After Texas joined the Union in December 1845, fighting broke out with Mexico, which had never recognized the new state's claim to be an

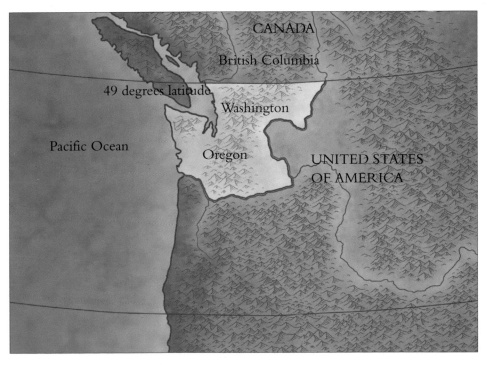

Left: The star among the stripes indicates Polk's support of the admission of Texas.

independent republic. In May 1846 Polk asked Congress for a Declaration of War, claiming that Mexican troops had attacked and killed US soldiers stationed on the Texas border under the command of General Zachary Taylor: "American blood had been shed on American soil." Not everyone was convinced by the president's argument. One member of the Whig party in Congress disputed whether the incident had indeed occurred on United States territory: his name was Abraham Lincoln. Congress nevertheless supported the president. Although there were some who opposed the United States' action – Henry David Thoreau became a famous protester – within two years, after a number of military setbacks, Mexico had admitted defeat.

Below: The gold rush quickly changed the balance of state populations but few became rich and many endured harsh conditions.

OREGON

Both Britain and the United States had territorial interests in the Oregon Country in the north-west, and the boundary had been the subject of dispute for several decades. Polk now hoped to admit Oregon as a free state, balancing the slave state of Texas. To gain the support of American expansionists, he had campaigned on the slogan 'Fifty-four Forty or Fight', calling for the entire territory up to the latitude of 54° 40' north to be claimed by the United States. But faced with the prospect of conducting two simultaneous wars (with Britain and Mexico) in June 1846, Polk compromised. A treaty was concluded with Britain, establishing America's north-west border with Canada along the 49th parallel. The United States gained what would become the states of Oregon, Montana, Washington and Idaho.

POPULATION BOOM

Iowa entered the Union in 1846, followed two years later by Wisconsin, both as free states. As its territory increased, so did America's attraction to European immigrants. During Polk's

SARAH POLK

Sarah Polk was born in Tennessee in 1803, and married James Polk in 1824. She had no children and devoted herself to her husband's career, becoming a widely respected and influential first lady. She survived the Civil War, dying in 1891 at the age of 87.

presidency, the Irish potato famine encouraged many to seek a new life across the Atlantic. Settlers swarmed over the continent.

In January 1848, gold was discovered in California, and the territory's population grew rapidly as a result of the rush to find more. As it applied for statehood, the need to resolve the controversy over whether slavery should be permitted to extend to the West became more pressing.

By then, Polk was no longer president. His health had deteriorated throughout his time in office. In 1848 he kept his promise not to seek re-election. The Whigs, many of whom had opposed the Mexican War, were its major beneficiaries. Their candidate, Zachary Taylor, won the election. In June 1849, less than four months after he had left the White House, Polk died.

HENRY DAVID THOREAU

An influential voice in the Transcendentalist movement of New England was Henry David Thoreau (1817–62). The adherents of transcendentalism believed that individuals should listen to their consciences rather than obey laws or respect policies that offend their morals. Jailed for a night for refusing to pay a tax that might contribute to the war against Mexico, Thoreau's essay *Civil Disobedience* (1849) argued for non-violent direct action to protest against injustices. He would influence many Americans, among them Martin Luther King jr.

WAR WITH MEXICO
1846–1848

Following America's declaration of war on Mexico in May 1846, General Zachary Taylor's US forces invaded. Although outnumbered by the Mexican army, the Americans won the Battle of Palo Alto, and by September Taylor had taken the city of Monterrey in northern Mexico. By that time another US army, commanded by General Stephen Watts Kearny, had occupied Santa Fe, in the region that would later become the American state of New Mexico. Kearny then led some of his troops into California to link up with forces under Captain John Fremont. Others fought their way into Mexican territory and through Chihuahua to meet with Taylor's army in spring 1847.

Meanwhile, the former Mexican president, Santa Anna, saw an opportunity to revive his turbulent political career. He returned from Cuba, where he had lived in exile following a coup in 1844. In return for a guarantee of safe passage, he had assured Polk that once restored to power he would negotiate a peace favourable to the Americans in

return for $30 million. He was bluffing. After regaining the presidency, he marched north from Mexico City with an 18,000-strong army to confront Taylor. On 22 February 1847, despite being once again heavily outnumbered, the Americans beat Santa Anna's forces at the Battle of Buena Vista.

The following month General Winfield Scott embarked on an ambitious expedition by sea and land, capturing the port of Veracruz in March and then fighting a six-month campaign, at the end of which he captured Mexico City. Santa Anna was deposed again and the new Mexican government surrendered. Under the terms of the Treaty of Guadeloupe, signed on 2 February 1848, Mexico ceded half its territory to the United States, agreeing to $15 million compensation for the loss of California and New Mexico and the establishment of the border along the Rio Grande.

It was a one-sided war. About 700 Americans died in battle, although 18 times that number succumbed to

Above: The Battle of Palo Alto was the first battle of the Mexican War: the United States won all the major engagements between the two sides.

disease. Mexico suffered almost 50,000 casualties. Of the US commanders and troops who took part, many would later find themselves on opposite sides during the Civil War.

Below: The war with Mexico was controversial in Congress, but its hero Zachary Taylor became America's next president.

CHAPTER FOUR

ZACHARY TAYLOR TO ANDREW JOHNSON

1849–1869

THE 20 YEARS BETWEEN 1849 AND 1869 BEGAN WITH THE ISSUE OF SLAVERY STILL DOMINATING AMERICAN POLITICS, CULMINATED IN THE CIVIL WAR, AND ENDED WITH A PRESIDENT ASSASSINATED AND HIS SUCCESSOR ESCAPING IMPEACHMENT BY A SINGLE VOTE. TWO WHIGS, TWO DEMOCRATS, THE FIRST REPUBLICAN PRESIDENT AND A SOUTHERN DEMOCRAT WHO HAD REMAINED LOYAL TO THE UNION WOULD OCCUPY THE WHITE HOUSE DURING TWO OF THE MOST DRAMATIC DECADES IN AMERICAN HISTORY. AS ABOLITIONISTS ARGUED FOR AN END TO SLAVERY, IN 1848 A CONVENTION, MEETING AT SENECA FALLS, NEW YORK, HAD ISSUED ITS 'DECLARATION OF SENTIMENTS', A DEFINING MOMENT IN THE LONG STRUGGLE FOR WOMEN'S EQUALITY. THE ELECTION OF ABRAHAM LINCOLN IN 1860 HASTENED THE SOUTH'S SECESSION AND THE OUTBREAK OF THE CIVIL WAR BUT BROUGHT TO THE WHITE HOUSE ONE OF AMERICA'S GREATEST PRESIDENTS.

Left: The Battle of Gettysburg, the turning point of the Civil War, saw the largest number of casualties.

ZACHARY TAYLOR

1849–1850

The fourth military hero to become president, Zachary Taylor's affiliation to the Whigs owed more to the party's desire to win back the White House than to his ideological convictions. Taylor tried to remain 'above politics', cultivating the image of an outsider and grazing his favourite old army horse, 'Whitey', on the White House lawn.

Taylor's father had been an aide to George Washington during the War of Independence. Taylor grew up in Kentucky on what became a prosperous plantation. He joined the military and by 1808 he was a lieutenant. He served under William Henry Harrison. Taylor briefly resigned his commission in 1815, but rejoined the army the following year and lived the peripatetic life of an army officer while his career steadily advanced. After his exploits during the Mexican War, he became a popular choice for the presidency in 1848. His defeat of the Democrat candidate, Lewis Cass, was helped, ironically, by the intervention of the Free Soil Party, a coalition of his opponents. Their candidate, the former president Martin Van Buren, split the Democrats' support, particularly in New York, delivering Taylor the White House by a margin of 36 electoral college votes.

THE ISSUE OF SLAVERY

As president, Zachary Taylor, who was a slave owner, had to confront the intractable problem that his success as a soldier had helped create: should slavery be extended west into the territories acquired as a result of the Mexican War? He disappointed Southerners, and advocated the entry of California and New Mexico into the Union as free states. When Southern leaders talked of secession, he threatened to hang those who conspired against the Union.

Extremism on both sides encouraged politicians to seek what little common ground remained. A compromise was being debated in the Senate when, on 4 July 1850, the president attended a ceremony at the still incomplete Washington Monument. He fell ill after consuming copious amounts of fruit, cold milk and iced water. Five days later, he died, after only 16 months in office.

Born: 24 November 1784, near Barboursville, Virginia
Parents: Richard (1744–1829) and Sarah (1760–1822)
Family background: Military, landowning
Education: Not formally educated
Religion: Episcopalian
Occupation: Soldier
Slave owner: Yes
Political career: No political office prior to presidency
Presidential annual salary: $25,000
Political party: Whig
Died: 9 July 1850, Washington DC

MARGARET TAYLOR

Born in Maryland in 1788, Margaret Smith married Zachary Taylor in 1810. The Taylors had six children. In 1820, two of them died of a fever that also affected their mother's health. Another daughter, Sarah, died shortly after marrying Jefferson Davis. In the White House Margaret avoided public functions. She died in Mississippi in 1852, aged 63.

Left: Taylor's military reputation helped the Whigs recapture the White House; as president his party allegiance was always weak.

THE COMPROMISE
1850

Victory in the Mexican War brought the United States more territory but focused attention once more on the problem of slavery. The Compromise of 1850 was Congress's attempt to provide a legislative framework in answer to a series of controversial questions. Should California be admitted as a free state, thereby disrupting the delicate balance of slave-owning and free states that had been the cornerstone of Clay's compromise 30 years earlier? Should Texas be allowed to claim more land from New Mexico? Should slavery be tolerated in the nation's capital?

Would more territory mean more slavery? This question was the divisive and decisive issue in government. The Compromise of 1850 represented the last great effort to hold the Union together. In the end it merely postponed what eight years later Senator William Seward from New York would call the "irrepressible conflict" between North and South. The complex negotiations involved politicians from both major

parties – Democrats and Whigs – who eventually worked their way to common ground. Once again the architect of the compromise was Henry Clay, who confronted several related problems.

THE COMPROMISE IS DEBATED

The Senate debate, which began in January, lasted nine months. The major protagonists were Clay, who was now 70, Stephen Douglas from Illinois, and, before he became Millard Fillmore's secretary of state, Daniel Webster from Massachusetts. Calhoun (a former vice president), who privately admitted that the South "cannot with safety remain in the Union … and there is little or no prospect of any change for the better", died aged 68 on 31 March, before a final agreement had been reached.

The Compromise postponed the decision as to whether slavery should be allowed in New Mexico, Nevada, Arizona and Utah. It was agreed that their inhabitants would resolve the issue after they had organized for statehood. In the event, none of these territories would reach the population thresholds

Above: Henry Clay was instrumental in putting together the Compromise of 1850, which delayed the crisis of secession for another decade.

that allowed them to enter the Union until after 1863, when Abraham Lincoln issued the Emancipation Proclamation signalling the end of slavery.

California was admitted as a free state. Texas gave up its territorial claims in return for $10 million. Slavery was still permitted in Washington DC, but the slave trade there – it was the largest market in the country – was ended.

The most controversial part of the agreement was the Fugitive Slave Act, passed to placate the South, which required that escaped slaves be returned to their owners. It enraged abolitionists. In 1852, one of them, Harriet Beecher Stowe, published *Uncle Tom's Cabin*, a searing indictment of slavery. Later, President Lincoln would acknowledge its impact in contributing to the popular mood that, despite the Compromise, would lead inexorably to the outbreak of the Civil War.

THE SENECA FALLS CONVENTION 1848

Around 300 people, including about 40 men, attended the first women's rights convention, which took place at Seneca Falls, New York, on 19 and 20 July 1848. Its principal organizers were Lucretia Mott and Elizabeth Cady Stanton. The meeting agreed the 'Declaration of Sentiments', written by Stanton and drawing its inspiration from the language used by Thomas Jefferson in 1776. The openness of American society had created opportunities for women to take up public roles, often as educators. Many of those involved in the struggle for women's rights were also active in the causes of abolitionism and temperance.

MILLARD FILLMORE
1850–1853

Millard Fillmore spent the first six months of 1850 presiding over the Senate as it debated the Compromise that it hoped might avoid the South's imminent secession. On 10 July 1850 he became the 13th president, following Zachary Taylor's death the previous night. He supported the Compromise of 1850, but his presidency imploded as political attitudes became polarized.

Born in 1800 in the frontier township of Locke, New York, Fillmore escaped a life of poverty through determined self-improvement, qualifying as a lawyer at the age of 23. He began his political career as a member of the single-issue Anti-Masonic party – which was gradually absorbed into the Whig party during the 1830s – in opposition to Andrew Jackson, who was a Mason. In 1843 he narrowly failed to become governor of New York; he was elected the state's financial comptroller in 1847, and the following year he was nominated as the vice-presidential candidate

Above: Fillmore replaced Taylor's Cabinet, with supporters of the 1850 Compromise.

for the Whigs, balancing the ticket headed by Taylor, whose home was then the slave state of Louisiana.

DEMISE OF THE WHIGS
Fillmore immediately restructured the Cabinet to include like-minded Whigs, including Daniel Webster who became secretary of state. In September 1850 he signed the Compromise measures into law, including the controversial Fugitive Slave Act, which, despite his anti-slavery sentiments, he felt he had the constitutional duty to enforce. His gesture boosted the activities of the Underground Railroad, which helped escaped slaves move north, and also stirred up abolitionist sentiment. This deepened political division within the Whig party, and in 1852, hopelessly disunited, they preferred to nominate another general, Winfield Scott, as their candidate. Fillmore would be the party's last president.

Fillmore was the second vice president to inherit the presidency, and like John Tyler he never won election to the White House. He was once again

attracted to the political fringe. In 1856, he became the presidential candidate of the strongly anti-immigrant and strangely named 'Know Nothing' party, winning only Maryland's eight electoral college votes. He died in 1874.

STATES ENTERING THE UNION DURING FILLMORE'S PRESIDENCY: CALIFORNIA

Entered the Union: 9 September 1850

Pre-state history: Claimed by Mexico following War of Independence against Spain (1821); proclaimed Independent Republic for one week during Mexican–American War (1846); ceded to US (1848)

Total population in 1850 census: 92,597

Total number of slaves in 1850 census: 0

Electoral College votes in 1852: 4

Born: 7 January 1800, Locke Township (now Summerhill), New York

Parents: Nathaniel (1771–1863) and Phoebe (1780–1831)

Family background: Farming

Education: Not formally educated

Religion: Unitarian

Occupation: Lawyer

Slave owner: No

Political career: New York State Assembly, 1828–31
US House of Representatives, 1833–5, 1837–45
Comptroller of New York, 1847
Vice president, 1849–50

Presidential annual salary: $25,000

Political party: Whig

Died: 8 March 1874, Buffalo, New York

ABIGAIL FILLMORE
Abigail Powers was born in 1798 in New York. She married in 1826 and had two children, a son named for his father, and a daughter called Mary. She founded the White House library. In 1842, an accident caused her health to deteriorate; she died of pneumonia in 1853, shortly after attending Franklin Pierce's inauguration. Her death was followed a year later by that of Mary.

FRANKLIN PIERCE
1853–1857

Franklin Pierce's family traced its ancestry to the Puritans. After graduation at the age of 20, he embarked on a career that mixed the law, politics, alcohol (he was a heavy drinker) and the military. He entered the New Hampshire State Legislature in 1829. Four years later he was elected to Congress, returning home in 1842 to practise law. Pierce volunteered for military service during the Mexican War of 1848, and at its end resumed his political career to become leader of New Hampshire's Democrat party. In the 1852 presidential election he defeated his former commanding officer, General Winfield Scott.

Between his election and inauguration, Pierce and his wife were involved in an accident which killed their son. The tragedy cast a cloud over their relationship and his presidency.

INEFFECTIVE GOVERNMENT

The first Northern Democrat since Martin Van Buren to win the White House, Franklin Pierce's four years in office were marked by increasing conflict between pro-slavery and anti-slavery forces. In Kansas, civil war broke out over the issue.

JANE PIERCE

Jane Appleton was born in New Hampshire in 1806 and married Pierce in 1834. Unlike her husband she believed in both temperance and abolitionism, and he periodically moderated his affection for liquor in respect of her commitment to the temperance movement. They had three sons, and the death of her youngest and only surviving boy just before she entered the White House plunged her into depression. She died in Massachusetts in 1863.

Above: Pierce was widely regarded as a 'doughface', a Northerner who tolerated slavery in the South. Democrats refused to nominate him for a second term.

In his inaugural address Pierce made his beliefs clear: "That the laws of 1850, commonly called the 'compromise measures', are strictly constitutional; and to be unhesitatingly carried into effect." To his critics, he was a 'doughface' – a Northerner with Southern sympathies.

Within six months of the Gadsden Purchase in 1853, Congress passed the Kansas–Nebraska Act, so that a northern railroad could be built from Chicago to the west coast. This repealed the Missouri Compromise, organizing these territories for statehood under the principle of 'popular sovereignty' and leaving the question of slavery to the inhabitants to decide. The battle lines crystallized. A guerrilla war broke out between pro- and anti-slavery settlers in the territory of Kansas – known as 'Bleeding Kansas' – over the question of whether it would enter the Union as a free or a slave state.

With the Whigs in terminal decline as an electoral force, the Democrats now faced opposition from the Republicans, a party formed from abolitionist Northerners who had opposed the

GADSDEN PURCHASE

With the aim of acquiring land south of the mountains to facilitate the building of a southern transcontinental railroad, James Gadsden was sent to Mexico by President Pierce to negotiate the purchase of an area of about 75,000 sq km (30,000 sq miles) in what is now southern Arizona and New Mexico. The treaty was signed in Mexico in 1853, agreeing a price of $10 million, but aroused controversy because abolitionists saw it as a way of expanding slave territory in the South.

repeal of the Missouri Compromise. Pierce lost his own party's confidence over his support of the Kansas–Nebraska Act and became the first elected incumbent not to be re-nominated by his party. Instead the 1856 Democrat convention nominated James Buchanan. Pierce retired into obscurity and died, all but forgotten, in 1869.

Born: 23 November 1804, Hillsborough (now Hillsboro), New Hampshire
Parents: Benjamin (1757–1839) and Elizabeth (1768–1844)
Family background: Military, farming, politics
Education: Bowdoin College (1824)
Religion: Episcopalian
Occupation: Lawyer, public official
Slave owner: No
Political career: New Hampshire Legislature, 1829–33
US House of Representatives, 1833–7
United States Senate, 1837–42
Presidential annual salary: $25,000
Political party: Democrat
Died: 8 October 1869, Concord, New Hampshire

JAMES BUCHANAN
1857–1861

By the time James Buchanan left the White House through the revolving door of presidential politics (since Andrew Jackson, no chief executive had managed to serve two terms) the United States had begun to disintegrate and the Democrat party had fallen apart. The combustible mixture of Northern abolitionism, Southern slavery and Western expansion ignited the fuse of secession that exploded into civil war. Faced with the impossibility of reconciling sectional differences, Buchanan did little to postpone what he and many of his contemporaries considered inevitable: the break-up of the United States.

James Buchanan volunteered for military service during the War of 1812, but did not see action, and afterwards

Below: Buchanan, an experienced politician and diplomat, could do nothing to prevent the nation's headlong rush towards civil war.

pursued a successful legal and political career. In 1819, following rumours that he had been seen with another woman, his fiancée, Anne Coleman, whose father had opposed their engagement, ended their relationship. She died a few days later: suicide was suspected. A devastated Buchanan never married.

Seeking solace in politics, he won election to Congress as a Federalist, and spent 10 years from 1821 in the House of Representatives. After his party's final collapse, he supported the Democrats. In 1832, President Jackson sent him to Russia as the US representative. Two years later he returned, becoming a member of the Senate until 1845 when President Polk appointed him secretary of state.

Buchanan had hoped for his party's presidential nomination in 1844 and tried for it again in 1852, only to lose out to Franklin Pierce, who appointed him ambassador to Britain. This enabled him to remain aloof from the political arguments resulting from the Kansas–Nebraska Act, but he was implicated in a controversial plan to acquire Cuba in order to allow the Southern slave economy to expand into the Caribbean. This made him suspect among those opposed to slavery, but his main rivals for the Democrats' presidential nomination in 1856, Franklin Pierce and Stephen Douglas, aroused even greater antipathy, and Buchanan emerged as the party's compromise candidate.

In a three-way contest against the Republican John Fremont and the former president Millard Fillmore, Buchanan won a minority of the popular vote. His convincing majority in the electoral college was built on solid support from the slave-owning South: he carried only four Northern states. The new president of the United States had been elected by an incontestably divided nation. He realized

Born: 23 April 1791, Cove Gap (near Mercersburg), Pennsylvania
Parents: James (1761?–1821) and Elizabeth (1767–1833)
Family background: Store keeping
Education: Dickinson College (1809)
Religion: Presbyterian
Occupation: Lawyer
Slave owner: No
Political career: Pennsylvania House of Representatives, 1815–16
US House of Representatives, 1821–31
Minister to Russia, 1832–4
United States Senate, 1834–45
Secretary of state, 1845–9
Minister to Britain, 1853–6
Presidential annual salary: $25,000
Political party: Democrat
Died: 1 June 1868, Wheatland (near Lancaster), Pennsylvania

what was at stake, predicting before he was inaugurated that: "Before many years the abolitionists will bring war upon this land. It may come during the next presidential term." During his term the United States began to disintegrate.

ADMINISTRATION

In his inaugural address Buchanan announced that he would not seek a second term in office. Two days later, the Supreme Court announced its decision in the case of Dred Scott v. Sanford. Its

DRED SCOTT V. SANFORD

In 1857, in the case of Dred Scott v. Sanford, the Supreme Court decided that African-Americans had no rights of citizenship, that slavery should be permitted in the western territories, and that the Missouri Compromise of 1850 was unconstitutional.

Above: Buchanan with his Cabinet of 1859, many of whose members resigned on the secession of the Confederate states.

pro-slavery stance galvanized abolitionist sentiment. In December a rigged referendum in Kansas approved the Lecompton Constitution, which would have permitted slavery in the state.

In 1858, Buchanan reiterated the language of expansionism, telling Congress, "It is, beyond question, the destiny of our race to spread themselves over the continent of North America." He also had overseas ambitions. Throughout his administration he encouraged plans to annexe Cuba, intensifying Republican opposition and confirming their assessment that like his predecessor he was a 'doughface' who favoured the expansion of slavery.

In 1859, the Republicans won a majority in the House of Representatives, but the Senate and the president's veto blocked any anti-slavery legislation and led to a political stalemate. With the next presidential election looming, the militant abolitionist John Brown launched a quixotic raid on the federal armoury at Harper's Ferry in Virginia, hoping to use the captured munitions in the slave uprising he was convinced his action would provoke. This action further polarized opinion in the North and South.

Buchanan retired in 1861. While in office he did nothing to prevent the South's secession and the formation of a new Confederacy of slave-owning states. Blamed by his critics for the outbreak of the Civil War, he maintained that it was the fault of the Republicans and his successor, Lincoln. He supported the cause of the Union, and survived to see the end of the war.

STATES ENTERING THE UNION DURING BUCHANAN'S PRESIDENCY:

MINNESOTA	OREGON	KANSAS

Entered the Union: 11 May 1858
Pre-state history: Minnesota Territory organized from lands remaining from Iowa and Wisconsin Territories (1849)
Total population in 1860 census: 172,023
Total number of slaves in 1850 census: 0
Electoral College votes in 1860: 4

Entered the Union: 14 February 1859
Pre-state history: Border dispute with Britain resolved by treaty (1846); organized as Oregon Territory (1848)
Total population in 1860 census: 52,465
Total number of slaves in 1850 census: 0
Electoral College votes in 1860: 3

Entered the Union: 29 January 1861
Pre-state history: Part of Louisiana Purchase (1803); organized as Kansas Territory (1854)
Total population in 1860 census: 107,206
Total number of slaves in 1850 census: 2
Electoral College votes in 1864: 3

THE PRESIDENTIAL ELECTION
1860

There were two presidential elections in 1860: one in the North and one in the South. The Democrats, the only party that had previously commanded support across the nation, were by then hopelessly split, finding it impossible to settle on another compromise candidate like Pierce or Buchanan who could bridge the sectional divide.

During the turbulent 1850s, as the Western territories had organized for statehood, the basis of Democrat unity had been the principle of popular sovereignty advocated by their leader in the Senate, Stephen A. Douglas. This meant leaving it to the settlers to decide for themselves whether a new state would be for or against an extension of slavery. But by 1860, interpretations of the idea were so different as to cause a schism.

NORTH AND SOUTH

Northerners thought that popular sovereignty simply kept decision-making out of the hands of Washington politicians, and that in practical terms the

Below: The four candidates each drew on different sectional support as the nation finally fell apart.

Above: Lincoln and his running mate, Hannibal Hamlin from Maine, had no appeal below the Mason–Dixon line.

new territories would prove unsuitable for the extension of the slave economy. Southerners, meanwhile, stood by what they considered was their constitutional right to bring slaves into the territories. Only after slavery had made its presence felt there could a final choice be made as to whether it should continue after statehood was achieved. 'Bleeding Kansas' dramatized the issue, as pro-slavery and anti-slavery forces battled for territorial control and the violence illustrated the failure of the compromise.

REPUBLICANS AND DEMOCRATS

In April 1860, the Democrats held their national convention in Charleston, South Carolina. Southerners proposed that a federal slave code be adopted, guaranteeing the right to take slaves into the territories. When their idea was rejected, the Southern delegates walked out. Two months later, two separate Democrat conventions, both held in Baltimore, rallied behind different candidates. The Northerners nominated Stephen Douglas from Illinois. The group of breakaway Southerners fielded Buchanan's vice president, John Breckenridge from Kentucky.

The Republicans opposed the idea of popular sovereignty. While not all were committed to abolitionism – many

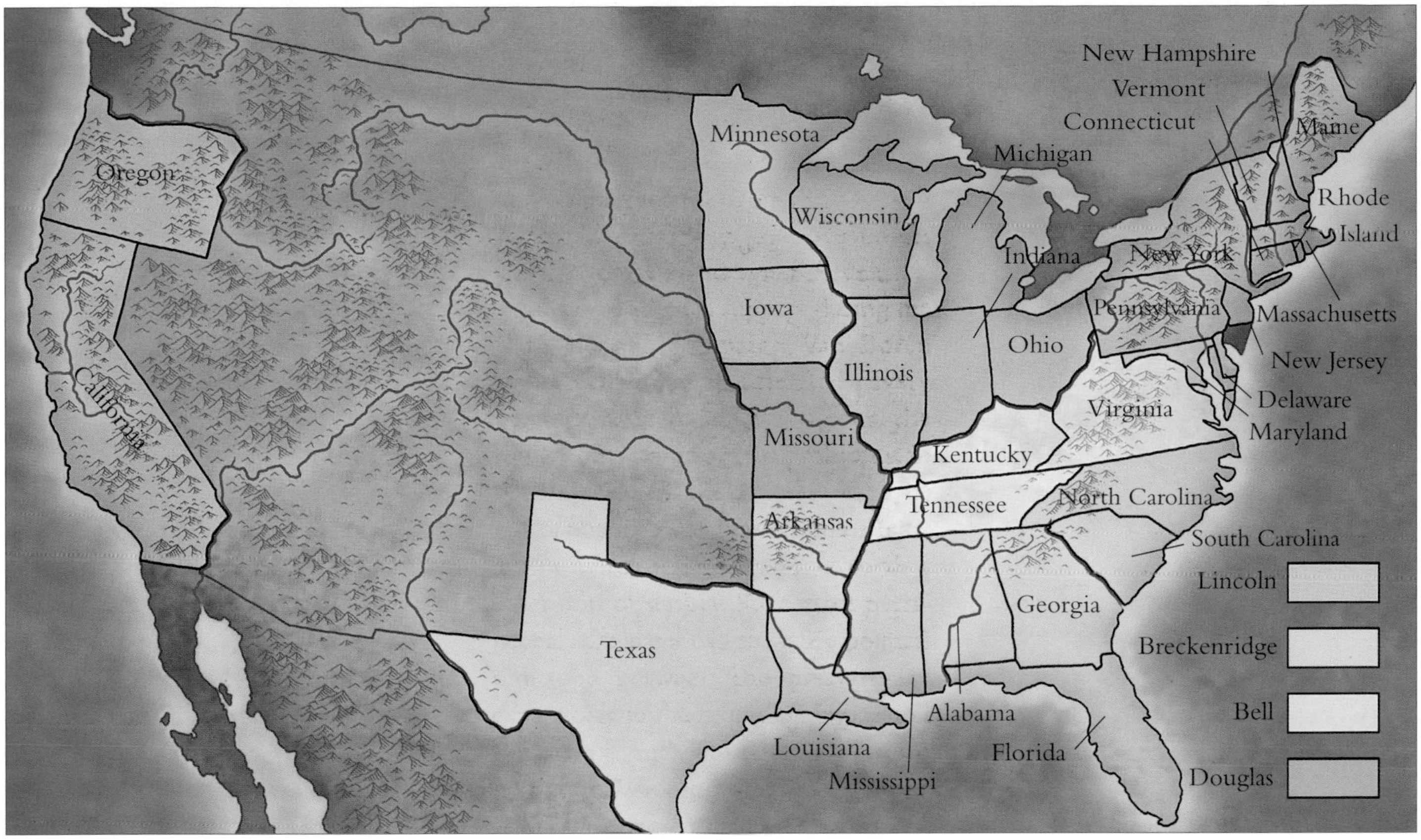
New Hampshire
Vermont
Connecticut
Maine
Minnesota
Michigan
Oregon
Wisconsin
Rhode Island
Indiana
New York
Iowa
Pennsylvania
Massachusetts
Ohio
Illinois
New Jersey
California
Virginia
Delaware
Missouri
Maryland
Kentucky
North Carolina
Tennessee
Arkansas
South Carolina
Lincoln
Georgia
Texas
Breckenridge
Bell
Alabama
Louisiana
Florida
Mississippi
Douglas

Republicans could tolerate the existing situation in the South – they nevertheless saw slavery as a moral rather than a political issue and were against its further expansion. The Republican party's candidate was Abraham Lincoln, whose electoral appeal was confined to the North.

The political landscape was further complicated by the new Constitutional Union party: a coalition of disaffected Whigs and the remnants of the Know Nothing party, hoping to appeal to those alienated by the acrimony of sectional politics. Lincoln's name did not appear on the ballot papers in most Southern states, where the Southern Democrat Breckenridge was opposed by the Constitutional Unionists' representative, John Bell, from Tennessee.

Of the 33 states then in the Union, 15 were slave-holding and 18 were free. Despite the South's over-representation in Congress and the electoral college, its electoral advantages were progressively unwinding as the North's population growth steadily outpaced it. By 1860 slave states had a total of 80 seats in the House of Representatives and 120 electoral college votes. Free states had 147 representatives in the House and 183 votes for the presidency.

With four candidates running for the White House in two distinct contests, the prospects of anyone gaining a majority of the popular vote were remote. Lincoln managed to gain around 40 per cent of it, without receiving a single vote in ten Southern states and only a small percentage in the remaining five slave states. Douglas received approximately 30 per cent, Breckenridge 18 per cent and Bell 12 per cent of the votes cast.

LINCOLN'S VICTORY

It was the electoral college that magnified the sectional divide. Lincoln's winning coalition was a result of his outright victory in 17 free states, which, together with the four additional votes he gained from New Hampshire, gave him a clear majority: 180 of the 303 electoral college votes cast. Douglas won Missouri, a slave state, and the support of the remaining three electors in New Hampshire. In the deep South, Breckenridge captured 11 states, while Bell took only Kentucky and Virginia in addition to his home state of Tennessee. In Congress, the Republicans kept their majority in the House of Representatives. The Senate, in which only a third of the members could potentially be changed, stayed in the hands of the Democrats.

With the Democrats so clearly divided, the logic of the electoral mathematics was compelling: in the electoral college the South had become, as John Calhoun had predicted, "a fixed and helpless minority" and in the Congress its position was being steadily eroded. The 1860 election was not a mandate for abolitionism – far from it – but it encouraged the Southern states to consider their next step: secession.

Above: Lincoln's election in 1860 dramatized the division between free and slave states and led to the rapid secession of the South. The states that seceded from the union formed a confederacy of states and elected their own president.

ABRAHAM LINCOLN
1861–1865

Left: Shortly after Lincoln entered the White House, the Civil War broke out. A week after it ended, he was assassinated.

London summed him up: "He was hardly a representative Republican so much as a representative American."

BEGINNINGS

Abraham Lincoln was born in a log cabin in the slave state of Kentucky. His father, Thomas, was a farmer who moved his family to Indiana when Lincoln was seven. Two years later, his mother died. He had a difficult relationship with his functionally illiterate father, and in contrast it was his stepmother, Sarah Bush Johnston, who taught Lincoln the value of education and self-improvement, although his formal schooling was sporadic.

As a youth, he enjoyed life on the Mississippi, taking produce on a flatboat to sell in New Orleans. In 1830 his family moved to Illinois, and in the following year, after another river trip to Louisiana, Lincoln left home to live in New Salem, Illinois. He had been

In 1860, the election of Abraham Lincoln precipitated a constitutional crisis that was only resolved by war. Lincoln changed America. Even before his first inaugural address, seven Southern states had seceded and formed the Confederacy. During his first three months in office, they were joined by four others, and less than six weeks after he entered the White House, there was civil war. Lincoln fought the war initially on the pretext of forcing the South back into the Union, but in issuing the Emancipation Proclamation he acknowledged its ever-present subtext: the abolition of slavery.

Lincoln explored the limits of his presidential power, creating precedents that his successors would exploit for different purposes. During four years of conflict, his considerable political skills, inspirational rhetoric and ability to read the public mood rallied support for the Union cause. At Gettysburg, he would give one of America's most inspiring and enduring orations. In his moment of victory, he was assassinated. In its obituary pages, *The Times* newspaper of

STATES SECEDING FROM THE UNION

South Carolina	20 December 1860
Mississippi	9 January 1861
Florida	10 January 1861
Alabama	11 January 1861
Georgia	19 January 1861
Louisiana	26 January 1861
Texas	1 February 1861
Virginia	17 April 1861
Arkansas	6 May 1861
North Carolina	20 May 1861
Tennessee	8 June 1861

Born: 12 February 1809, Hardin (now Larue) County, Kentucky
Parents: Thomas (1778–1851) and Nancy (1784–1818)
Family background: Farming, wood-working
Education: Not formally educated
Religion: Not proclaimed
Occupation: Lawyer
Slave owner: No
Political career: Illinois State Legislature, 1834–42
US House of Representatives, 1847–9
Presidential annual salary: $25,000
Political party: Republican
Died: 15 April 1865, Washington DC

there only six months when he was
encouraged to run for election to the
state legislature. Lincoln's first campaign
for state office was unsuccessful (he was
to win a seat in 1834). During the
election campaign he volunteered to
fight in the Black Hawk War against
local American Indians. He did not see
action, but was elected captain of his
local militia during the conflict in
which Zachary Taylor, then a colonel in
the regular army, also served.

By 1837 Lincoln had qualified as
a lawyer, and he moved to a practice
in Springfield, Illinois. In 1840 he

MARY LINCOLN
Born into a prominent Kentucky
family in 1818, Mary Todd married in
1842 and had four sons. Edward, her
second born, died in 1850 at the age
of four, and when William, born later
that year, contracted typhoid fever and
died while at the White House, the
depression from which she was prone
to suffer returned. Her mental health
declined following Lincoln's death and
she attempted suicide twice before her
death in 1882.

supported William Henry Harrison for
president, and was selected as one of the
Whig representatives in the electoral
college when the party managed to
elect its first successful candidate.
Lincoln remained active in state politics,
serving in the legislature until 1842.

As an Illinois Whig, Lincoln twice
decided against running for governor in
what was then a predominantly
Democrat state. Instead he campaigned
for a seat in the federal Congress,
securing the nomination by pledging to
serve only a single term. In 1846 he was
elected to the House of Representatives.
He vehemently opposed the conflict
with Mexico in 1848, challenging
President Polk to produce evidence of
the provocation he had used as an
excuse to demand a declaration of war.

Back in Illinois, Lincoln remained
active in Whig politics but failed in an
attempt to return to Washington as a
senator. In 1856 he joined the new
Republican party. At its convention in
Philadelphia that year Lincoln's name
was put forward as a vice-presidential
candidate, but the nomination eventually went to William Dayton from New
Jersey. Two years later he again ran for
the Senate and his debates with his

opponent, the incumbent, Stephen
Douglas, to whom he eventually lost,
clarified the debate over slavery, and
brought Lincoln national attention.
By 1860 he was one of the leading
contenders for the Republicans' presidential nomination, which he won at
the party's convention in Chicago that
May. Facing a weakened and divided
Democrat opposition, Lincoln was
elected president.

IMPENDING CRISIS
Lincoln's was not the only inaugural
address that year. On 18 February,
Jefferson Davis, who had been unanimously endorsed as the provisional
president of the Confederacy, had
spoken in Montgomery, Alabama. He
was in no doubt that "a reunion with
the States from which we have separated
is neither practicable nor desirable".
Lincoln disagreed. In his address on 4
March 1861, with Stephen Douglas,
aware of the looming crisis, murmuring
his approval, the new president appealed
to the South. He had "no purpose … to

*Below: Lincoln delivers his Gettysburg
address. He is just visible, wearing a top
hat, in the centre of the photograph.*

HABEAS CORPUS

Lincoln controversially suspended the right of habeas corpus early in the Civil War. The Constitution permitted this when "in Cases of Rebellion or Invasion the public safety may require it", but the president faced legal challenges to his action, which he ignored, allowing his critics to argue that he had abused his presidential powers. Suspension gave the administration the right to arrest suspects without subsequently producing them before a court to determine if they had been legally detained. In the Confederacy, Jefferson Davis also suspended habeas corpus and declared martial law.

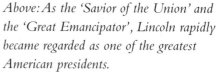

interfere with the institution of slavery in the States where it exists. I believe I have no lawful right to do so, and I have no inclination to do so." At the same time, Lincoln was adamant that the Confederacy had no constitutional status: "No State upon its own mere motion can lawfully get out of the

Below: Lincoln (centre) and his bodyguard Pinkerton (left) and General McClellan at Antietam, 1862.

Union … the central idea of secession is the essence of anarchy." Furthermore, "In your hands, my dissatisfied fellow-countrymen, and not in mine, is the momentous issue of civil war."

CIVIL WAR

Little more than a month later, on 12 April, the war started. Following a Confederate bombardment, federal forces in Fort Sumter, South Carolina, surrendered. There were no fatalities.

Above: As the 'Savior of the Union' and the 'Great Emancipator', Lincoln rapidly became regarded as one of the greatest American presidents.

On 15 April Lincoln issued a proclamation calling on the states to raise a 75,000-strong militia. Two days later, Virginia announced it would secede. The decision was endorsed in a popular referendum held the following month. Arkansas, North Carolina and Tennessee followed. In a bold extension of presidential authority, Lincoln suspended habeas corpus, blockaded Southern ports, and increased the size of the regular army and navy. At the end of April, the Confederate Constitution was ratified, and Jefferson Davis called Lincoln's proclamation mobilizing the militia a "declaration of war".

On 4 July Lincoln sent a message to Congress, focusing on events in a Southern state bordering Washington DC: "The people of Virginia have thus allowed this giant insurrection to make its nest within her borders, and this Government has no choice but to deal with it where it finds it." Thomas Jefferson's home state was about to become the principal theatre in America's Civil War.

THE EMANCIPATION PROCLAMATION

On 1 January 1863, President Lincoln issued the Emancipation Proclamation, declaring that "all persons held as slaves" in the states that had seceded "are, and henceforward shall be free". It did not extend to those slaves in the border states that had remained loyal and those parts of the Confederacy that the Union had occupied. Nevertheless, the Proclamation changed the character of the Civil War, which became not only a struggle against secession but also one for the freedom of those whom the South had enslaved.

It began badly for the Union. There was little to celebrate in 1861, as Confederate forces consolidated their hold on Virginia. There was no telling how it would end, but in his Annual Message to Congress in December, Lincoln made it clear that, "In considering the policy to be adopted for suppressing the insurrection, I have been anxious and careful that the inevitable conflict for this purpose shall not degenerate into a violent and remorseless revolutionary struggle." From the Confederacy's perspective, that is what it became.

In 1862, North and South traded blows at the Battles of Shiloh, Bull Run (for a second time), Antietam and Fredericksburg. It was after Antietam, on 22 September, that Lincoln announced his intention to issue the Emancipation Proclamation on the forthcoming New Year's Day. On 1 January 1863, he was true to his word: the slaves would be free, provided he won the war.

In July 1863 the Battle of Gettysburg proved to be a turning point in the war: the Union victory forced the Confederacy on to the defensive for the remainder of the conflict. In his Gettysburg address at the ceremonies dedicating the battlefield as a military cemetery, Lincoln gave a powerful and compelling justification of the need to fight and to preserve the principles of America's republican democracy.

Still the war dragged on. In 1864, Lincoln was re-nominated for a second term. His Democrat opponent was one of his former generals, George McClellan, and with Union morale at a low ebb, it seemed that the president might lose the election. In September, Confederate forces abandoned Atlanta, and Lincoln's political fortunes revived. In November, he defeated McClellan decisively in the election. By the time of his second inauguration in March

Above: Lincoln conferring with his military commanders. As commander-in-chief, he took responsibility for Union strategy.

1865, he looked confidently to the future: "With malice towards none, with charity for all ... let us strive to finish the work we are in, to bind up the nation's wounds." A month later the Civil War was over. The Confederate surrender at Appomattox Courthouse in Virginia came on 9 April. Abraham Lincoln had succeeded.

Five days later, the president was immortalized by an assassin's bullet. President Abraham Lincoln died on 15 April 1865.

STATES ENTERING THE UNION DURING LINCOLN'S PRESIDENCY:

WEST VIRGINIA	NEVADA

Entered the Union: 20 June 1863
Pre-state history: Part of Virginia; remained in Union after outbreak of Civil War (1861)
Total population in 1870 census: 442,014
Electoral College votes in 1864: 5

Entered the Union: 31 October 1864
Pre-state history: Part of western Utah Territory; organized as Nevada Territory (1861)
Total population in 1860 census: 42,491
Electoral College votes in 1864: 2

JEFFERSON DAVIS
CONFEDERATE PRESIDENT

Around the time that Abraham Lincoln was born in a log cabin in Kentucky, the Davis family left the state. Unlike the Lincoln family, who later moved north, they headed south, eventually settling in the state of Mississippi. With them was the youngest of their ten children: Jefferson Davis, born in June 1808 and named for the author of the Declaration of Independence.

Davis's great-grandfather had emigrated from Wales to Pennsylvania in the 18th century, and his grandfather had settled in Georgia. During the War of Independence, his father, Samuel Davis, joined the Patriot militia, taking part in the Siege of Savannah. Two of his elder brothers served with Andrew Jackson's forces in the War of 1812. Davis had more formal education than Lincoln, returning to Kentucky and completing his studies at Transylvania College before entering the United States Military Academy, at West Point, as a cadet in 1824.

In 1831 he was involved in the Black Hawk War, in which Abraham Lincoln had volunteered for the militia. Three

Above: The Confederacy existed for four years and during that time Jefferson Davis was its only president.

years later, he resigned his commission, not least because his future wife's father, Zachary Taylor, who had first-hand experience of the difficulties of family life in the military, opposed her involvement with a career soldier. He married Sarah Taylor in June. Three months later she died from malaria.

Davis spent the next decade growing cotton on his plantation near Vicksburg Mississippi, where he owned more than a hundred slaves. In 1845 he went to Washington as a member of the House of Representatives, and in the same year he married Varina Howell. They had six children.

Unlike Lincoln, Davis favoured the annexation of Texas. When war broke out with Mexico, he resigned his seat and rejoined the military. He fought alongside his former father-in-law, General Taylor, at the Battle of Buena Vista, where he was badly wounded.

In 1847, he entered the federal Senate. Although firmly identified with the politics of pro-slavery, he still favoured the South staying within the

United States, although he opposed elements of the 1850 Compromise. In 1851 he left Washington, contesting and narrowly losing the election for governor of Mississippi.

Returning to federal politics as Franklin Pierce's secretary of war, he was a leading supporter of the Kansas–Nebraska Act. When James Buchanan took office, Davis went back to the Senate and remained there until 21 January 1861. After Mississippi had voted for secession, he made his farewell speech. The South, he said, had history on its side: "When you deny us the right to withdraw from a Government which … threatens to be destructive of our rights, we but tread in the path of our fathers when we proclaim our independence and take the hazard."

A LOSING BATTLE
Given his military experience, Davis would have preferred to have been made commander-in-chief of the

Below: Davis had argued against secession while a senator, but was nevertheless inaugurated as president of the Confederacy.

Born: 3 June 1808, Christian County, Kentucky
Parents: Samuel (1756–1824) and Jane (1759–1845)
Family background: Farming
Education: West Point (1824)
Religion: Episcopal
Occupation: Soldier, planter
Slave owner: Yes
Political career: US House of Representatives, 1845–6
US Senate, 1847–51
Secretary of War, 1853–7
US Senate, 1857–61
Political party: Democrat
Died: 6 December 1889, New Orleans, Louisiana

Above: In 1862, Davis appointed Robert E. Lee (seated at table) as his chief military advisor in planning the Confederacy's campaigns.

Confederacy's armies rather than its president. Instead he was first appointed to that office in February 1861, and then elected, without opposition, in November that year. He could not overcome the problems of infrastructure, economics and politics that would ultimately undermine the Confederacy. There was no integrated transport network: railroads had been constructed merely to allow cotton to be exported, rather than to facilitate movement between Southern states. The South's predominantly agricultural economy could not compete with the North's industrial production once that was organized to support the Union war effort.

During the Civil War the South's financial position lurched from precarious to parlous as it experienced rampant inflation.

Believing that Britain, which relied on the South for most of its cotton, would be a natural ally, Davis underestimated the opposition to slavery across the Atlantic, where British workers had little sympathy for the Confederate cause. Foreign governments refused to recognize his administration, which remained isolated throughout the Civil War. Within the Confederacy, he found it difficult to exercise centralized authority, as rival states jealously guarded their political autonomy.

Davis toured the South trying to boost morale, but he could not postpone its complete political, economic and military collapse. Having escaped Union forces advancing on Richmond, he was captured on 10 May 1865 and imprisoned at Fort Monroe in Virginia. Indicted for treason the following year, he was released on bail in 1867. In 1868, the case was dropped. He survived for 21 years, widely respected in the South as a symbol of its 'Lost Cause'. On 6 December 1889 Jefferson Davis died in New Orleans.

THE 'LOST CAUSE'

Soon after the surrender at Appomattox, the South began to rationalize its defeat and to recover its sense of honour through the concept of the 'Lost Cause'. This movement emphasized the leadership qualities of Davis, Robert E. Lee and 'Stonewall' Jackson, among others, together with the endeavours of Confederate troops as they had heroically resisted the Union's attack on their homeland. With the United States anxious to avoid recriminations over slavery, the defeated Confederacy emerged victorious in the battles over how the Civil War was to be remembered.

Above: Lee surrendered to Grant at the end of the Civil War. Though the battle was lost, Lee's stature was assured.

THE CIVIL WAR
1861–1865

Why did they fight? For the Union, Southern secession threatened to destroy the 'idea of America' expressed in the Declaration of Independence and enshrined in the Constitution of 1787: a republic based upon the democratic principles of equality and liberty. For the South, the prospect of invasion from the North, in order to force it back into the political and constitutional framework that it had finally rejected, mobilized its resistance and explained its persistence. Early in the conflict a Confederate prisoner of war was asked why he had taken up arms. His reply was simple: "I'm fighting because you're down here." For almost four years, the Blue and the Gray – the colours adopted by the Union and the Confederacy – battled with one another in what remains the fiercest and most compelling conflict in American history.

START OF THE WAR

After the Battle of Fort Sumter, in which the Union troops surrendered, no serious confrontations took place until July 1861. Then, at the Battle of First Manassas (Bull Run) in Northern Virginia, the Confederates, commanded by General Pierre Beauregard, won, forcing Union troops and civilian spectators who had come from Washington to witness the action into a disorderly retreat. In Southern mythology, this was where one of its most famous generals, 'Stonewall' Jackson, won his nickname. Appearing not to panic in the confusion

Above: In April 1863 the price of wheat tripled, leading starving women to riot over the price of bread.

of the battlefield, he set an example to the rest. Lincoln swiftly removed General Irving McDowell, who was held responsible for this setback as commander of the army of the Potomac. His replacement, George McClellan, proved reluctant to engage the enemy and risk further failure. The momentum of the conflict stalled.

By January 1862, Lincoln faced increasing public discontent over the lack of military action. There were concerns about the rising costs of keeping a 700,000-strong army in the field. McClellan was suffering from typhoid fever. In conversation with Montgomery Meigs, the quartermaster general of the Union army, the president gloomily observed: "The bottom is out of the tub."

In March, the architecture of naval warfare changed. 'Ironclads' (armour-plated ships) were used for the first time. The *Merrimack*, an old Union frigate salvaged by the Confederates and renamed the *Virginia*, was fitted out with armour plating and took on with ease the Union navy's wooden ships that

---

KEY BATTLES OF THE CIVIL WAR

Fort Sumter: 12–13 April 1861, near Charleston, South Carolina. Bombardment of Union fort that began Civil War.

First Manassas (Bull Run): 21 July 1861, Virginia. Confederate victory.

Wilson's Creek: 10 August 1861, Springfield, Missouri. First major battle west of the Mississippi, won by Confederates and the Missouri State Guard.

Fort Donelson: 12–16 February 1862, Stewart County, Tennessee. Union victory.

Pea Ridge: 7–8 March 1862, near Bentonville, Arkansas. Union victory, gaining control of Missouri.

Hampton Roads: 8–9 March 1862, naval battle, notable as the first encounter between ironclads.

Shiloh: 6–7 April 1862, south-west Tennessee. Union victory.

New Orleans: 25 April–1 May 1862. Bloodless capture of largest Confederate city.

Seven Days Battles: 25 June–1 July 1862, near Richmond, Virginia. Confederate victory.

Second Manassas (Bull Run): 28–30 August 1862. Confederate victory.

Antietam: 17 September 1862, near Sharpsburg, Maryland. First major battle on Northern soil.

Fredericksburg: 11–15 December 1862, Virginia. Confederate victory.

Chancellorsville: 30 April–6 May 1863, Spotsylvania Courthouse, Virginia. Confederate victory.

Gettysburg: 1–3 July 1863, Pennsylvania. Union victory and turning point of the war.

Vicksburg: 18 May–4 July 1863, Mississippi. Union victory.

Chattanooga: 23–25 November, 1863, Tennessee. Union victory.

Atlanta: 22 July 1864. Union victory. City razed on 11 November.

Five Forks: 1 April 1865, near Petersburg, Virginia. Union victory leading to Confederate retreat.

were enforcing Lincoln's blockade of Southern ports, until the Union's equivalent, the *Monitor*, purpose built and better designed, arrived. The blockade was preserved.

The following month, at Shiloh in Tennessee, Union forces commanded by Ulysses S. Grant survived a surprise Confederate attack. It established the pattern of war: battles were decided by a combination of the competence, or lack of it, of the generals on both sides and the heroic, sometimes futile, sacrifice of their troops: the number of casualties, killed and wounded, was both appalling and terrifying.

ROBERT E. LEE

In June 1862, the most talented of the Confederacy's generals, Robert E. Lee, took command of the army of Northern Virginia. He replaced Joseph Johnston, who had been wounded at the Battle of Seven Pines, and whose reluctant approach to the war had made him an apt opponent for the equally

THE CONFEDERATE FLAG

The Confederate states had more than one flag in the four years between 1861 and 1865. The first flag (pictured top right) known as the Stars and Bars was shown with between seven and 15 stars. The second flag, the Stainless Banner (held by the soldier) was also the battle flag. It was displayed on a white background (middle right), but at sea was thought to look like a flag of truce, so the red vertical bar was added (bottom right).

Above: The second Battle of Bull Run involved tens of thousands of men on each side and was a major engagement in the Civil War.

cautious McClellan, whose army of the Potomac remained aloof from the conflict. Two months later Lee inflicted a crushing defeat on General John Pope's army of Virginia at the Battle of Second Manassas (Bull Run). In September he took the fight to the North, but at the Battle of Antietam in Maryland, amid scenes of widespread slaughter on both sides, the Union claimed victory. Lincoln sacked McClellan for refusing to press home his advantage, only to see his replacement, General Ambrose Burnside, advance into Virginia and lose the Battle of Fredericksburg.

During 1862 the war in the West ebbed and flowed. Grant's campaign, deep in Confederate territory, was disrupted by the guerrilla tactics of Nathan Forrest, who became one of the most successful cavalry commanders during the war, and forced Grant to abandon an attempt to capture the strategically important town of Vicksburg on the Mississippi River. In May 1863, Grant regained the initiative, winning five battles in three weeks, but his exploits appeared as supporting acts to the unfolding drama in the East. The fighting in Northern Virginia, between Washington and the Confederate capital of Richmond, was coupled with the occasional Southern foray into Union

territory. It was here that the most important battle of the war took place, not on Confederate soil but in Pennsylvania, at Gettysburg.

DEATH OF A GENERAL

In Virginia in May 1863, Lee defeated Burnside's replacement, Joseph Hooker, at the Battle of Chancellorsville. The victory was marred by the death of Stonewall Jackson, who was a victim of friendly fire. Afterwards, Lee moved his army north. By invading Union territory he hoped to relieve the military pressure being exerted by Grant in the West, finally to destroy the army of the Potomac, and maybe to capture Washington itself, forcing European powers to recognize the Confederacy as an independent nation.

Meanwhile Hooker clashed with Henry Halleck, whom Lincoln had appointed general in chief of the Union armies in July 1862. Forced to choose between them, the president replaced Hooker with General George Meade. Within three days he faced Lee at Gettysburg.

Left: During the Civil War new and lethal weapons used in close quarters combat caused battlefield carnage. The similarity of the flags of the Union (shown held by the Union army in blue) and the Confederacy (held by the Confederate army in grey) may have unwittingly caused the death by friendly fire of General Stonewall Jackson at Chancellorsville.

GETTYSBURG

The battle began on 1 July. For two days, the Union army resisted Confederate attacks. When the battle recommenced on the afternoon of 3 July, in Lee's words it "raged with great violence until sunset". During this decisive phase, General James Longstreet, who later claimed he had been reluctant to do so, gave Lee's order to attack Union forces ranged on Cemetery Ridge. Pickett's charge was Lee's military gamble, and he lost. Union artillery and troops repulsed the assault, with the Confederates sustaining heavy casualties. It was the beginning of the end.

UNION ADVANCES

It rained at Gettysburg on Independence Day that year and no significant fighting took place there. In the West, however, Grant finally captured Vicksburg. On 5 July the survivors of the Confederate army in Pennsylvania started the retreat to Virginia. Southern morale received a temporary boost with victory at the Battle of Chickamauga in Tennessee in September, but before the year ended, Grant won the Battle of Chattanooga and the state was in Union hands.

In March 1864, Grant became only the second officer to be promoted to the rank of lieutenant general; the first had been George Washington, taking overall command of the armies of the United States.

The Civil War had entered its final phase. In Virginia, the Wilderness Campaign became a relentless struggle of attrition. The army of the Potomac sustained more than 50,000 casualties as it advanced slowly into Confederate territory, and some of Lee's key generals were killed, wounded or captured as his Confederate army suffered proportionately similar losses.

On 2 September, General William Tecumseh Sherman captured Atlanta, a critical Confederacy citadel. He wrote to Grant, outlining his next move: "If you can whip Lee and I can march to the Atlantic, I think Uncle Abe will give us twenty days leave of absence to see the young folks". Grant's grim struggle in Virginia was complemented by Sherman's purposeful destruction of Confederate resources further South during his famous 'march to the sea' in the closing months of 1864.

THE END OF THE WAR

The final acts of war were swift. On 3 April 1865, Union troops occupied Richmond. President Lincoln visited the former Confederate capital, spending time in Jefferson Davis's study less than two days after his rival had hastily vacated it. On 9 April he arrived back in Washington. On the same day, in Virginia, at Appomattox Courthouse, a mud-spattered Lee surrendered to Grant, who was resplendent in his military uniform.

It was just under four years since the war had begun with the shelling of Fort Sumter. General Lee wrote to Jefferson Davis: "I did not see how a surrender could be avoided. We had no subsistence for man or horse, and it could not be gathered in the country. The supplies could not reach us, and the men, deprived of food and sleep for many days, were worn out and exhausted." So, too, was the Confederacy.

Grant would later recall the end of the war as a low-key affair in which he had been careful to treat Lee with respect, refusing to demand that the defeated leader give up his sword as a symbol of the Confederacy's capitulation. The hope was that the two sides could embark on a path towards reconciliation after what had been, for both of them, a brutal and costly conflict. Binding up the nation's wounds would not be easy. On 11 April Lincoln gave what proved to be his last public address. He was aware that "the re-inauguration of the national authority – reconstruction – which has had a large share of thought from the first, is pressed much more closely upon our attention. It is fraught with great difficulty." Among his audience was John Wilkes Booth. Three days later he fired the fatal shot: Abraham Lincoln, who had done so much to ensure that the United States survived the Civil War, became its most famous casualty.

THE ASSASSINATION OF LINCOLN

On the evening of 14 April 1865, Good Friday, Abraham Lincoln, accompanied by his wife, went to Ford's Theatre in Washington to watch a performance of the comedy, *Our American Cousin.* Ulysses S. Grant had turned down an invitation to share the president's box. In the play's third act, the 26-year-old John Wilkes Booth shot Lincoln in the head at close range. He jumped down on to the stage, catching his spur on the American flag decorating the box and injuring himself in the process, shouted the motto of Virginia, "*Sic semper tyrannis*" ("Thus always to tyrants") and escaped. This was an assassin who never intended to remain anonymous, and an actor who would be forever remembered for that one performance.

Lincoln did not regain consciousness. He died at 7.22 a.m. the following morning. Edwin Stanton, the secretary of war, witnessed the president's final moments, and observed: "Now he belongs to the ages." The news caused consternation in the South, which expected both blame and reprisals when it became evident that the assassin had not acted on a whim nor alone.

THE SEARCH FOR THE MURDERERS

Booth was hunted down and killed while trying to resist arrest. Private John Millington was present when the assassin was cornered in a barn near Port Royal, Virginia: "He refused to come out … I heard a shot and a moment later saw the door was open. Booth had been shot through the neck."

Afterwards the conspiracy was pieced together. On 13 April, a stranger had appeared at Edwin Stanton's house, where General Grant was visiting. He had asked that both the secretary of war and his guest be pointed out to him. The following evening Booth had visited the hotel where the vice president, Andrew Johnson, was staying, leaving a card and

the message: "Don't wish to disturb you. Are you at home? J. Wilkes Booth." While the well-mannered assassin went to find Lincoln, two accomplices, Lewis Powell and David Herold, arrived at the home of the secretary of state, William Seward. Powell forced his way into Seward's bedroom and stabbed him a number of times before escaping.

In the immediate aftermath of the assassination, Stanton sent investigators to the home of Mary Surratt, where Booth was known to stay while in Washington. When they returned to question her late on the night of 17 April, Powell arrived with a pick-axe. Surratt refused to corroborate his story that she had hired him to dig a gutter, and both were arrested. Powell was quickly identified as Seward's assailant.

By then there had been three other arrests: Edman Spangler, seen with Booth before the assassination, Samuel Arnold, also linked to Booth by incriminating correspondence, and Michael O'Laughlen, a childhood friend of Booth's, who had allegedly been given the task of assassinating Stanton, but had not carried it out.

On 20 April George Atzerodt, who was suspected of being a conspirator, was taken into custody. He had been

seen at the vice president's hotel on the day of the assassination and evidence was found connecting him to Booth. Samuel Mudd, the doctor who treated Booth's broken leg, was arrested as a member of the conspiracy and David Herold, who had helped Booth to Mudd's house, was also captured.

They were tried by a military commission. On 30 June 1865 all were found guilty of at least one of the conspiracy charges brought against them. Surratt, Powell, Atzerodt and Herold received the death sentence. Arnold, Mudd and O'Laughlen were given life imprisonment with hard labour. Spangler was jailed for six years. The remaining suspect, Mary Surratt's son, John Jr, was apprehended in Egypt the following year.

Lincoln's funeral took place on 19 April 1865. After ceremonies in the East Room of the White House, his body lay in state at the Capitol before being taken back to Springfield, Illinois, where he was finally laid to rest.

Below: Lincoln's assassination ensured his reputation as one of America's finest presidents. For his successors, the political landscape had been permanently changed as a result of the catharsis of Civil War.

ANDREW JOHNSON
1865–1869

Andrew Johnson was born in a log cabin in North Carolina. He had less formal education than Lincoln, but he did have a trade. Johnson was the first president not to have pursued a career in either the law or the military. He was apprenticed as a tailor in 1822, and four years later, not yet 18 and still illiterate, arrived in Greeneville, Tennessee, where he opened for business. In 1827, he married Eliza McCardle, the 16-year-old daughter of the local cobbler. She helped him learn to read and write.

By 1834, he had become an alderman, then mayor of Greeneville. A southern Democrat and a slave-owner, his career in state and national politics took him first to the Tennessee State Legislature, then to the House of Representatives in Washington, then back to the office of state governor for

Above: Andrew Johnson was from that part of Tennessee which remained loyal to the Union despite the state's secession. His presidency was not highly regarded.

Tennessee, and in 1857 to the federal Senate. East Tennessee, Johnson's home, was an area of the country where there was a strong abolitionist sentiment and a majority of the local population were opposed to the state's secession. It stayed loyal to the Union. In 1861, Johnson remained in Washington, the only southern senator not to resign his seat. The following year he was appointed military governor of Tennessee.

In 1864, seeking to broaden his electoral base among pro-Union Democrats, President Lincoln sacked his vice president, Hannibal Hamlin, in favour of Johnson, who served in that position for just 11 days. He inherited the office on 15 April 1865, and with it the problems of post-Civil War reconstruction, where his approach ran aground on the implacable rock of congressional opposition. He faced several political disadvantages. As a southerner who had remained loyal to the Union, he was mistrusted in the former Confederacy and by Northern

Republicans alike. Above all, Andrew Johnson was not Abraham Lincoln.

Extreme Republicans expected the defeated Confederacy to suffer. More moderate opinion favoured the Southern states' restoration to the Union under terms decided by the federal Congress. Lincoln himself had considered the simple option of using the executive power of pardon to bring the South back into the Union, believing that constitutionally the rebel states had never ceased to be part of the United States.

RECONSTRUCTION MEASURES
Johnson adopted Lincoln's agenda for reconstruction and swiftly moved it forward. Provisional governors were appointed in the former Confederacy, new constitutions abolishing slavery were written and, once they were ratified, states were allowed representation in Washington. This strategy fell apart as soon as Congress reconvened: the Republicans refused to admit Southern representatives or to recognize the reconstituted state governments.

The legislature was reasserting its power after deferring to the executive during the war years. In April 1866, Johnson's veto of a Civil Rights Act giving citizenship to all those born in the United States (it had also included Native Americans but had not given them voting rights) was overturned.

Born: 29 December 1808, Raleigh, North Carolina
Parents: Jacob (1778–1812) and Mary (1783–1856)
Family background: Labouring
Education: Not formally educated
Religion: Not proclaimed
Occupation: Tailor, public official
Slave owner: Yes – but not while president
Political career: Alderman, Greeneville, Tennessee, 1830–3
Mayor, Greeneville, Tennessee, 1834
Tennessee State Legislature, 1835–43
US House of Representatives, 1843–53
Governor of Tennessee, 1853–7
US Senate, 1857–62, 1875
Military Governor of Tennessee, 1862–5
Vice president, 1865
Presidential annual salary: $25,000
Political party: Democrat
Died: 31 July 1875, Carter's Station, Tennessee

ELIZA JOHNSON
Eliza McCardle was born in Tennessee in 1810 and married Andrew Johnson in 1826. They had five children. Illness restricted her public appearances as first lady, so her daughters took on that role. She died in 1876, six months after her husband, and four months before their 50th wedding anniversary.

Two months later, Congress enshrined this principle in the Fourteenth Amendment to the Constitution and made Southern states' acceptance of it a pre-condition for readmission. In that year's mid-term elections, Republicans won two-thirds majorities in the House and the Senate.

The following year Johnson's veto of the Reconstruction Act, introducing military government and martial law

Below: In 1864 Johnson, a southern Democrat, broadened the Republican ticket's appeal at a critical stage of the war.

in the South, was also overturned. Congress assumed the right to decide when former Confederate states might rejoin the Union. Seven had met the strict criteria for readmission by June 1868. Only Virginia, Mississippi, Texas and Georgia were still excluded.

IMPEACHMENT

In the acrimonious political atmosphere, Johnson provoked his own impeachment trial by reasserting the president's power to remove federal officials without congressional approval. He sacked Edwin Stanton as secretary of war.

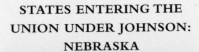

STATES ENTERING THE UNION UNDER JOHNSON: NEBRASKA

Entered the Union: 8 February 1867
Pre-state history: Organized as Nebraska Territory (1854)
Total population in 1870 census: 122,993
Electoral College votes in 1868: 3

On 24 February 1868, the House of Representatives approved the articles of impeachment by a vote of 126 to 47. In the Senate trial, with the chief justice of the Supreme Court, Salmon Chase, presiding, Johnson's opponents three times fell short by a single vote of the two-thirds majority necessary for conviction. Although it failed, impeachment achieved Congress's desired result: the president had no effective political influence for the remainder of his time in office. Following his impeachment, he failed to gain the Democrats' nomination in the 1868 presidential election.

Johnson died in July 1875, a few months after he had returned to the Senate, where his impeachment trial had so nearly brought an ignominious end to his presidency.

Below: Johnson survived impeachment when the Senate vote fell one short of the majority needed for conviction.

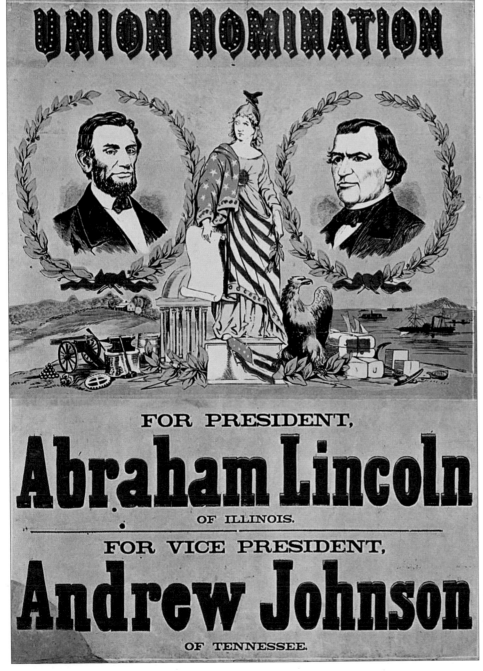

RECONSTRUCTION

Could the South change? Would the society that had embraced slavery be able to transcend its history of discrimination? Confederate ghosts continued to haunt many Southern attics: it would be another century before the Civil Rights movement forced fundamental alterations to the attitudes that were preserved there.

THE FREEDMEN'S BUREAU

With President Johnson encouraging the initial pace of reconstruction during 1865, restoring the Confederate states to the Union was more important than establishing civil rights for former slaves. Congress established the Bureau of Refugees, Freedmen and Abandoned Lands, known as the Freedmen's Bureau, to assist them. Its most notable achievement was the setting up of schools and colleges for the children of freedmen, but it was underfunded and faced mounting opposition.

Below: The Ku Klux Klan used tactics of violence and intimidation in its campaign for white supremacy.

Several Southern states implemented strict 'Black Codes' to ensure the continued social, political and economic exclusion of the black population. Most of these codes left only agricultural labour and domestic work open to blacks. They were not allowed to raise their own crops, to lease land or to live in towns and cities without the consent of a white employer.

The Ku Klux Klan was formed, with former Confederate officers among its leaders – Nathan Forrest was its first Grand Wizard – and Southern white supremacists persisted in their acts of racial terrorism until, in 1871, congressional action temporarily curbed their activities. The Ku Klux Klan reformed in 1915: its intimidating white-hooded regalia, its practice of burning crosses and its predilection for lynchings became powerful symbols of the South's continuing violent reaction to any prospect of racial integration.

CARPETBAGGERS AND SCALAWAGS

The collapse of the Confederate National Government and many state governments had left a legislative vacuum. The 1867 Reconstruction Act passed by the Radical Republicans reorganized ten former Confederate states into five military districts, each under the direct control of a US army general. The army either appointed its own officers to government posts or supervised elections and safeguarded the elected officials.

Meanwhile, a host of Northerners travelled south to take part in the reconstruction. They were characterized as 'carpetbaggers' because they travelled light – implying that they were not intending to stay long – carrying their possessions in inexpensive luggage. Some were abolitionists full of reforming zeal, who went to join the struggle

Above: 'Carpetbaggers' travelled south with all their worldly possessions, often hoping to exploit the economic opportunities of reconstruction.

for racial equality, others were teachers and missionaries who worked with the freed slaves and their children, often as the employees of the Freedmen's Bureau. But there were many others, including former Union soldiers, who were attracted by the economic opportunities opening up in the South, where the infrastructure had been left in a state of chaos, and it was from them that the term 'carpetbagger' derived its derogatory sense of an outsider who meddles in the politics of a region for personal gain.

The incomers made fortunes by buying up cotton plantations and using freedmen as hired labour, and largely took control of the Southern railroads. They formed the basis of the Republican party in the South, and together with indigenous white Republicans (who were pejoratively known by their opponents as 'scalawags', a term for disreputable and unprincipled scoundrels) and blacks elected to political office, they monopolized positions of political power.

A PLACE APART

The Fourteenth Amendment to the Constitution had extended citizenship to blacks in 1866; the Fifteenth Amendment gave them the right to vote, though most of the Southern states found ways to restrict these rights. But by 1870, the Radical Republican effort to reconstruct the South was faltering. President Ulysses S. Grant and many of his contemporaries, as well as the generations succeeding them, accepted the price of a lasting peace: recognition that the South's sense of honour could ultimately only be recovered if the Civil War was seen as the Confederacy's valiant but losing fight for self-determination – the myth of the 'Lost Cause' – rather than as a struggle to end slavery.

Economic recession resulting from the panic of 1873 hit the Southern economy hard, as the price of cotton halved and small planters and merchants were bankrupted. Carpetbaggers returned to the North, and the Republican party in the South, which had given blacks a political voice,

Above: Supporters of the former Confederacy suffered under military occupation and resented the influx of carpetbaggers.

PLESSY V. FERGUSON

The case of Plessy v. Ferguson (1896) was brought to test the constitutionality of a statute of Louisiana, which required railroads to provide separate accommodation for white and coloured passengers. Plessy had been arrested for refusing to move to the coloured section of the car.

The Supreme Court decided that if facilities were "separate but equal", then no constitutionally protected civil rights were infringed. In practice, this allowed the system of segregated institutions established in the South after the Civil War to remain in place. It was not until almost 60 years later that the Civil Rights movement finally managed to overturn the legal protection the Court had given to racial discrimination, forcing Southern states into desegregation.

dwindled. As *The Nation*, which had begun publishing weekly in 1865 and which sympathized with the cause of civil rights, correctly prophesied after the election of President Rutherford B. Hayes: "The negro will disappear from the field of national politics. Henceforth, the nation, as a nation, will have nothing more to do with him." Shortly after Hayes entered the White House in 1877, the remaining federal troops in Southern states were recalled. Without their protection, black political participation came to an end, and Republicans were replaced by newly elected white Southern Democrats. Reconstruction, along with Republican political influence in the former Confederacy, was over.

As the 'Lost Cause' myth gained historical traction, the region, which was now dominated by conservative

Democrats who would not vote for the party of Lincoln, continued to define itself in cultural and political terms as a place apart from the nation as a whole. Although slavery had been abolished, racism remained as a fundamental fault line in American politics, permeating attitudes on both sides of the Mason–Dixon line.

In 1896, the Supreme Court legitimized racial segregation throughout the American South in the case of Plessy v. Ferguson. It was a decision that the then president, Grover Cleveland, from New York, did not oppose. Black civil rights were ignored. The Confederate states had lost the war, but in many ways they had won the peace.

CHAPTER FIVE

ULYSSES S. GRANT TO WILLIAM MCKINLEY

1869–1901

Seven presidents entered the White House between 1869 and 1901. Six were Republicans, five were born in Ohio, and four had served in Congress. Three were re-elected, two were assassinated. None of them was from the former Confederacy. From the end of the Civil War to the turn of the new century, the United States experienced rapid industrialization and urbanization, fuelled by another wave of predominantly European immigration. It was the 'Gilded Age', in which the wealthy saw capitalism as confirming Charles Darwin's theory of evolution: "the survival of the fittest". Violent confrontations between workers and employers became commonplace. Within the federal government, Congress assumed a dominant role, but as the 19th century drew to a close, presidents began to take the lead in the political transitions that accompanied the USA's emergence as a world power.

Left: The meeting of the railways in Utah ensured westward expansion and heralded a new industrial era.

ULYSSES S. GRANT

1869–1877

After a turbulent military career, during which his critics alleged that his longest battle had been with the bottle, in 1868 General Ulysses S. Grant spent the accumulated political capital from his military defeat of the Confederacy in becoming the first president elected after the Civil War. He became the highest-ranking general in the United States army and the first president since Andrew Jackson to serve two full terms in the White House. Grant's political skills never matched his abilities as a soldier and he proved as incapable of mastering the intricacies of US politics as he had been successful in fighting the South's secession.

Born in Ohio in 1822, he won a scholarship to West Point Military Academy and embarked on an army career. With his natural affinity for horses and peerless skill in riding, Grant seemed destined for the cavalry, but disciplinary problems, coupled with low academic achievement (he graduated in 1843 in the bottom half of his class),

Above: A brilliant general but an unskilled politician, Grant's reputation was tainted by the widespread corruption in his administration.

meant he was assigned to the infantry instead. He served under Zachary Taylor in the Mexican War, and another of his superior officers was Robert E. Lee. By 1854, he had been promoted to captain, but his inability to accept army discipline, coupled with rumours of excessive drinking, led to a request for his resignation. He tried farming, but lost his land after a succession of crop failures. Then the Civil War came.

Back in the army, Grant impressed Lincoln with his coolness under fire, and his willingness to fight brought him regular promotions to positions of increasing military responsibility. In 1865 he accepted Robert E. Lee's surrender when the Confederacy collapsed. His status as a national hero made him an obvious choice as the Republican nominee for the presidential election of 1868. Grant won a

convincing victory, defeating the Democrat candidate, Horatio Seymour, the governor of New York.

SCANDAL IN GOVERNMENT

Apart from Hamilton Fish, a former governor of New York who became his secretary of state, most of Grant's cabinet appointments did not serve him well. As president he proved vulnerable to manipulation by those less honest than himself. Two unscrupulous businessmen, Jay Gould and Jim Fisk, gained access to the president through his brother-in-law, Abel Corbin, and convinced him that he should restrict the sale of gold, while they cornered the market. When Grant finally worked out the scheme, he instructed the Treasury to sell government gold reserves, but there was financial panic on 24 September 1869 – 'Black Friday' – as the price of gold plummeted.

Born: 27 April 1822, Clermont County, Ohio
Parents: Jesse (1794–1873) and Hannah (1798–1883)
Family background: Leather tanning
Education: West Point Military Academy (1843)
Religion: Methodist
Occupation: Soldier
Slave owner: One slave inherited from father-in-law (later freed)
Political career: None prior to presidency
Presidential annual salary: $25,000, increased to $50,000 (1873)
Political party: Republican
Died: 23 July 1885, Mount McGregor, New York

Right: The 1868 presidential election campaign was the first that took place during the reconstruction of the south.

JULIA GRANT

Born Julia Dent in 1826 on a Missouri plantation, she married Grant in 1848; her cousin, the future Confederate general James Longstreet, was one of the groom's attendants. The Grants had four children. Julia Grant revelled in being first lady, leaving the White House reluctantly. Her memoirs were finally published 73 years after her death in 1902.

Right: Julia Dent Grant, while first lady.

designs on the White House, and tried unsuccessfully to regain the Republican nomination in 1880. By 1884, speculative investments had failed. Facing mounting debt, and terminally ill with cancer of the throat, Grant took the advice of a friend, Mark Twain, and wrote the story of his remarkable life. He died just after he had completed his task, and the profits from the posthumous publication of his memoirs restored his family's fortune.

Other scandals emerged. In 1872, it became evident that the cost of building part of the Union Pacific Railroad had been massively inflated by the construction company, Credit Mobilier of America. The action created windfall profits for its owners, who also happened to be major stockholders in Union Pacific and some of whom either were or had been senior members of Grant's administration. As Grant's campaign for re-election entered its last weeks, newspapers reported that many leading politicians, including Schuyler Colfax, his vice president, who had failed to gain re-nomination, Colfax's replacement, Henry Wilson, and the future president James Garfield, were implicated in the affair. Grant survived: profiting from a divided Democrat opposition, he was re-elected in an electoral college landslide, but his presidency collapsed under the weight of charges of cronyism and corruption.

A WORSENING CRISIS

Renewed financial panic in 1873 led to economic recession. Two years later members of the administration, including Grant's private secretary, were exposed as members of the 'Whiskey Ring', diverting tax revenue from liquor into their own pockets. In 1876, William

Right: The election campaign of 1872 was designed to appeal to the working classes.

Belknap, secretary of war resigned rather than face impeachment charges relating to bribes received from American Indian agents. Later that year, Grant, who had been dissuaded from seeking a third term, admitted in his final message to Congress that: "It was my fortune, or misfortune, to be called to the office of Chief Executive without any previous political training … Failures have been errors of judgment, not of intent."

RETIREMENT

After his presidency Grant embarked on a successful world tour that served to rehabilitate his reputation. He still had

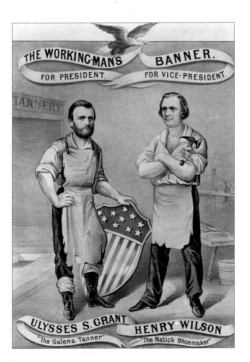

STATES ENTERING THE UNION DURING GRANT'S PRESIDENCY: COLORADO

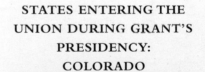

Entered the Union: 1 August 1876
Pre-state history: Part of Louisiana Purchase (1803) and land acquired from Mexico (1848); organized as Colorado Territory (1861)
Total population in 1880 census: 194,327
Electoral College votes in 1876: 3

'ROBBER BARONS'

The scandals that occurred during President Grant's administration were in part the product of the freewheeling world of post–Civil War US capitalism. Fortunes were made from industrialization, transportation, speculation and exploitation. Those able to take advantage of the opportunities on offer became either famous or notorious: sometimes both. In common with Andrew Carnegie, they started poor, or, like John Pierpoint Morgan, they inherited fortunes that they promptly increased. Their business empires, like those of John D. Rockefeller or Cornelius Vanderbilt, brought them wealth and power.

PHILANTHROPISTS

To their admirers, these architects of the USA's industrial economy were role models, demonstrating the potential of the 'American Dream': the myth that it was possible for everyone to rise in American society through talent and opportunity alone. Although some became famous for their philanthropy, to their critics they remained 'Robber Barons' – the economic opportunists who prospered in the free-for-all capitalism of the 'Gilded Age'.

ANDREW CARNEGIE

Born in 1835, Andrew Carnegie and his family emigrated from Scotland to Pennsylvania when he was 13. After initially working in a textile mill, in 1847 he became a telegraph messenger. He later joined the Pennsylvania Railroad as a telegraph operator, and by the time the Civil War broke out he had become superintendent of its Western Division. After spending the war in charge of Union telegraph communications, he saw the opportunities opening up in the steel industry to supply the track as the railroads expanded westwards. In 1875 he

Above: Carnegie realized that steel would replace iron as the metal of the future and built his fortune through investing in its production.

opened his first steel plant in Braddock, Pennsylvania, and his business interests expanded as his profits multiplied. By 1889 he was able to pay himself an annual salary of $25 million.

In 1900, at the age of 65, having built up the Carnegie Steel Company, Carnegie sold the business to J. P. Morgan for more than $400 million. Believing that "the accumulation of wealth should be followed by its distribution in the form of public endowments", he then proceeded to donate his fortune to numerous charitable causes, notably the foundation of libraries and other educational institutions. He died in 1919, one of the wealthiest and most generous philanthropists in American history.

Right: Rockefeller revolutionized the oil industry and amassed his personal fortune as the demand for oil increased.

J. P. MORGAN

During the Civil War, John Pierpoint Morgan was involved in a scheme to buy 5,000 obsolete rifles which, when refurbished, were resold to the Union army for a considerable profit. Born in 1837, the son of a financier, he inherited a fortune and increased it tenfold, using the family bank as the foundation of his

110

business empire. In 1891 he formed General Electric, the USA's principal manufacturer of electrical equipment.

In 1895 Morgan's financial influence was such that in order to save the USA's gold reserves, President Grover Cleveland was forced to allow him temporary but exclusive and hugely profitable control of the nation's gold trade. Having acquired Carnegie's steel company, Morgan created the United States Steel Corporation – the first billion-dollar industrial conglomerate.

At one time, Morgan held 72 directorships in 47 corporations. He was a passionate collector of books, works of art and gemstones. He died in 1913, having once confessed that "America is good enough for me." The comment provoked the Democrats' presidential candidate, William Jennings Bryan, to observe: "Whenever he doesn't like it, he can give it back to us."

JOHN D. ROCKEFELLER

The radical journalist Henry Demarest Lloyd once wrote that Standard Oil, John D. Rockefeller's corporation, had done everything to the Pennsylvania State Legislature except "refine it". Born in 1839, by the time he was 20 Rockefeller had set up in business for himself. After the Civil War he saw the potential of oil as the lubricant of the new industrial economy. In 1870 he established the Standard Oil Company of Ohio, and was its major shareholder. Within two decades, he had created a virtual monopoly.

Rockefeller's problem was not making money, but finding ways of spending it. He retired in 1897 and devoted himself to philanthropy: he was a major benefactor of the University of Chicago. By the time he died in 1937 he had succeeded in giving away most of his fortune.

CORNELIUS VANDERBILT

A member of an earlier generation than Carnegie, Morgan or Rockefeller, Cornelius Vanderbilt was born in 1794 and made his first fortune from steamboats on the Hudson River. Thenceforward known as 'the commodore', he turned his attention to railroads and by 1873 had established the rail link between New York and Chicago, creating one of America's most important transportation networks. During the economic depression of the same year, he built New York's Grand Central Station, providing employment for thousands of his fellow citizens. He died in 1877, leaving a fortune estimated at $100 million, at that time the largest in the United States.

Below: Vanderbilt built his fortune on the back of the industrial expansion that produced a need for steamships and railways.

THE DEVELOPMENT OF THE RAILROADS

In 1865 George Pullman built a sleeper car that set a new standard in comfort for long-distance rail travel. When one was attached to the funeral train carrying President Abraham Lincoln's body back to Illinois, it acted as an advertisement: the products of the Pullman Palace Car Company, based in Illinois, would become synonymous with transcontinental journeys by rail.

Railroads were the arteries of the USA's industrial age. Entrepreneurs, contractors and land speculators profited from building them. The Reno gang, from Indiana, had the dubious distinction of being the first to realize that railroads offered another source of income: in 1866 they boarded and robbed a train belonging to the Ohio and Mississippi Railroad.

THE TRANSCONTINENTAL RAILROAD

In 1850, Millard Fillmore approved the first Railroad Land Grant Act, allowing federal land to subsidize the construction of railroads in order to promote economic development and the settlement of the nation's interior. Abraham Lincoln, who had been a railroad lawyer in Illinois, granted more land to them than any other president. In 1862 he approved the first Pacific Railway Act, a critical step in creating the rail network that would link the east and west coasts of the United States. In deciding that the route west would start out from Omaha and be built by the newly formed Union Pacific, Lincoln enabled one of his former clients, Thomas Durant, the pivotal figure in

the Credit Mobilier scandal during Grant's presidency, to profit hugely from the government subsidies associated with the railroad's construction.

Initially, Durant was more concerned with financial wheeling and dealing than building the track, but eventually, using principally Irish immigrant workers, the Union Pacific Railroad began to make progress. The Central Pacific track was started in 1863 and was built east from Sacramento, mostly by Chinese immigrants. In 1869, the two tracks met at Promontory Summit in Utah. Further work was necessary before New York and San Francisco

Below: The Union Pacific and Central Pacific railroads met at Promontory Summit in Utah in 1869.

Above: The building of the railroads heralded the USA's industrial expansion.

Above: Luxury Pullman cars carried affluent Americans across the US.

were connected, but by June 1876 it was possible to travel between the two cities by train in less than four days.

SPECULATORS AND RAILROAD WORKERS

By the end of the 19th century, the US railroad system employed one in 20 of the nation's workforce. It had benefited from the gift of nearly 650,000 sq km (250,000 sq miles) of government land, and billions of dollars had been invested. Fortunes were made, mostly through the buying and selling of stock or by mergers and acquisitions.

The profits were in the construction rather than the operation of the rail network. From time to time, speculation and over-building helped to cause the economic recessions that recurred throughout the post-Civil War period. Many railroads went bankrupt, and they became political targets for those who saw them as rife with corruption. During his first term in the White House, Grover Cleveland made the railroads return more than 32 million ha (80 million acres) of government land

granted in the West, and also involved the federal government in trying to regulate the industry.

In 1893, as Cleveland began his second term and as another economic depression was deepening, 50 railway workers, meeting in Chicago, formed the American Railway Union. One of its leaders was Eugene Debs, born in

Below: As transport links increased the government used the railways as an incentive to move settlers west.

Indiana in 1855. He had been working on the railroads since the age of 14. In April 1894, soon after its formation, the union flexed its industrial muscle with a successful strike against the Great Northern Railway. A month later, the American Railway Union supported industrial action by Pullman workers protesting against a wage cut. In July, President Cleveland sent in federal troops to break the strike. The union's leaders, including Debs, were arrested. The following year they served seven months in jail for contempt of court.

The potential of the railroads seized the public's imagination. Nothing so dramatically symbolized the industrial and economic expansion of the United States as the building of an integrated rail network that linked its major cities. Travelling from coast to coast no longer required the heroic sacrifices of the pioneers who had struggled west in their covered wagons. Instead, it would be steel rails, steam locomotives and Pullman cars that opened up new opportunities for those restless to explore the North American continent.

THE GROWTH OF CITIES
AND POLITICAL MACHINES

When Thomas Jefferson became president in 1800, America was predominantly an agricultural nation. By 1896, when William McKinley occupied the White House, almost half the population of the United States lived in its cities, creating not only an energetic, dynamic and mobile society but also, in many urban centres, a new form of politics appropriate to the industrial age.

NEW YORK

From 1886 onwards, the first sight of America for the millions who came to the United States through the gateway of New York's Ellis Island immigration depot was the Statue of Liberty. Those who stayed in the city would soon find that it was the Democrat party organization, Tammany Hall, that dominated New York's political life.

The leaders of Tammany Hall saw what they did as 'honest graft': finding homes and jobs for newly arrived immigrants in return for their electoral support. That in turn brought them political capital and sources of patronage, and they became rich. To their critics, their organization and

Below: A newspaper cartoon depicting corrupt 'Boss' Tweed welcoming illness and disease into America.

Above: The United States opened its doors to European immigrants, who entered through the processing depot on Ellis Island, New York.

exploitation of those fresh from the boats was a corrupting influence in US democracy.

One of Tammany's most infamous leaders was William 'Boss' Tweed, who effectively controlled New York City's finances before being convicted of fraud and sentenced to 12 years in prison. With Tweed jailed, the city's Irish Catholic community, which had fought long and hard against prejudice and exclusion, finally took over the machine. Irish 'bosses' controlled Tammany Hall from 1872 onwards, giving them a voice not only in the city, but also in state and national politics.

CHICAGO

The city of Chicago began as a frontier fort in the midst of some farmhouses. It became a town in 1833. By the 1870s Chicago's population was 300,000, and by the end of the century it would be well on the way to two million. After 1871, rising from the ashes of a destructive fire, Chicago rivalled New York in developing the iconic symbol of the US city: the skyscraper.

During the 19th century, Chicago did not develop any highly organized political 'machines' like New York's Tammany Hall. It would not be until later in the 20th century that the Democrats managed to dominate the

---

TAMMANY HALL

Founded as a charity in 1789, within a decade the Tammany Society had become part of Aaron Burr's opposition to the Federalist party in New York. By the 1820s, it had established the practice of using the promise of delivering its members' votes as a way of gaining influence and political benefits. In 1830, the society moved its headquarters to Tammany Hall, the name that became synonymous with the Democrats' political machine in New York City.

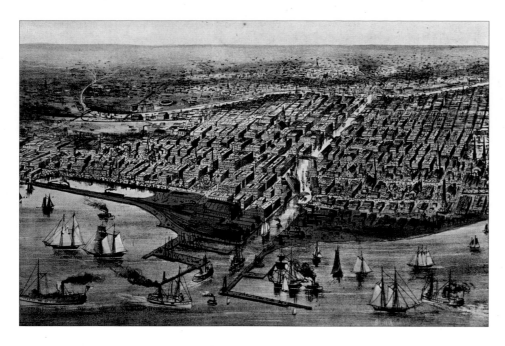

Above: New York in 1850 was a prosperous city for many.

Above: Chicago grew rapidly throughout the 19th century. Home to the world's first skyscraper, it revolutionized city planning.

mayor's office. Sometimes the city's politics seemed as combustible as its buildings had once been: in 1886, the Haymarket Riot led to the arrest and execution of anarchists accused of throwing a bomb that killed and injured police and protestors.

SAN FRANCISCO

Early in 1848, only a few hundred people lived in San Francisco; by the end of 1849 there were more than 30,000. It was built on the back of the Gold Rush. Over the next two years, six major fires destroyed it almost as quickly as it could be rebuilt. 'The wickedest city in the world' was a freewheeling place: in its red-light district, the Barbary Coast, brothels jostled with bars and dance halls competed with gambling houses, and in Chinatown there were thriving opium dens.

By the end of the 19th century, San Francisco had developed into a sophisticated city and had become the major urban financial and cultural centre of the Pacific coast. Its politics remained as corrupt as some of its morals. Nowhere was this better illustrated than in the career of Christopher Buckley, the city's 'Blind Boss' (he had lost his eyesight at the age of 30). He never held an elected office, but as the acknowledged leader of the San Francisco Democrats he ran the city's government for the last two decades of the century from his bar, the Alhambra, which was popularly known as 'Buckley's City Hall'.

POLITICS AND THE CITY

New York in the East, Chicago in the Midwest and San Francisco on the Pacific coast were three of the many US cities that grew as immigration, industrialization and the lure of the West transformed the landscape and shaped new forms of democratic politics. Cities meant votes. Political machines like Tammany Hall could deliver vital support for favoured local and national candidates. They were also where a new generation of US politicians learned their trade. Rising through the ranks of the Boston Democrat machine, in 1888 a second-generation Irish–American would give a nomination speech for Grover Cleveland at the Democrats' national convention. Seventy-two years later, Patrick Kennedy's grandson, benefiting from critical votes delivered by his party's Chicago political machine, became America's first Catholic president.

Left and below: Between 1850 (left) and 1875 (below) San Francisco's population burgeoned with the discovery of gold.

THE PRESIDENTIAL ELECTION
1876

The disputed presidential election of 1876 was one of the last convulsive aftershocks of the political earthquake of the Civil War. Unlike the two previous occasions when the electoral college had 'misfired', it was neither a tied vote nor the lack of a clear winner that confused the outcome. Having dissuaded Ulysses S. Grant from running for a third term, the Republicans won the disputed election only after an electoral commission that arbitrated the result voted on party lines and gave the White House to Rutherford B. Hayes.

The House of Representatives was not called upon to make the final decision. Instead Congress decided that a commission with five members from the House of Representatives, five members from the Senate and five Supreme Court justices would decide who should occupy the White House. Their choice of Hayes, the Republican candidate, was an accurate reflection of their partisan loyalties, but it was a distortion of democracy: his Democrat opponent, Samuel Tilden, had beaten him at the polls.

THE ELECTION AND ITS OUTCOME

Republican President Grant's administration, scandal-ridden and accident-prone, had grappled with the problems of reconstruction and a deteriorating economic climate and had lost the confidence of the nation. It had been 16 years since a Democrat had occupied the White House but in 1876, the party, which was increasingly entrenched in the South, made an electoral comeback in the rest of the country. The Democrats had the political sense to nominate Samuel Tilden for president. Not only was he from New York, which had the largest number of votes in the electoral college, he also had a reputation as a crusader against corruption, having successfully prosecuted 'Boss' Tweed of Tammany Hall. Thomas Hendricks from Indiana was selected as his running mate.

Rutherford Hayes was the former governor of Ohio, a Republican party stronghold. At the party's national convention, held in Cincinnati, he emerged as the compromise candidate, while

William Wheeler from New York – inevitably – became the party's vice-presidential nominee.

The election campaign was close fought as well as controversial. Invective and insult dominated the debate. The Democrats seized on the issue of Republican corruption and the Republicans replied with an unsubtle reminder of recent history, goading their opponents with the slogan, "Not every Democrat was a Rebel, but every Rebel was a Democrat."

Tilden won the popular vote. He swept the South. With the support of New York and Indiana among other Northern and Midwestern states, he had 184 certain electoral college votes, one short of a majority. If he could gain the votes of South Carolina, Louisiana and Florida, which, like the rest of the former Confederacy, were regarded as Democrat states, he would be the clear winner. But there was one problem: those three states remained under military rule while reconstruction continued there. They also remained under Republican control.

Another controversy involved Oregon, where the Republican Hayes had won the popular vote. In the electoral college, one of the electors committed to vote for him held a federal office and so was disqualified from the proceedings on those grounds. The state's governor, who was a Democrat, appointed a substitute elector from his own party.

On 6 December, the electoral college convened in each state capital. In the three Southern states where both parties claimed that they had won the election, and in Oregon, Republican and

Left: Tilden being congratulated on becoming president: it was initially thought that he had won the election until events proved otherwise.

Democrat electors met and cast their votes separately, submitting two different ballot papers to Congress and leaving it to politicians in Washington to decide which one should be accepted as valid. Congress compromised, setting up the electoral commission that would arbitrate the result. Its members were carefully selected: there would be seven Democrats and seven Republicans who could be expected to vote on party lines. The 15th member, Supreme Court Justice David Davis, was appointed as an independent who would have the casting vote. Then he resigned amid charges of bribery and corruption. His replacement, Joseph Bradley, who was seen as the next most impartial justice after Davis, was nevertheless inclined towards the Republicans. His deciding vote meant that the commission awarded the disputed electoral college votes to Hayes. In such extraordinary circumstances, the Republicans retained control of the White House.

THE AFTERMATH

The result of the election was so transparently fraudulent that it immediately robbed Hayes of any semblance of political legitimacy as president. The Democrats initially threatened to obstruct the formal counting of the votes in the Senate, potentially leaving the outcome of the contest still undecided when Grant's term came to an end on 4 March 1877. It was not simply an act of political pique. There were rumours of a deal, although no official negotiations took place. Still, the circumstances of the election gave Southern Democrats some leverage. Soon after Hayes entered the White House, the remaining federal troops were recalled from the former Confederacy. Reconstruction was at an end. The Republicans effectively abandoned the South to the Democrats. Tilden retired from public life. As he observed, he had: "been elected to the highest position in the gift of the people, without any of the cares and responsibilities of the office."

Above: Congress determined that the presidential election should be decided by a specially appointed electoral commission.

Below: Democrats and Republicans contested electoral college votes mainly in Southern states still under military rule.

Key
C = Connecticut
D = Delaware
M = Massachusetts
Md = Maryland
N J = New Jersey
PA = Pennsylvania
R I = Rhode Island

Hayes

Tilden

RUTHERFORD HAYES

1877–1881

Rutherford Hayes was born in Ohio in October 1822 and was named in memory of his father, who died three months before his second son was born. His mother's brother helped to support the family thereafter. After obtaining his law degree from Harvard in 1845, Hayes returned to Ohio and became a successful criminal lawyer. In 1852, he married Lucy Webb, a graduate from a women's Methodist college in Cincinnati. They had eight children, five of whom survived to adulthood.

In 1853, influenced by his wife's anti-slavery convictions, Hayes began defending runaways escaping to the free state of Ohio across the Ohio River from Kentucky. He worked with Salmon Chase, later Lincoln's secretary of the treasury and chief justice of the Supreme Court. He served with distinction during the Civil War.

After the Whigs disintegrated, Hayes helped to organize the Republican party in Ohio, and won election to the

Above: Hayes, who had a distinguished military and political career, worked to restore the presidency's prestige, despite the controversy surrounding his election.

federal House of Representatives after the war. He resigned in 1867 to serve two terms as governor of Ohio. In 1872, he retired temporarily from political life, before winning the Republican presidential nomination and the bitterly contested election of 1876.

RESTORATION OF TRUST

Although lacking a mandate, Hayes began to re-establish the political prestige of the presidency, which had been buffeted by Lincoln's assassination, Johnson's impeachment and Grant's incompetence. Responding to political realities in the South, where the Republicans were losing the battle to eradicate racism and establish civil rights for former slaves, Hayes formally ended reconstruction. Federal troops were withdrawn on condition that Southern Democrats pledged to preserve black voting rights. The 'party of Lincoln' retreated with the troops and Democrats dominated Southern politics well into the 20th century.

LUCY HAYES

The first president's wife to have a college degree, Lucy Webb was born in Ohio in 1831 and married Hayes in 1852. Despite his controversial election, she was a popular first lady. She died in 1889.

Hayes supported the USA's return to the Gold Standard (by which the dollar was supported by the guarantee that it was convertible to a fixed weight of gold), predicting correctly that it would help to revive the economy. After the Democrats won control of Congress in 1878 he won a constitutional battle to preserve the executive's veto power over legislation. In 1880, he became the first president to visit America's west coast while in office.

Hayes honoured his pledge to serve only one term. He died in 1893. His funeral procession was led by Grover Cleveland, the president elect, along with William McKinley, then governor of Ohio, who had served in Hayes's regiment during the Civil War.

THE GOLD STANDARD

To help finance the Civil War the government began printing dollar notes, known as 'greenbacks', in 1862 and established a national currency. How to deal with the inflationary pressures this produced provoked bitter postwar arguments. The Greenback party favoured expanding the currency. Advocates of 'free silver' wanted a currency based on silver as well as gold, and 'goldbugs' argued for the Gold Standard: the government's guarantee that the paper money in circulation could be redeemed at a fixed value against the precious metal.

Born: 4 October 1822, Delaware, Ohio
Parents: Rutherford (1787–1822) and Sophia (1792–1866)
Family background: Farming, whiskey distilling
Education: Kenyon College (1842), Harvard Law School (1845)
Religion: Not proclaimed
Occupation: Lawyer
Military career: Major-General, Civil War
Political career: US House of Representatives, 1865–7
Governor of Ohio, 1868–72 and 1876–7
Presidential annual salary: $50,000
Political party: Republican
Died: 17 January 1893, Fremont, Ohio

JAMES GARFIELD
1881

James Garfield was born in Ohio in 1831. An early seafaring ambition remained unfulfilled when, as a teenager, his tendency to fall off canal boats while trying to work on them led him to return home after six weeks with no more to show for his efforts than a fever. An academic life beckoned. Garfield went to the newly established Western Reserve Eclectic Institute in Hiram, Ohio, and then to Williams College in Massachusetts, graduating with honours in 1856. He returned to teach at Eclectic Institute, becoming its principal from 1857 to 1860. In 1858 he married Lucretia Rudolph, whom he had first known as a student there. Their first daughter and last-born son both died in infancy, but their eldest son survived until 1942, and four other children lived through World War II.

Not content with academic life, Garfield studied law privately and was admitted to the Ohio Bar in 1860, by which time he was already active in politics. A Republican, in 1859 he

Above: Garfield was assassinated before he could make any impact on the presidency.

became the youngest member of the Ohio State Senate. Following two years' military service as an officer during the Civil War, he was elected to the House of Representatives.

PRESIDENTIAL NOMINATION
He remained a Washington politician, rising to become House minority leader during Hayes's presidency. In 1880 the Ohio State Legislature elected him to the Senate. Later that year, at the Republican convention in Chicago, Garfield emerged as a compromise candidate and secured the presidential

nomination. In the election he beat the Democrat, Winfield Hancock, narrowly in the popular vote but convincingly in the electoral college.

Garfield was president for slightly more than six months. On 19 September 1881, he died of complications following an assassination attempt the previous July. He was a victim of the spoils system, the system of political patronage that had become entrenched in government at all levels. Charles Guiteau, a deranged and disgruntled office-seeker, whom Garfield had refused to appoint to a diplomatic post in Paris (on the basis that he was completely unqualified for it), shot the president as he prepared to leave Washington from the Baltimore and Potomac railway station. Even Alexander Graham Bell's new device – the metal detector, hastily invented for the purpose – could not trace the bullet, which was lodged in his pancreas, and his doctors failed to remove it. Garfield died from blood poisoning in the same New Jersey hospital in which his wife was then being treated for malaria.

Born: 19 November 1831, Orange, Ohio
Parents: Abram (1799–1833) and Eliza (1801–88)
Family background: Farming
Education: Williams College (1856)
Religion: Disciples of Christ
Occupation: Teacher
Military career: Major-General, Civil War
Political career: Ohio State Senate, 1859–61
US House of Representatives, 1863–80
US Senate, 1880
Presidential annual salary: $50,000
Political party: Republican
Died: 19 September 1881, Elberon, New Jersey

LUCRETIA GARFIELD
Born in 1832 in Ohio, Lucretia Rudolph married James Garfield in 1858. Of her seven children, five survived to adulthood. She was a conscientious and hospitable first lady, but was convalescing from malaria and nervous exhaustion when her husband was assassinated. She survived him by 36 years, until her death in 1918.

SPOILS SYSTEM
'To the victor go the spoils' describes the system in the United States by which a political party winning power gave government positions to its supporters, rewarding loyalty rather than appointing on merit. The drawback was that an incoming administration would be besieged by office-seekers, whose various demands it could not possibly hope to satisfy. The response to the assassination of Garfield was the passing of the Pendleton Civil Service Reform Act in 1883, establishing a Civil Service Commission that made an increasing number of federal appointments according to merit.

CHESTER ARTHUR

1881–1885

His political career was forged in the corrupt world of New York machine politics, but as president, Chester Arthur transcended his background, making honesty and integrity central to the conduct of his administration.

Chester Arthur was born in Vermont in 1829. His father was a Baptist minister and a committed abolitionist, who moved his family to New York. In 1848, Arthur graduated from Union College in Schenectady. After a few years' teaching he became a lawyer, and acted in some high-profile civil rights cases, including one leading to the desegregation of New York's streetcars. In 1859, he married Ellen Herndon. They had three children.

Arthur had relatives by marriage in the Confederacy. During the Civil War he was appointed quartermaster general of the state of New York, so did not see active service. In 1863 following the war, he resumed his law practice and became involved in politics as an influential member of the Republican party machine, working for Roscoe Conkling, the party's leader in New

York and a US senator. From 1871 to 1878 Arthur was collector of the Port of New York, a lucrative post that involved supervising the receipt of import duties. Some of the revenue was routinely diverted to the coffers of the state Republican party, which had close ties with the Customs House. During Rutherford Hayes's administration, the president eventually managed to reform the New York customs house. Conkling, who Hayes saw as a political rival in the Republican party, lost his source of patronage. Arthur was suspended from office.

In 1880, anxious to improve their prospects of winning New York, Garfield's supporters offered Arthur the vice-presidential nomination. The offer was accepted. Chester Arthur, the only Republican president in the late 19th century not to come from Ohio, was included on the party's ticket in 1880 principally because he was from New York, the state that then had the most electoral college votes.

He became president on 20 September 1881. Once again a vice president inherited the office but was never elected to it. In 1883, he signed the Pendleton Civil Service Reform

Left: As president, Arthur confounded his critics by supporting the reform of the spoils system.

Act, an attempt to insulate the federal bureaucracy from political influence. When his Tariff Commission suggested deep cutbacks in protectionist taxes, a nervous Congress failed to support it, passing a compromise 'Mongrel Tariff', which lowered duties on some items but raised them on a wide variety of manufactured goods. He was more successful in persuading Congress to fund the rebuilding of the navy and the refurbishment of the White House (by Louise Comfort Tiffany) as symbols of national power and prestige.

In 1882, he was diagnosed with Bright's Disease, a progressive illness affecting the kidneys. His condition remained unpublicized but two years later it played a part in his reluctant decision not to pursue the Republican presidential nomination. In 1886, two years after leaving the White House, Chester Arthur died in New York, at the age of 57.

Born: 5 October 1829, Fairfield, Vermont
Parents: William (1796–1875) and Malvina (1802–69)
Family background: Baptist ministry
Education: Union College (1848)
Religion: Episcopalian
Occupation: Lawyer
Military career: Brigadier general, Civil War
Political career: Vice president, 1881
Presidential annual salary: $50,000
Political party: Republican
Died: 18 November 1886, New York

ELLEN ARTHUR

Chester Arthur married Ellen Herndon in 1859. Born in Virginia in 1837, her first child died aged three, but a son named for his father and a daughter called after her mother survived to adulthood. Ellen died from pneumonia in 1880, the year before her husband became president, and he deeply mourned his loss: Arthur had a stained glass window erected in St John's Episcopal Church and a light kept burning inside so that he could see the window from his desk. Arthur's sister assumed the duties of hostess in the White House and looked after his children.

GROVER CLEVELAND

1885–1889

After five Republican presidents it was time for a change. The first Democrat to be elected since James Buchanan, in 1884 Grover Cleveland benefited not only from the party's revival in the South but also from the fact that, like his predecessor, he came from New York. His achievement remains unique: he is the only president to serve non-consecutive terms, winning back the White House in 1892 after losing his first re-election campaign four years previously.

When Cleveland was 16, his father, a Presbyterian minister, died. Cleveland supported his family, forgoing a college education, but still qualified as a lawyer. During the Civil War, in which, like others, he avoided military service by paying a substitute to fight in his place, he became a district attorney in Erie County, New York, and from 1870 to 1873 he served as its sheriff. In 1882 he embarked on his political career: in a

Below: Grover Cleveland was the only president to have a wedding at the White House, though the second to marry in office.

year he had moved from the mayor's office in Buffalo to the governor's mansion in Albany.

A Democrat populist (known to some as 'Uncle Jumbo'), with a reputation for confronting Tammany Hall's corruption, the fact that he might win New York made him an appealing choice for a party that had lost seven presidential elections in a row. In 1884 he faced the Republican, Senator James Blaine, an unpopular candidate even within his own party. During the campaign, Republican attacks on Cleveland's character centred on the possibility that he had fathered an illegitimate child. But in a close contest, his 1200-vote winning margin in New York finally broke the Republican stranglehold on the presidency.

POLITICAL UNPOPULARITY

Using his veto power liberally, Cleveland notably refused to sanction pensions for Civil War veterans. His economic policies, commitment to 'sound money', belief in the Gold Standard and tariff reduction, were politically divisive. Democrats in the South and West disagreed with his conviction that paper money should be backed by gold. Even though some within the party supported tariff reform, the president failed to provide strong leadership on this issue.

In 1886 his marriage to Frances Folsom, 27 years his junior, was a major event: the first presidential wedding in the White House. If the 1888 election

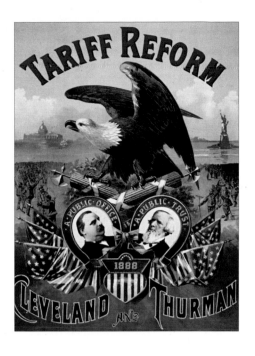

Above: In 1888, Cleveland lost his home state and the electoral college, despite winning the popular vote.

had been decided by the popular vote, he would have won his second term then. Electoral college defeat, including the loss of New York, forced him to wait four years for the re-match.

FRANCES CLEVELAND

Born Frances Folsom in 1864, she was the youngest ever first lady and survived longest after leaving the White House. She had five children. Frances died in 1947 at the age of 83.

Born: 18 March 1837, Caldwell, New Jersey
Parents: Richard (1804–53) and Anne (1806–82)
Family background: Presbyterian ministry
Education: Not formally educated
Religion: Presbyterian
Occupation: Lawyer
Military career: None
Political career: Sheriff, Erie County, New York, 1870–3
Mayor, Buffalo, New York, 1882
Governor of New York, 1883–5
Presidential annual salary: $50,000
Political party: Democrat
Died: 24 June 1908, Princeton, New Jersey

BENJAMIN HARRISON
1889–1893

Named for his great-grandfather, who had signed the Declaration of Independence, Benjamin Harrison was seven years old when his grandfather, President William Henry Harrison, died. Forty-eight years later, he entered the White House at a challenging time: political and economic turbulence had led to a succession of one-term presidencies. Harrison did not break the trend. His brief Republican interlude merely interrupted Cleveland's political tour de force.

Harrison's robust attitude to foreign affairs did not detract from the unpopularity caused by his domestic policies. He grappled with the onset of the deepest economic depression that the United States had experienced up to that time, which caused irreparable damage to his prospects for a second term and helped ensure Cleveland's triumphant return to office.

Harrison was born in Ohio in 1833, and graduated from Miami University in 1852. The following year he married

Below: Harrison fought in the Civil War, where he received rapid promotion and served with distinction.

Above: Harrison controversially approved congressional spending of a billion dollars, hoping to improve the USA's economic infrastructure.

Caroline Scott and they had three children. After qualifying as a lawyer, in 1854 he moved to Indiana. He joined the Republican party and entered politics in 1857, when he won election as attorney for the city of Indianapolis. During the Civil War he rose to become a brigadier general and was involved in Sherman's Atlanta campaign.

In 1876 Harrison lost an election for state governor, but four years later he entered the federal Senate. In 1888 he won the Republicans' presidential nomination and his victory in the critical swing states of New York and Indiana gave him the necessary electoral college votes to become president, despite receiving 90,000 fewer votes than Grover Cleveland. The Republicans also gained control of Congress.

SHERMAN ANTI-TRUST ACT

In terms of domestic policy, 1890 was the key year of Harrison's presidency. As well as signing into law an act providing benefits for Union veterans, he saw through the Sherman Anti-Trust Act, the first federal law of its kind

Born: 20 August 1833, North Bend, Ohio
Parents: John (1804–78) and Elizabeth (1810–50)
Family background: Farming
Education: Miami University, Ohio (1852)
Religion: Presbyterian
Occupation: Lawyer
Military career: Brigadier general, Civil War
Political career: US Senate, 1881–7
Presidential annual salary: $50,000
Political party: Republican
Died: 13 March 1901, Indianapolis, Indiana

aimed at regulating the activities of US corporations, and the Sherman Silver Purchase Act, which increased the supply of silver coinage in circulation. This backfired as the Treasury was required to buy the additional silver with notes that could be redeemed with either silver or gold: most investors demanded gold for their silver notes, causing a run on gold reserves.

BILLION DOLLAR CONGRESS

Most controversially, President Harrison supported the punitive McKinley Tariff, which imposed duties averaging more than 48 per cent on a wide range of imported goods. The tariff, which was the highest in US history, was designed to safeguard US agriculture, but it

CAROLINE HARRISON

Born in Ohio in 1832, Caroline Scott married Benjamin Harrison in 1853 and had three children, the last of whom was stillborn. She died in the White House from pneumonia in 1892.

STATES ENTERING THE UNION DURING HARRISON'S PRESIDENCY:

NORTH DAKOTA

Entered the Union: 1889
Pre-state history: Part of Louisiana Purchase (1803); organized as Dakota Territory (1861)
Total population in 1890 census: 182,719
Electoral College votes in 1892: 2

MONTANA

Entered the Union: 1889
Pre-state history: Part of Louisiana Purchase (1803); organized as Montana Territory (1864)
Total population in 1880 census: 132,159
Electoral College votes in 1892: 3

IDAHO

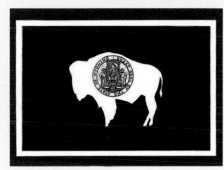

Entered the Union: 1889
Pre-state history: Part of Oregon and Washington Territories; organized as Idaho Territory (1863)
Total population in 1880 census: 84,385
Electoral College votes in 1892: 3

SOUTH DAKOTA

Entered the Union: 1889
Pre-state history: Part of Louisiana Purchase (1803); organized as Dakota Territory (1861)
Total population in 1880 census: 328,808
Electoral College votes in 1892: 2

WASHINGTON

Entered the Union: 1889
Pre-state history: Part of Oregon country (1846); organized as Washington Territory (1853)
Total population in 1880 census: 349,390
Electoral College votes in 1892: 4

WYOMING

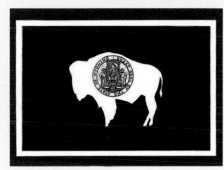

Entered the Union: 1890
Pre-state history: Part of Louisiana Purchase (1803), Oregon country (1846) and land acquired from Mexico (1848); organized as Wyoming Territory (1868)
Total population in 1880 census: 60,705
Electoral College votes in 1892: 3

had the effect of raising prices sharply all round and in its wake caused widespread economic hardship.

Republicans dominated the 'Billion Dollar Congress', so-called because of its lavish spending plans, which cost the party much public support. In November 1890, the Democrats regained control of the House of Representatives in the mid-term elections, weakening Harrison's position within his own party.

With his secretary of state James Blaine, Harrison pursued an activist foreign policy: threatening war against Chile and standing firm in diplomatic confrontations with European powers. He supported the annexation of Hawaii when its monarchy was overthrown and a republic set up in 1893, but the treaty he put forward was later withdrawn by Grover Cleveland. (Hawaii eventually became a US territory in 1900.)

Harrison's wife Caroline died during his unsuccessful re-election campaign. After leaving office, he married Mary Dimmick, his first wife's niece, with whom he had a daughter. He became a well-regarded elder statesman, and died in 1901 in Indianapolis.

THE CHICAGO WORLD'S FAIR

1893

On 1 May 1893, less than eight weeks after his second inauguration, President Grover Cleveland was in Chicago. The occasion was the opening ceremony of the Chicago World Exposition, marking the 400th anniversary of the discovery of America by adventurers from Europe. Due to construction delays it was a year late, but that seemed scarcely to matter. The president's speech made it clear that the fair was really to be a celebration of America's contemporary achievements rather than a nostalgic look at the nation's past: "I am here to join in congratulations which are appropriate to this day. Surrounded by the remarkable results of American entrepreneurship and American energy and in view of the outstanding examples of American skills and intelligence we do not need to fear that our congratulations will be exaggerated."

Then the president pressed a button on a table decorated with the United States flag and the fair came to life: fountains shot into the air, waterfalls tumbled back to the earth, flags unfurled and bells rang out. The thousands gathered on the 240ha (600 acre) site at Jackson Park near Lake Michigan were the first among the 27.5 million visitors who would see the attractions before the World's Fair closed almost six months later on 30 October.

Chicago had beaten off challenges from St Louis, New York and Washington DC to host the event. The fair became a showcase for the city as well as for the United States. Other nations were represented there, but it was the sheer scale of the American achievement in creating the White City that housed the exhibition halls that captured the public imagination. In addition, there was Midway Plaisance, the prototype amusement park that would influence successors from Coney Island in New York to Disneyland.

It was dominated by George Ferris's invention: the 'observation wheel' to which he gave his name and which, after it opened in June, gave more than 1.5 million people a unique perspective on the fair below.

THE POWER OF ELECTRICITY

Electricity was supplied by the Westinghouse power company. For many visitors the sight of an electric light bulb was a novelty, but other

Above: The Chicago World's Fair was visited by more than 27 million people.

potential applications of electricity were more amazing still in household appliances such as irons and sewing machines. An early version of a fax machine was on display, and Alexander Bell's telephone company demonstrated the potential of long-distance calls between Chicago and New York. In addition to his phonographs, Thomas Edison presented a new invention, the kineto-graph, which impressed his audiences with short (they lasted less than half a minute) moving picture shows.

The fair was not only about invention. Lectures were organized as part of the daily programme of events. A future president, Woodrow Wilson, delivered one. So too did the historian, Frederick Jackson Turner. His talk, 'The Significance of the Frontier in American History', became the most influential interpretation of America's past, linking the experience of settlement with the development of national identity. Turner argued that life on the frontier shaped the American character. European immigrants, through the experience of taming the wilderness, developed the

Below: The original Ferris wheel was the centre of attraction at the fair, providing entertainment and far-reaching views.

Above: Buffalo Bill's Wild West was the most popular show of its time.

qualities of 'rugged individualism' that were uniquely American. As a reminder of the expansion across the continent, as they left, the crowds could visit

Buffalo Bill's Wild West, the show that was then in its tenth year of touring the United States and which had been set up on a site near the fair.

In his opening remarks, the president suggested that the USA had come of age: "In the presence of the oldest nations on Earth we point to our achievements that are shown here and do not need to ask for forbearance on account of our youth. The enthusiasm for our own work forms the welcome that we extend to those who have come to us from far away to demonstrate, together with us, growth and efforts in the area of civilization."

The Chicago World's Fair was a visible sign of the USA's growing self-confidence and sense of its potential achievement. Barely a century old, the United States was still recovering from the Civil War that had threatened its existence as a federal democratic republic. Its history had been one of ter-ritorial expansion. Economic growth, industrialization and increasing urban-ization had changed the face of society as immigration and migration spread America's population throughout the continental United States. In Chicago in 1893 it looked to the future: through a combination of commercial flair and technological invention, it would increasingly influence and shape the politics, economic life and popular culture of the modern world.

GROVER CLEVELAND

1893–1897

By the time Grover Cleveland returned to the White House in 1893, the first of his five children had been born, and two more daughters were born while he was president. His second inauguration took place two weeks before his 56th birthday. He had won the election convincingly, despite the impact of the Populist Party – which won 22 electoral college votes in six states – on the result. Cleveland inherited an economy that was heading into recession, and it was this situation that determined the fortunes of his second administration.

DOMESTIC CRISIS

In 1894, almost one in five of the US workforce was unemployed. Cleveland's forceful intervention in the 'Pullman strike' on the Chicago railroad lost him support among Northern workers. His repeal of the Sherman Silver Purchase Act, which he argued had helped to cause the economic depression, alienated Democrats in the South and the West, who had seen agricultural prices

Right: Rioters burn rolling stock in the strikes of 1894. The president called in the infantry to end the strikes.

Left: Cleveland's second term in office began with a financial panic on the stock exchange.

rise as a result of the inflationary pressures the Act had caused. Cleveland's continued determination to maintain the Gold Standard, the basis of 'sound money', led him to rely on J. P. Morgan to broker the necessary deals, leaving him open to the criticism that he was a puppet of Wall Street financiers. The 1894 mid-term elections were a predictable disaster for the Democrats: their only electoral support came from the Deep South.

In foreign policy, Cleveland did not intervene when Cuba rebelled against Spanish imperial control, and he reversed Harrison's policy in favour of annexing Hawaii. Where he did exert US power it was in support of the precepts of the Monroe Doctrine: threatening war in order to force Britain to accept an arbitrated solution in a boundary dispute with Venezuela.

Cleveland ended his second term deeply unpopular within his own party and in the nation as a whole. He took no part in the 1896 presidential campaign, in which the Democrats chose the populist candidate William

STATES ENTERING THE UNION UNDER CLEVELAND'S PRESIDENCY: UTAH

Entered the Union: 1896
Pre-state history: Acquired from Mexico (1848); organized as Utah Territory (1850)
Total population in 1880 census: 210,779
Electoral College votes in 1896: 3

Jennings Bryan and lost the White House to the Republicans and William McKinley.

In 1908, he died. Throughout his career in public service he had set great value on his reputation for integrity and political independence. His last words were a plea for understanding: "I have tried so hard to do right."

THE DEVELOPMENT OF NEWSPAPERS

During the 19th century the newspaper industry in the United States expanded rapidly, helped by new technologies including the steam press and the telegraph. News agencies such as Associated Press gathered and distributed news with increasing efficiency, both nationally and internationally: Britain, for example, first became aware of Abraham Lincoln's assassination in 1865 from reports carried in London by the Reuters News Agency. After the Civil War, two American newspaper tycoons came to dominate national headlines: Joseph Pulitzer and Randolph Hearst.

JOSEPH PULITZER

Born in Mako, Hungary in 1847, Pulitzer emigrated to the United States in 1864, seeking a military career, and served in the final year of the Civil War. He launched his career as a reporter on a German language paper in St Louis, which had a large German-American community, and in 1879 he became sole proprietor of a daily paper. In 1877 he married Kate Davis, a niece of the former president of the Confederacy.

In 1883 Pulitzer bought the *New York World* from Jay Gould, and set about increasing its circulation by combining news and sensational stories with serious crusades against corporate excesses and abuses of political power. He was elected to Congress as a Democrat but served only a year, resigning to concentrate on his newspaper business.

Overwork led to ill health and at the age of 40, he lost his sight. When eventually he gave up managing newspapers, he became a philanthropist, establishing the prizes for journalistic and literary achievement that are still associated with his name. In 1911, he died on board the yacht he had named *Liberty*: arriving a penniless immigrant, he had achieved the 'American Dream'.

RANDOLPH HEARST

Born into a wealthy Californian family in 1863, Randolph Hearst studied journalism at Harvard, returning home to publish his father's newspaper, the *San Francisco Examiner*, which he transformed into a popular success by modelling it on Pulitzer's *New York World*. In 1895 he acquired the *New York Morning Journal* and embarked on a circulation war with Pulitzer, employing the sensationalism and disregard for truth for

Above: Randolph Hearst built a newspaper empire and had hopes of becoming president of the United States.

which the term 'yellow journalism' was coined at the time. In 1898 when Frederic Remington, whom he had sent to Havana to provide pictures of rumoured Spanish atrocities, reported back that there was nothing much to sketch, Hearst, who like Pulitzer advocated American intervention in Cuba, allegedly sent him a telegram: "You furnish the pictures and I'll furnish the war."

Hearst represented the Democrats in Congress and campaigned unsuccessfully for the 1904 Democrat presidential nomination. The previous year he had married Millicent Willson, but it would be the actress Marion Davies who lived with him at San Simeon, the spectacular Californian castle he began building in 1919. The model for Orson Welles in his 1941 film *Citizen Kane*, Hearst died in 1951. His media empire survives.

Left: Newspapers revolutionized communication, and better transport links ensured their speedy distribution.

WILLIAM McKINLEY
1897–1901

By the end of the century, the Republican party had strayed from its roots in the radical cause of abolitionism to become the preferred choice of those who believed that the business of the United States was business. William McKinley's election campaign in 1896 was the first in which money played a decisive role. His populist opponent, William Jennings Bryan, mixed a powerful cocktail of support among the hitherto politically dispossessed in the South and the West. In a hard-fought contest, McKinley easily outspent Bryan and won, a feat he was to repeat with slightly more ease against the same opponent four years later.

William McKinley not only announced America's arrival on the world stage as a potential rival to European imperial powers, he also helped to lay the foundations for the 20th-century development of the presidency as the focal point of the United States political system.

After an education disrupted by ill health and financial problems, the

Below: McKinley's election campaign was the most expensive of its time.

Above: McKinley presided over an era of prosperity, winning a second term before falling victim to an assassin's bullet.

18-year-old McKinley joined the Ohio Volunteers when the Civil War broke out. He served as an aide to Rutherford Hayes, seeing action at Antietam. After the war, he became a lawyer and went into Republican politics. In 1871 he married Ida Saxton. They had two daughters, who both died in childhood.

POLITICAL CAREER

In 1876 McKinley won election to the federal House of Representatives. He remained in Washington for six years. Rejected by the voters in 1882, he was re-elected two years later, spending another six years in Congress until swept away in the mid-term Democrat landslide during the administration of his political mentor, President Hayes. McKinley returned to Ohio and in 1891 became governor. By 1896 he was the front-runner for the Republican presidential nomination. Helped by his campaign manager, Mark Hanna, a businessman from Ohio, McKinley was chosen as his party's candidate on the first ballot at the Republican convention in St Louis.

His election looked doubtful. The Democrats, strengthened by the support of the Populist party, had a potentially winning electoral college coalition in the South and West and a formidable candidate: William Jennings Bryan. On the principal political issue of the day – preserving the currency based on gold, or increasing the money supply by allowing the coinage of 'free silver' – Bryan was in no doubt. His appeal not to "crucify mankind on a cross of gold" was echoed by many ordinary voters.

The prospect that Bryan would become president both shocked and galvanized the business community. A gold-backed currency favoured industrial interests in the north-east and the developing cities of the Midwest. Silver inflation might appeal to the agricultural producers of the South and West but could cause financial instability. Business favoured McKinley, and money assumed its central role in presidential elections. Mark Hanna was able to raise $7 million in contributions; Bryan, with only $300,000 to spend, and despite more vigorous campaigning, was comprehensively defeated.

Born: 29 January 1843, Niles, Ohio
Parents: William (1807–92) and Nancy (1809–97)
Family background: Iron manufacturing
Education: Allegheny College
Religion: Methodist
Occupation: Lawyer
Military career: Major, Civil War
Political career: US House of Representatives, 1877–91
Governor of Ohio, 1892–6
Presidential annual salary: $50,000
Political party: Republican
Died: 14 September 1901, Buffalo, New York

Above: With a successful term in office behind him, McKinley won the election of 1900 comfortably.

In 1896 gold had been discovered in the Klondike. Prospectors rushed to Alaska and the Yukon and the first shipments arrived in the United States the following year. The production of gold doubled during the 1890s, undermining the argument for 'free silver'. In 1900, McKinley committed the United States to the Gold Standard.

Later that year he was re-elected, again beating William Jennings Bryan, this time by an even greater margin. His vice president, Garret Hobart, had died in 1899. In his place, the Republican nominee was the governor of New York: Theodore Roosevelt.

THE US GOES TO WAR

Although as a Republican McKinley was firmly identified with business interests, he also courted labour leaders, appointing some to positions in his administration. But the key to rallying national support lay in his decision to go to war. As president, he flexed the USA's military muscle overseas: the Spanish–American War would bring the United States an empire of its own, in the Philippines, and also Cuba, closer to home and long coveted.

On 15 February 1898, the US battleship *Maine* exploded in Havana harbour. Though probably an accident, the US took it to be an act of provocation by the Spanish, who were then fighting against Cuban revolutionaries supported by US interests. On 23 April, with McKinley's diplomacy exhausted, Spain declared war on the United States: two days later, Congress reciprocated. It was over by December. Cuba gained a form of independence: it would be under US military occupation until 1902 and a protectorate until 1934. In addition to acquiring Puerto Rico and Guam, the United States bought the Philippines for $20 million. The investment immediately turned sour, as a nationalist insurgency there involved the USA in another four years of fighting.

END OF AN ERA

On 6 September 1901 McKinley travelled to Buffalo, New York, to attend the Pan-American Exposition. As he shook hands with well-wishers, he was shot at close range by Leon Czolgosz, an anarchist. Despite initial optimism that he would recover, eight days later he died at the age of 58. The last chief executive elected in the 19th century, McKinley was the first 20th-century president to be assassinated. He was succeeded by Theodore Roosevelt.

Below: McKinley was shot twice, but doctors never retrieved the second bullet.

IDA McKINLEY

Ida Saxton was born in 1847 and married William McKinley in 1871. Her health deteriorated after her marriage and she suffered from epilepsy. Devoted to her husband, she survived for six years after his assassination, dying in 1907 in her birthplace of Canton, Ohio.

THE SPANISH–AMERICAN WAR

1898

John Hay, writing to his friend Theodore Roosevelt, called it a "splendid little war". As Abraham Lincoln's secretary almost 40 years previously, during a far more dramatic conflict, he was well placed to pass judgement. Following the Spanish and US declarations of war in April 1898, the fighting lasted less than four months. A peace treaty was concluded by the end of the year. US combat fatalities amounted to fewer than 400, although disease and illness killed more than ten times that number.

By the 1890s, Spain's empire in the Caribbean and the Pacific was crumbling. In Cuba and the Philippines, leaders such as Jose Marti and Emilio Aguinaldo fought against increasing Spanish repression. US sympathy for these independence movements was fuelled by humanitarian concerns, missionary fervour and the popular press. There was also a strategic motive: those in favour of US expansion overseas argued that establishing bases in the Caribbean, the Philippines and Hawaii

Above: 'Remember the Maine' became a popular slogan after its sinking precipitated war.

would protect the trading interests of the United States. While Republicans favoured annexing Hawaii, President Grover Cleveland disagreed. It was left to McKinley to approve such action during the war with Spain, giving the United States a permanent naval base at Pearl Harbor.

Below: The Spanish fleet (in the distance) was systematically destroyed by the superior US navy at the Battle of Santiago de Cuba.

After the sinking of the *Maine* in February 1898, Roosevelt, then assistant secretary to the navy, issued orders to the Pacific fleet to prepare for hostilities. The first action of the war took place at sea on 1 May: Commodore George Dewey destroyed the Spanish fleet in Manila Bay. In August, the main US invasion force reached the islands. Neither the United States nor Spain wanted Filipino independence. The day after a truce had been signed in Washington DC, a battle was engineered to keep insurgents from taking power. The Spanish surrendered and the Americans occupied Manila, but the subsequent insurrection, led by Aguinaldo, would last another four years and cost almost 4,500 American lives.

CUBA AND EXPANSIONISM

In Cuba, Roosevelt and the 'Rough Riders', the volunteer cavalry that he had helped to organize, took part in the assault on San Juan Hill on 1 July. It made him a national hero. Two days later the US navy sank enemy ships in the harbour of Santiago de Cuba, and on 17 July the remaining Spanish forces there surrendered. After the war, US forces continued to occupy the island. In 1902, the United States recognized limited Cuban independence. The following year, a treaty with the new Cuban government gave the United States a base on the island at Guantanamo Bay.

The United States, having proclaimed its support for those resisting European imperialism, had now replaced Spain as the dominant power in the Caribbean and the Pacific. Some leading Americans, including Mark Hanna, Andrew Carnegie and Mark Twain, opposed what they saw as an

Above: A general explosion ripped through the front section of the Maine, *killing more than 270 men.*

imperial adventure. For Twain, the "Person Sitting in the Darkness" would conclude that "There must be two Americas: one that sets the captive free, and one that takes a once-captive's new freedom away from him, and picks a quarrel with him with nothing to found it on; then kills him to get his land."

The Philippines provided a base for increased trade in the Far East. In 1899, John Hay, now McKinley's secretary of state, announced the 'Open Door' policy, which attempted to preserve the USA's commercial interests while the European powers and Japan sought to consolidate their influence in China. During the Boxer Rebellion the United States joined an international military force to relieve the siege of diplomatic legations in Beijing.

There were other considerations. Missionaries had long seen the religious enlightenment of the Chinese as their greatest challenge; US business interests had different ambitions. John D.

Rockefeller's company wanted to provide oil for every lamp in China.

Marti died during the Cuban struggle against Spain. Aguinaldo lived to see Philippine independence, dying in Manila in 1964. America's "splendid little war" gave Roosevelt the opportunity to use his reputation as a military hero to advance his political career, first

as governor of New York, and then as McKinley's vice president. Just over three years after fighting his way up San Juan Hill, an assassin's bullet would take him to the White House.

Below: The Rough Riders were one of three volunteer cavalries raised for the war, and the only one that saw action.

PART TWO

LATTER-DAY PRESIDENTS FROM 1901

Since 1901, 19 presidents have held office: eleven Republicans and eight Democrats. Only three of these thus far have established historical reputations that match the most distinguished of their predecessors. At the same time as the United States became increasingly dominant on the world stage, the presidency became the focus of its global power and influence.

Left: The Statue of Liberty, an enduring symbol of freedom and opportunity.

CHAPTER SIX

THEODORE ROOSEVELT TO WOODROW WILSON

1901–1921

THEODORE ROOSEVELT LIKED THE IDEA OF US IMPERIALISM. WILLIAM TAFT HAD BEEN AN ADMINISTRATOR IN PART OF ITS EMPIRE. WOODROW WILSON BELIEVED IN THE IMPERIALISM OF AN IDEA: DEMOCRACY. FOR THE THREE PRESIDENTS ELECTED BETWEEN 1904 AND 1920, IT WAS A TIME OF DOMESTIC POLITICAL TURBULENCE, WITH THE DEMOCRATS PROFITING FROM DIVISIONS IN THE REPUBLICAN PARTY TO WIN BACK THE WHITE HOUSE FOR THE FIRST TIME IN 16 YEARS. THE EARLY 20TH CENTURY WAS THE AGE OF PROGRESSIVISM, BRINGING GOVERNMENT'S POWER TO BEAR IN THE STILL LARGELY UNREGULATED WORLD OF US CAPITALISM. IT WAS ALSO A PERIOD OF INTERNATIONAL TENSIONS, CULMINATING IN EUROPEAN EMPIRES FIGHTING WORLD WAR I: THE 'WAR TO END ALL WARS'. THE LEAGUE OF NATIONS, THE AMERICAN PRESIDENT'S LAST BEST HOPE FOR A FUTURE WITHOUT GLOBAL CONFLICT, FAILED TO KEEP WHAT PROVED TO BE A FRAGILE PEACE.

Left: The Great White Fleet was a demonstration of the USA's naval power and the country's arrival on the world stage.

THEODORE ROOSEVELT

1901–1909

Republican bosses thought Theodore Roosevelt was a maverick, appropriately enough for a one-time rancher out West, and conspired to place him where he could not do much political damage: the vice presidency. An anarchist's bullet then put him in the White House. In 1904 he defied tradition, becoming the first president who had inherited the office to be elected to it in his own right. He did not run for re-election in 1908 and during the administration of his successor, William Taft, he spent four years regretting his public commitment only to serve one full term. So in 1912 he ran again as the candidate of his own

Below: Roosevelt's was a high-energy presidency. Aged 42, he was the youngest president to take office.

Progressive party. He came second. Theodore Roosevelt was an elemental and unquenchable political force, whose impact upon the United States and the presidency was profound.

EARLY LIFE

Born in 1858, into a wealthy New York family, he was named for his father, a prominent businessman. The elder Theodore supported Lincoln during the Civil War, avoiding active service because Roosevelt's mother, Martha, came from a slave-owning family in Georgia and had relatives fighting for the Confederacy.

Roosevelt Jr was asthmatic, and as a teenager he worked to overcome his illness through a programme of rigorous physical exercise. It was an early

Born: 27 October 1858, New York, New York
Parents: Theodore (1831–78) and Martha (1834–84)
Family background: Business
Education: Harvard College (1880)
Religion: Dutch Reformed
Occupation: Author, public official
Military service: Colonel, US army, Spanish–American War
Political career: New York State Assembly, 1882–4
Civil Service Commision, 1889–95
Assistant secretary of the navy, 1897–8
Governor of New York, 1898–1900
Vice president, 1901
Presidential annual salary: $50,000
Political party: Republican
Died: 6 January 1919, Oyster Bay, New York

example of his self-discipline and obsession with what he called "the strenuous life". In 1876, he entered Harvard and beside academic pursuits took up wrestling and boxing. While he was there, in 1878, his father died. Roosevelt married Alice Hathaway Lee in 1880, the year he graduated. Two years later he dropped out of Columbia Law School to begin the first of two terms in the New York State Assembly as its youngest elected member.

His private life and a career in public service seemed settled, but on Valentine's Day 1884, it all fell apart. Roosevelt's mother died from typhoid fever and a few hours later his wife succumbed to a fatal kidney infection, dying in his arms. His diary entry for that day, written under a large cross, was devastatingly simple: "The light has gone out of my life." His first child, a daughter named Alice, was just two days old.

Leaving Alice with his sister, Roosevelt spent the next two years in the Badlands of Dakota, ranching, hunting and laying down the law as a local deputy sheriff. On his return to the city, in November 1886, he campaigned unsuccessfully to become mayor of New York. A month later, in London, he married his second wife, Edith Carow.

At home in Oyster Bay, New York, Roosevelt resumed a writing career that had started with the publication of his first book, *The Naval War of 1812* in 1882, publishing among other works the first volume of *The Winning of the West* (1889), a romanticized version of the USA's expansion across the continent. In 1897, following appointments to the United States Civil Service Commission and as president of the New York City Police Commission, he became assistant secretary of the navy in President McKinley's administration. He resigned to fight in the Spanish–American War.

Elected governor of New York, in November 1898, he rapidly became a nuisance to the party. His mistake, in the eyes of the state's Republican bosses, was

to support taxes on the public utility companies, which were important donors to the party machine. The Republican leader in New York, Thomas Platt, consulted with Mark Hanna, President McKinley's influential political adviser, and Roosevelt was manoeuvred into reluctantly accepting the vice-presidential nomination for the 1900 election. Nobody anticipated the assassination that would make "that damned cowboy", as Hanna dismissively called him, the youngest president to assume the office. On 14 September 1901, Theodore Roosevelt became chief executive at the age of 42.

A NEW CENTURY

When Roosevelt came to the White House in 1901, the United States had taken its place among the most industrialized nations of the age, and he aimed to demonstrate its potential to wield an unprecedented influence in world affairs. His energies were now focused on his ambition: an administration of unparalleled achievement. It was a compelling performance. Roosevelt

Above: Roosevelt's charge with the 'Rough Riders' (a volunteer regiment) up San Juan Hill in Cuba, carrying a revolver salvaged from the US battleship Maine, *was the stuff of heroic legend. The action was pivotal in propelling him to elective office as governor of New York in 1898.*

knew the political value of dramatic gestures: just over a month after taking office he invited Booker T. Washington, the prominent black civil rights activist, to the White House for dinner. He appreciated the persuasive power of what he called the "bully pulpit" of the presidency. He courted the press, and had the priceless talent of providing them with a memorable quote, the pre-radio equivalent of a sound bite. "Speak softly and carry a big stick" not only described his foreign policy, but also provided a gift for commentators and newspaper cartoonists.

THE PANAMA CANAL

During 1901 the USA and Britain negotiated a treaty opening the way for the construction of a canal across the

Central American isthmus. There were two possible routes to link the Atlantic and Pacific Oceans: through Nicaragua or Panama. Roosevelt backed the second option. After some complex financial, political and diplomatic manoeuvrings, together with a judicious US naval blockade to establish Panama as an independent republic, in 1904 work began.

TRUST-BUSTING
In February 1902, President Roosevelt announced that the federal government would prosecute the Northern Securities Company for violations of

---

Left: Constructing the Panama Canal, connecting two oceans, was one of the most difficult engineering tasks ever undertaken.

the Sherman Anti-Trust Act (which aimed to curb the activities of cartels and monopolies), taking on the world's leading banker, John Pierpont Morgan, one of the 20 or so financiers and industrialists who controlled the US economy. The *Detroit Free Press* observed, "Wall Street is paralyzed at the thought that a President of the United States should sink so low as to enforce the law." Two years later, by a one-vote majority, the Supreme Court ruled that Northern Securities should be broken up. Roosevelt's 'trust-busting' – more cases followed – gained him widespread popular support. In all, 44 lawsuits were initiated against major US corporations.

CONSERVATION
Roosevelt's abiding interest in the natural world and the memories of his experiences living on the US frontier combined in his commitment to conservation. In May 1902, he signed the bill establishing Crater Lake in Oregon as a National Park, the first of the five that he would create while president. Unpopular with business interests at the

---

time, his policy of bringing the USA's wilderness lands under public protection, and preventing their destruction through the exploitation of natural resources, proved to be of immeasurable benefit to future generations.

THE SQUARE DEAL
In 1902, hoping to use the persuasive powers of the presidency to end a coal strike in Pennsylvania that threatened the nation's heating supplies, Roosevelt met mine owners and union leaders at the White House. Negotiations stalled. The president threatened to use a big stick domestically: he suggested that federal troops could be used to take over the mines, which would then be run by the government. The negotiations were resumed, and both sides accepted arbitration. Roosevelt called it a "Square Deal" and coined the slogan for his 1904 election campaign. Surfing a wave of popular support, he won easily, admitting himself "glad to be elected President in my own right".

SECOND ADMINISTRATION
Before he took the oath of office for a second time, in December 1904, he announced the 'Roosevelt Corollary' to the Monroe Doctrine (which had been announced in 1823 and asserted

---

EDITH ROOSEVELT
Born in Connecticut in 1861 and a childhood friend of Roosevelt's sister Corrine, Edith Carow was a teenager when he proposed marriage: she refused. A year after his first wife died, he asked again and she accepted. Edith raised her stepdaughter, Alice, and five children of her own. As first lady, she supervised the White House's restoration, organizing it to reconcile the competing demands of public and family life. She died in 1948 aged 87.

Right: The French first tried building the Panama Canal. After the loss of 22,000 lives, they gave up.

Left: Slum-living in squalid, cramped conditions was a reality of life for many in the early years of the 20th century.

that the United States had a sphere of influence that included its neighbours to the south). Under Roosevelt's amendment, the United States assumed the right "to the exercise of an international police power" in Latin America. This more interventionist policy towards its neighbours provoked increasing resentment at 'Yankee Imperialism' but reflected what Roosevelt saw as the USA's necessary involvement in what was widely regarded as its backyard.

Below: Crater lake lies in a volcanic basin in Oregon. It was protected by legislation brought in by Roosevelt.

At home, the United States still needed cleaning up. Investigative journalists, whom Roosevelt characterized as "muckrakers", after the character in *Pilgrim's Progress* "who could look no way but downward, with a muckrake in his hand", highlighted the unsafe industrial practices and squalor that prompted the progressive politics of the period. In 1906, the president read the scathing exposure of corruption in Upton Sinclair's book, *The Jungle*, which portrayed with grim accuracy the sickening malpractices of the meat-packing factories. With public approval the president approved the first legislation regulating the industry, paving the way for the creation of the Food and Drug Administration. It was among the last of his significant domestic reforms.

In 1905, he used personal diplomacy to end the war that had broken out between Russia and Japan the previous year, mediating peace talks in New Hampshire. His efforts were recognized with the 1906 Nobel Peace Prize: the first time it had been awarded to a recipient outside Europe. The following year, Roosevelt sent the US fleet,

painted white for the occasion, on a voyage around the world. It symbolized the USA's sea power: only the British navy was now superior in size.

Roosevelt left the White House in 1909, at the age of 50. He had explored the possibilities of presidential power and made the office the focus of national attention in a manner unrivalled since the Civil War.

AFTER THE PRESIDENCY
Declaring himself "as fit as a Bull Moose", the popular name given to his insurgent political party, Roosevelt returned to the political arena in the presidential election of 1912. He split the Republican vote. Woodrow Wilson won. After that, he was a spent political force. He wrote, travelled, and when the United States entered World War I, volunteered to be part of the action. The government refused his offer. In 1919, Theodore Roosevelt's remarkable life ended: he died in his sleep on 6 January. According to *The New York Times* his last words were to his black servant: "Please put out that light, James."

THE INVENTION OF FLIGHT
THE WRIGHT BROTHERS

On 17 December 1903, after a first attempt at flight had ended when his elder brother Wilbur stalled on take-off, Orville Wright flew a powered heavier-than-air machine above an isolated beach at Kitty Hawk, North Carolina. The flight lasted 12 seconds. Wilbur tried again: another 12-second flight. The third flight, Orville's turn, was three seconds longer. Finally, Wilbur managed almost a minute in the air, travelling about 1km (more than half a mile) and landing before a gust of wind destroyed the brothers' successful prototype.

Orville sent a telegram to his father: "Success four flights Thursday morning … started from level with engine power alone … longest 57 seconds inform Press home Christmas." Laconic words, an eye for publicity and a dash of domesticity described the historic achievement: the Wright brothers had invented an aeroplane.

Having mastered the technology of flight, the Wright brothers tried to capitalize on their inventive genius. From the outset, they believed that the military would be interested in aeroplanes. In January 1905, they approached the US War Department. A letter outlined their previous year's achievements, linking one of them with President Roosevelt's election success:

Above: In 1904 the Wright brothers were able to fly a complete circle, and stay in the air for more than five minutes.

"The first of these record flights was made on November 9th, in celebration of the phenomenal political victory of the preceding day, and the second on December 1st, in honour of the one hundredth flight of the season."

The government remained unconvinced. Three years later, after the brothers had tried to interest Europeans by exhibiting their aeroplane in a number of countries, the Roosevelt administration finally invited tenders for a contract to supply a machine. In September 1906, Orville made a series of demonstration flights at Fort Myers, Virginia, witnessed by spectators including Theodore Roosevelt Jr. The following year, the army bought the Wright brothers' aeroplane.

Wilbur died in 1912, but Orville lived until 1948, through the two World Wars in which air power became increasingly important. Air warfare would claim the life of President Roosevelt's youngest and favourite son, Quentin, who joined the US Army Air Corps and was shot down over France in July 1918.

Below: The Wright brothers' first flight covered less distance than the wingspan of a Boeing 747 jet.

THE SAN FRANCISCO EARTHQUAKE
1906

"Hear rumors of great disaster through an earthquake in San Francisco but know nothing, or the real facts. Call upon me for any assistance I can render." The telegram to the governor of California, George Pardee, came from President Roosevelt. San Francisco had

Below: To restore business confidence the extent of the damage to the area was played down.

always been vulnerable. At just after 5 a.m. on Wednesday 18 April 1906, the earthquake struck. Chinatown was obliterated. Countless buildings collapsed. Fires raged and by Saturday morning, the city was a scrap yard. Even though news from the West Coast was sketchy, Roosevelt discussed the government's response with his Cabinet. Victor Metcalf, his secretary of commerce and a Californian, was sent to San Francisco to report back.

The president refused offers of foreign aid, but donations from other US cities and individuals including John D. Rockefeller and Andrew Carnegie were welcomed. Congress approved $2.5 million to support the relief efforts. Roosevelt, aware of the city's history of municipal corruption, announced on 22 April that funds would be channelled through the Red Cross, although subsequently he agreed that they should also go to the city's finance committee, set up as part of its co-ordinated response to the disaster.

Above: As the earth collapsed vertically and shifted horizontally along the San Andreas fault, San Francisco suffered one of the greatest urban catastrophes in American history. The fire ignited by the quake raged for three days.

On 26 April Metcalf sent the president a lengthy account of the damage done to the city and the progress of the relief effort: "It is almost impossible to describe the ruin wrought by the earthquake and especially the conflagration ... The people however, are confident and hopeful for the future and have not in any sense lost their courage. They feel under deep obligations to you and the national Government for the prompt and efficient assistance rendered them."

The death toll was eventually estimated at more than 3,000. In 1915, the city hosted the Panama-Pacific International Exposition. Eighteen million visitors came to see the rebuilt metropolis on America's West Coast.

WILLIAM TAFT
1909–1913

William Taft achieved his lifetime's ambition after serving in an office in which he never felt at home. For many years his career was a reflection of the expectations and aspirations of others: his parents and his wife. His predecessor's inability to stay away from the political arena destroyed their friendship and wrecked the Republicans' prospects of winning a fifth consecutive presidential election. Unlike Theodore Roosevelt, William Taft later found that fulfilment and fresh horizons existed beyond the White House.

Taft was born in 1857 in the Republican stronghold of Ohio. His father went to Yale, became a lawyer, served as secretary of war in Grant's Cabinet and was briefly attorney general before spending time in Europe as a diplomat. Taft followed dutifully in

Born: 15 September 1857, Cincinnati, Ohio
Parents: Alphonso (1810–91) and Louisa (1827–1907)
Family background: Law and public service
Education: Yale College (1878); Cincinnati Law School (1880)
Religion: Unitarian
Occupation: Lawyer, public service
Military service: None
Political career: Ohio Superior Court judge, 1887–90
US solicitor general, 1890–2
US circuit court judge, 1892–1900
Governor of the Philippines, 1901–4
Secretary of war, 1904–8
US Supreme Court chief justice, 1921–30
Presidential annual salary: $75,000
Political party: Republican
Died: 8 March 1930, Washington DC

his father's footsteps, graduating from Yale in 1878 and embarking on a legal career. In 1886 he married Helen Herron, a judge's daughter. They had three children.

A superior court judge at the age of 30, Taft was appointed solicitor general by Benjamin Harrison. He hoped to become a Supreme Court justice. Instead President McKinley asked him

Above: Taft became president reluctantly – his lifetime's ambition was to be chief justice of the Supreme Court.

to govern the Philippines. He returned to Washington in 1904 as secretary of war, overseeing the construction of the Panama Canal and supervising the federal government's response to the San Francisco earthquake. His wife

HELEN TAFT

After visiting the White House as a teenager, Helen Herron aspired to become first lady. Born in Ohio in 1861, she married William Taft in 1886. Having achieved her life's ambition, in May 1909 she suffered a stroke. Her influential role in public life remained undiminished. She was 81 when she died in 1943.

STATES ENTERING THE UNION DURING TAFT'S PRESIDENCY:
NEW MEXICO
ARIZONA

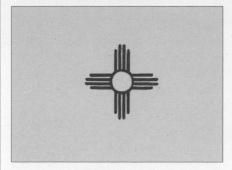

Entered the Union: 1912
Pre-state history: Land acquired after Mexican War (1848) added to as a result of 1850 Compromise; organized as Territory (1850) supplemented by Gadsden Purchase (1853)
Total population in 1920 census: 360,350
Electoral College votes in 1912: 3

Entered the Union: 1912
Pre-state history: Land acquired through Gadsden Purchase (1853); part of Confederacy (1861); organized as Arizona Territory (1863)
Total population in 1920 census: 334,162
Electoral College votes in 1912: 3

wanted him to succeed Roosevelt, as did, initially, the president himself. Taft duly obtained the Republican nomination in the 1908 presidential election and easily defeated William Jennings Bryan, who was then making his third attempt to win the White House for the Democrats.

TARIFF REFORM

William Taft tackled an issue that Roosevelt, knowing its potential to cause political problems, had deftly avoided: his attempt at tariff reform antagonized Congress. But he proved a relentless 'trust-buster'. At this time much of the US economy was controlled by a system of trusts: virtual

monopolies run by large groups of businesses. Taft ended many of them. He was a believer in the benefits of 'dollar diplomacy' – using the USA's economic power as leverage in international affairs, rather than displays of military might and imperial hubris – and his foreign policy promoted trade relations and sought to promote world peace.

He could never escape his predecessor's ambition, and it was this that sealed his fate in the 1912 election. After

leaving the White House, Taft taught at Yale Law School. In 1920 President Warren Harding gave him the job he had always really wanted: chief justice of the Supreme Court, a position he held until just before his death in 1930. He is the only president to have been chief justice.

Below: Taft tackled issues that his predecessor had chosen to ignore, and continued Roosevelt's trust-busting policy.

Below: Taft forged ahead with 80 trust-busting suits, benefiting less well-off people, but alienating business leaders.

HENRY FORD AND THE MODEL 'T'
THE DEVELOPMENT OF THE MOTOR CAR

Not only did Henry Ford make a motor car that was affordable – changing it from an object of desire to an ordinary purchase – he also revolutionized industrial practices in the process. His innovation was a moving assembly line: by 1914, it took less than 100 minutes to make a Model 'T'. Rivals employed five times as many workers as did Henry Ford in order to construct their automobiles.

Mass production and low overheads were the key to increasing supply. Demand was created by another innovation. In 1914 the Ford Motor Company announced that it would pay its workers $5 an hour, more than double the minimum wage. This shocked his competitors, but for the workers it meant that working for Ford made it possible to buy one of his cars. High wages compensated for the drudgery of the work. Within two years Ford's company profits had doubled to

Above: Ford revolutionized the motor car industry, with the first assembly line production of vehicles.

$60 million and Henry Ford became rich while putting his fellow Americans behind the wheel of a car.

First launched in 1908, the Model 'T' sold for $850. It was reasonably reliable and easy to drive. The basic design of the 15 million that were made remained unchanged during its 19 years of production. Capable of reaching a speed of 30 miles an hour on a good road, of which there were then few, its versatile engine was useful for powering saws or grinding corn when its innovative steel alloy chassis was not transporting people and goods across the United States.

Ford became famous. He dabbled in politics, initially professing himself a Democrat, but revealing himself as an unreconstructed apostle of religious intolerance – he was accused of anti-semitism – and notoriously hostile to trade unions. His most quixotic political gesture came in 1915 when, having failed to persuade a sceptical President Wilson of his plan, he sponsored a 'Peace Ship' to Europe to try to stop World War I.

Henry Ford's monument was the massive Rouge River factory in Detroit, where raw materials were moulded into rows of black Model 'T's. He was an industrial alchemist whose cars transformed American society.

Below: The 'peace ship' Oscar II, sponsored by Henry Ford, visited European nations to try to end the war.

Below: The Model 'T' was the first cheaply available motor car, which was within the means and aspirations of many households.

THE NAACP

The 100th anniversary of Abraham Lincoln's birth fell on 12 February 1909. The date was marked by the first meeting of the National Association for the Advancement of Colored People (NAACP). The previous year, William Walling, who had strayed far from his family's roots as wealthy slave-owners in Kentucky, and had emerged from the University of Chicago as a committed socialist, had witnessed the brutality of the lynching and killing taking place during a riot in Lincoln's home town of Springfield, Illinois. Walling's description of these events, published in an article entitled *The Race War in the North*, ended with a plea for black equality, and posed the question: "Who realizes the seriousness of the situation, and what large and powerful body of citizens is ready to come to their aid?"

Mary White Ovington, a fellow socialist and civil rights campaigner, was one who answered the call. She agreed with Walling that, in her words, "the

spirit of the abolitionists must be revived". Along with another civil rights activist, Henry Moskowitz, they met in New York in January 1909 and agreed to form the NAACP. Another member was W. E. B. Du Bois, the first African

Above: The NAACP's campaign for equality of treatment under the law finally succeeded in the 1950s.

American to obtain a doctorate from Harvard, who in 1910 became the NAACP's director of publicity and research. He was the founding editor of its principal publication, *The Crisis*. In the first issue, he defined its purpose: "To set forth those facts and arguments which show the danger of race prejudice, particularly as manifested today toward colored people." The NAACP became the major pressure group for black civil rights, leading protests against segregation wherever it existed, whether in Wilson's administration or in the South with its entrenched labyrinth of 'Jim Crow' laws. Its 45-year fight for racial justice led to the 1954 Supreme Court ruling that "separate but equal" facilities in the South were unconstitutional, a triumph for the "spirit of the abolitionists".

Below: The NAACP opposed the activities of the Ku Klux Klan, including the widespread practice of lynching.

THE DEVELOPMENT OF SILENT FILM
ENTERTAINING AMERICA

California had a reliable climate in which to shoot movies and its scenery was exotic and varied, making it especially suitable for the increasingly popular genre of the Western. It was also a more favourable business environment: workers were less expensive to hire in what was already a labour-intensive industry. The land was cheaper for building studios, and it was far away from those dominating the fledgling industry in New York. After 1908, when the Motion Picture Patents Company attempted to monopolize the industry on the East Coast, independent film-makers escaped across the continent, settling in California, in a suburb of Los Angeles: Hollywood.

In 1910, D. W. Griffith, who had started his movie career as an actor and then a director with the Edison Moving Picture Company before moving to the Biograph Company, directed the first Hollywood movie, *In Old California*. It was not until the following year that the first film studio was established there. Other independents soon followed.

In 1913, Griffith returned to establish his own studio. Shortly after, he started work on the film that was to revolutionize the industry.

Released in 1915, Griffith's *Birth of a Nation* remains a landmark in the history of US cinema. It was the first Hollywood blockbuster, an epic tale of

Left: Griffith's The Birth of a Nation *proved the persuasive power of cinema.*

the Civil War and its aftermath, based on *The Clansman*, a novel by Thomas Dixon. Its claims to historical authenticity soon aroused great controversy. President Woodrow Wilson, after seeing it at the White House, allegedly remarked that it was like "writing history with lightning and my only regret is that it is all so terribly true". But its positive portrayal of the activities of the Ku Klux Klan led the NAACP to describe the film as "three miles of filth". For the audiences sitting in the darkness of nickelodeons across the United States, Griffith presented a version of the nation's past that was filtered through his own experiences growing up in rural poverty in the post-Civil War American South.

Hollywood became synonymous with film-making, and before long worldwide audiences could escape into the 'American Dream' simply by paying for a ticket to the movies.

NICKELODEON

The name 'nickelodeon' was coined by combining the price of admission – five cents – and the Greek word for a covered theatre. All over the United States, and particularly in the cities, these small neighbourhood cinemas screened the latest Hollywood productions. The films were silent, so newly arrived immigrants with limited command of the language could still enjoy the melodramas and slapstick comedies, without having to concentrate on dialogue. Nickelodeons brought movies as popular entertainment to the American masses.

Right: Piano accompaniment added to the impact of silent movies.

WOODROW WILSON
1913–1921

Woodrow Wilson believed in the ideal of democracy. He led the nation into World War I because he was convinced that "the world must be made safe for democracy". Determined that "peace must be planted upon the tested foundations of political liberty", he was the architect of an international organization that aimed to avert future conflicts. Like Theodore Roosevelt, President Wilson was awarded the Nobel Peace Prize. The United States initially rejected his vision, retreating into isolationism. Nevertheless his idealism would still influence US foreign policy and the rhetoric of his successors as the United States aspired to fulfil the destiny Wilson had envisaged for it: spreading its democratic values throughout the world.

EARLY LIFE
He was born in 1856 in Staunton, Virginia. Eight months before his fifth birthday, the state seceded from the Union: Thomas Woodrow Wilson's early childhood memories were of war.

Born: 28 December 1856, Staunton, Virginia
Parents: Joseph (1822–1903) and Jessie (1826–88)
Family background: Presbyterian ministry
Education: College of New Jersey (Princeton) (1879)
Johns Hopkins PhD (1886)
Religion: Presbyterian
Occupation: Academic, public service
Military service: None
Political career: Governor of New Jersey, 1911–13
Presidential annual salary: $75,000
Political party: Democrat
Died: 3 February 1924, Washington DC

His father was a Presbyterian minister, originally from Ohio, who, upon moving to the South in 1849, became a convert to the Confederate cause. His mother, from whom he gained his middle name, and the one by which he preferred to be known, was a minister's daughter. Wilson's character was shaped by his family's strong Christian values.

At 16 he went to Davidson College in North Carolina, but ill health – he had never been physically robust – contributed to his decision to drop out after a year. In 1875, he went north, enrolling at the College of New Jersey, yet to be renamed Princeton University. Four years later, he graduated and began to study law, eventually qualifying as a lawyer in Georgia and setting up a practice in Atlanta. It was the wrong career choice. Within a year he had returned to study for a doctoral degree in political science and history at Johns Hopkins University. Wilson's academic career progressed through appointments at Bryn Mawr College and Wesleyan University. His publications on US government and politics were well received. In 1890 he returned to his

Left: As the United States became a world power, Woodrow Wilson imbued its foreign policy with an idealistic fervour and a missionary ambition to spread the values of US democracy abroad.

alma mater in New Jersey. Six years later it became Princeton University, and in 1902 Professor Wilson was chosen as its 13th president.

Initially popular with both the University's trustees and its faculty, his plans to reform Princeton bitterly divided both the academic community and the graduates, whose continuing financial commitment to the institution was often based on their nostalgic affection for its traditions.

POLITICAL CAREER
In the 1910 mid-term elections he left academic life, graduating to state politics as New Jersey's first Democrat governor for 14 years. Two years later, Wilson, the Southerner who had made his political career in the North, won his party's presidential nomination. Running on a reform platform, he beat both Taft and Theodore Roosevelt to become the first Democrat to win the White House in the 20th century.

The Democrats were no longer the party of the South: for the first time since the Civil War they controlled both Houses of Congress. Wilson was in no doubt as to who was responsible for his

ELLEN WILSON
Born in Georgia in 1860 and married to Woodrow Wilson in 1885, Ellen Axson, like her husband, came from a Presbyterian minister's family. They had three children. Her strong social conscience led her to work to improve the slum conditions in which many of Washington's black community lived. She died from kidney failure in 1914.

Above: The passengers of the luxury liner
Lusitania *were unaware that it carried a*
deadly cargo of munitions.

victory. He told William McCombs, his
campaign manager, "Remember that
God ordained that I should be President
of the United States."

RADICAL REFORM
Not since John Adams had addressed
Congress in person in 1797 had a
president come to Capitol Hill as
Wilson did in April 1913, a month after
his inauguration, to enlist support for his
progressive legislative agenda. He confronted head-on the issues that had
divided generations of US politicians:
tariff reform, the currency and the
banking system. Within the year, Wilson
achieved the first significant reduction
in the tariff in almost 70 years, moving
the United States towards accepting the
benefits of free trade. He also signed
legislation allowing him to appoint
members to the Federal Reserve Board,
which would exercise central control
over the nation's banking system. In
1914, the Federal Trade Commission
was established, with powers to
intervene when businesses were
suspected of abusing anti-trust laws.

Wilson's domestic legislative achievements during his first year in office
consolidated his reputation both as a
progressive and as a president prepared

to use the powers of his office to
promote his reform agenda. When war
broke out in Europe in August 1914,
it would be the problem of how
America should react to the conflict

that increasingly preoccupied its president. He also faced a personal tragedy:
his wife, Ellen, died from kidney disease
on 6 August.

OUTBREAK OF WAR
As the fighting in Europe escalated,
Wilson argued for US neutrality. After
the Cunard liner *Lusitania* was sunk by
a German torpedo in May 1915, with
more than 1,000 passengers, including
128 Americans, losing their lives, the
president demanded that Germany's
indiscriminate submarine warfare
should cease, involving the United
States publically in the war. This proved
too provocative for his secretary of state,
William Jennings Bryan, who resigned
over the issue. Wilson then made
strenuous efforts to mediate between
the European belligerents. He failed.

EDITH WILSON
Edith Bolling was born in Virginia in 1872. Her first husband, Norman Galt, died
in 1908 and she married Wilson in 1915. Four years later, following his stroke, she
began what she called her "stewardship" of his administration, determining the flow
of public papers to him and acting as his intermediary with the Cabinet. She successfully kept the American people unaware of his incapacity for the remainder of
their time in the White House. Her last public appearance was at John F. Kennedy's
inauguration in 1961. She died later that year, on the 105th anniversary of her late
husband's birth.

Below: Edith Bolling Galt may well have been the 'first woman to run the American
government', during the debilitating illness of her husband.

In December 1915, he married Edith Bolling Galt. The following year he became the first Democrat to be elected to two consecutive terms in the White House since Andrew Jackson.

SECOND ADMINISTRATION

In February 1917, Germany abandoned any commitment to restrict the operations of its submarines. Neutral vessels – including US ships – were counted as legitimate targets. At the same time, the German foreign minister, Arthur Zimmermann, instructed his ambassador in Mexico to suggest that if the US abandoned its neutrality, Germany would help Mexico "reconquer" territory lost during the Mexican-American war. The British intercepted his telegram and revealed its decoded content to the Americans. The following month, Wilson took the oath of office for a second time. On 2 April, he asked Congress to declare war against Germany. The United States would help to "bring peace and safety to all nations and make the world itself at last free". Although US troops did not begin crossing the Atlantic in numbers until the following year, the potential military resources that the United States offered its European allies helped to hasten the end of the war.

In January 1918, Wilson outlined the basis of a peace settlement in which European empires should respect the rights of those whom they ruled. The organizing principle of his 'Fourteen Points' was the idea of "justice to all peoples and nationalities, and their right to live on equal terms of liberty and safety with one another, whether they be strong or weak". The following year Wilson arrived in Paris to participate in the peace negotiations at Versailles. While he was there, he ignored representations from a French colonial subject, Ho Chi Minh, who had been

Right: Army officers stand on chairs to see into the room where the Treaty of Versailles is being signed on 28 June 1919.

FOURTEEN POINTS

Wilson's list of fourteen principles for a lasting peace included ending "private international understandings", ensuring freedom of navigation in international waters, promoting free trade, and encouraging disarmament. The president argued for the rights of colonial peoples to be recognized and proposed solutions to the specific disputes over territory that had led Europe into war. He also advanced his idea of "a general association of nations" to guarantee "political independence and territorial integrity" for all the nations of the world.

inspired by his democratic rhetoric to request help in liberating his country from imperial control. Many years later, Vietnam would demand rather more of the USA's attention.

European leaders had different agendas as they discussed the terms and conditions of the Treaty of Versailles. They had no intention of deferring to the democratic idealism of the president of the United States when it came to the details of the settlement, although they did accept his proposal to establish the League of Nations.

When Wilson left Europe it was with a treaty that many Americans thought betrayed the principles for which they had been persuaded to fight, and the country was now in no mood to give its support to his international organization for preserving peace. The postwar reaction at home was isolationism: the United States was reluctant to involve itself with international politics. It was this that undermined the architecture of the League of Nations, Wilson's vision for a lasting democratic peace.

Taking his case to the people caused Wilson's health to collapse. He suffered a massive stroke, and was no longer capable of taking part in the administration of the country. It became Washington's best-kept secret: for more than a year his wife and closest advisers maintained the charade that he was still in control. The world was one that he no longer understood. The United States rejected the Treaty of Versailles, the League of Nations and international engagement; instead it prepared to indulge itself in the heady materialism of the 1920s.

Despite this defeat, Wilson had achieved great things. His liberal progressivism brought about significant economic and social reforms. He was opposed to prohibition, which became law during his last year in office. He once wrote: "The President is at liberty both in law and conscience to be as big as he can." Woodrow Wilson had tried his best to live up to his ideal.

WORLD WAR I
1914–1918

When Congress declared war on Germany on 6 April 1917, the United States was not ready for a fight. Given the casualties being inflicted on the killing fields of Europe at the time, the regular army could muster only enough troops to take part in a single battle. The United States mobilized. Like Abraham Lincoln before him, Woodrow Wilson assumed a broad range of executive powers to lead the nation into war.

In May 1917, Congress passed the National Conscription Act. Few had volunteered immediately for active service. Now, on 5 June 1917, all men aged between 21 and 30 were required to register for the draft. A wave of patriotic fervour persuaded 10 million to do so; by the end of the war, another 14 million Americans had joined them.

Their commander was John 'Black Jack' Pershing. His nickname derived from his command of a regiment of black troops in Cuba. Among the forces he led in France would be more than 350,000 African-Americans who,

Below: Uncle Sam, the personification of the United States, calls the people to arms to join the war effort.

although they fought in segregated units, found that Europe was more racially tolerant than the USA, as well as being receptive to their music: jazz. They returned to the United States with renewed demands for the recognition of their civil rights.

Pershing and the first units of the American Expeditionary Force arrived in France in June 1917, with orders from the secretary of war that included the requirement "to co-operate with the forces of the other countries … But in so doing the underlying idea must be kept in view that the forces of the United States are a separate and distinct component of the combined forces, the

Above: General Pershing arrives in France with the first US troops to fight in World War I.

identity of which must be preserved." This, together with delays caused by the need to train Americans in the tactics of trench warfare, caused friction between the allies.

For the British and French, US replacements in existing units would mean a fresh infusion of troops in a grim war of attrition. Pershing resisted this idea: he wanted his forces to operate effectively and independently in battle. In October 1917 he did allow some battalions to spend short periods of time

alongside a French division. Three soldiers were killed: the first US casualties of the war.

It was not until the spring of 1918 that US infantrymen, known as 'doughboys' (there is no definitive explanation for this nickname), participated in battlefield action. On 20 April in the Lorraine region of France, the 26th Division fought to defend and then regain the village of Seicheprey. In May, US troops fought at Cantigny and in June at Chateau-Thierry and Belleau Wood. They were also involved in the second Battle of the Marne during the last major German offensive. By 4 July Pershing commanded a million troops in France, a number set to double during the following four months. General Pershing's army could now fight as equals beside those of France and Britain against the depleted and war-weary Germans.

In October, it was the US president whom the German Chancellor first approached with the proposal of an armistice. In answer to Wilson's request for clarification, Germany accepted the terms outlined in his 'Fourteen Points' speech of the previous January. Wilson's reply recognized that it would be the Allies who would dictate how the war would end, and if the United States was to respond to "the military masters and … autocrats of Germany now, or if it is likely to have to deal with them later in regard to the international obligations of the German Empire, it must demand, not peace negotiations but surrender".

The following month it was all over. With Germany in the throes of revolution, the armistice was signed on 11 November. US casualties stood at more than 300,000 in a war that had cost the lives of 8.5 million – the 'Lost Generation'. General Pershing and the American Expeditionary Force returned to the United States as heroes. On his retirement, he was given the title 'General of the Armies'. He died in July 1948, having witnessed another war in which US troops gave their lives fighting for the same ideal as those who had joined him on the battlefields of France in 1918.

Above: In August 1918, US forces planned their first independent action, at St Mihiel, France. Their limited offensive was successful, although the retreating Germans burnt down the town. Three months later the war ended when the armistice was signed.

US PARTICIPATION IN WORLD WAR I

1917

6 April: The United States declares war on Germany

25 June: First US Troops land in France

1918

8 January: Woodrow Wilson sets out his plan for peace in Europe ('Fourteen Points')

11 November: Armistice ends fighting in Europe

1919

18 January: Peace conference opens at Versailles

25 January: Proposal for League of Nations accepted

THE TREATY OF VERSAILLES
AND THE LEAGUE OF NATIONS

Having crossed the Atlantic on the USS *George Washington* the month after the armistice had been signed, Woodrow Wilson was the first president to meet with his counterparts in France, Britain and Italy face to face. The US idealist encountered European realists.

Wilson joined the European leaders in Paris to take part in the great power bargaining that would shape the Treaty of Versailles and enshrine his vision of the League of Nations. His political base at home had been shaken after the Republicans regained control of Congress in the 1918 mid-term elections. Worse was to come. Despite his widespread international popularity – the result of his clear commitment to the principles of a democratic peace – and the air of hopeful expectation that accompanied his arrival in Europe, Wilson and his allies sat down to

Below: Vittorio Orlando (second left) walked out of the Versailles negotiations. The remaining Allied leaders agreed the terms of peace.

negotiate in an atmosphere of mutual misunderstanding, their attitudes moulded by their different experiences of the war.

The French president, Georges Clemenceau, aged 77, had twice witnessed the consequences of German belligerence: the invasion of his country during the Franco-Prussian war of 1871 and the carnage of the previous four years of fighting on French soil. He was determined that the defeated enemy should no longer threaten its European neighbours. Britain's liberal prime minister, Lloyd George, came to Versailles having won an election on the promises to 'Hang the Kaiser' and 'Make Germany Pay'. More than five million Britons had served in France and almost half that number had become casualties of war. Lloyd George was prepared to compromise, but not at any price.

Italy had changed sides during the war. Vittorio Orlando, who had, ironically, become prime minister as a result of his country's heavy defeat at the hands of the Germans in the Battle of

Above: British prime minister Lloyd George, French premier Georges Clemenceau and President Woodrow Wilson during talks at Versailles.

Caporetto in 1917, wanted control of the Croatian port of Fiume as a reward for joining the winners. He failed in his objective and took no further part in the discussions.

President Wilson held to his unwavering commitment to preserve his ideal of the League of Nations. He encountered scepticism in Paris and at the same time was being buffeted by political turbulence from his opponents back in the United States. Although he achieved his aim, it was at the expense of accepting his European allies' demands for a punitive peace.

Although the British prime minister and the French president almost came to blows at one stage, and were prevented only through the intervention of the American president, it was Lloyd George who presented himself as the pragmatist, bridging the Atlantic divide between Wilson, who was fired with missionary zeal, and Clemenceau, the stubborn defender of his national interests. Always adept at conjuring a

Right: An artist's impression of the United States of Europe, which might encourage world harmony and peace.

memorable image, when he was asked to rate his performance during the negotiations, Lloyd George described with characteristic self-confidence how he felt he had done: "Not badly, considering I was seated between Jesus Christ and Napoleon."

The Versailles negotiations satisfied no one, least of all the Germans, who were excluded from them. They were presented with crippling demands for reparations and the loss of territory they had held before the war. Wilson was forced to accept his co-signatories' territorial demands and the punitive terms of the peace. On his less than triumphant return to the United States, he personally presented the treaty to the Senate. It would be sent back to him, unratified. The League of Nations, the Covenant for which he had fought so tenaciously to include in the Treaty of Versailles, would go ahead but without US involvement.

THE LEAGUE OF NATIONS
It was not only the Americans who did not join. Germany, defeated and humiliated, was excluded. So too was Russia: its new communist leaders were not invited to be members of the international organization, which from January 1920 was based in Geneva. The League's mission was "to promote international co-operation and to achieve international peace and security", but with three major powers relegated to the sidelines, its chances of promoting global harmony were slim. It was a forum for the diplomatic resolution of international conflict, backed by the threat of economic sanctions, but it had no independent military force that could act in a peacekeeping capacity. Successful in encouraging co-operation between nations in the areas of health and welfare policies, the League failed to prevent what many saw as the inevitable outcome of the treaty agreed in Paris in 1919. Two decades after Wilson's transatlantic voyage to Versailles, Europe went to war once more.

Below: Those who agreed the Treaty of Versailles and ended World War I soon saw their efforts undermined by events.

THE PALESTINIAN MANDATE
In 1922, the League of Nations gave the British government a mandate to govern Palestine. It recognized the need for "a national home for the Jewish people", a commitment independently endorsed by Congress. To honour wartime pledges to the Arabs, Britain divided the mandate, creating the Transjordan, an area where Jewish settlement was forbidden. These conflicting priorities fuelled the competing and irreconcilable claims of Arabs and Jews for sovereignty over the territory.

PROHIBITION
1920

The Eighteenth Amendment to the Constitution famously failed in its attempt to prevent Americans drinking alcohol. Prohibition was introduced for medical, social, political and economic reasons. It was agreed by Congress in December 1917, and its introduction banned "the manufacture, sale, or transportation of intoxicating liquors" in the United States as well as prohibiting their import and export to and from the country. After ratification by the states, many of which had already introduced measures banning the production and sale of alcohol, legislation was necessary to enforce the amendment. A teetotal member of the House of Representatives, Andrew Volstead, gave his name to the act, which was passed by Congress on 28 October 1919, ushering in the age of national prohibition.

President Woodrow Wilson, who was still incapacitated in the immediate aftermath of his stroke, opposed the Volstead Act, but Congress immediately overturned his veto. Prohibition went into effect in January 1920. While he was in favour of temperance, Wilson, like many others at the time, saw that a constitutional amendment would not

ANTI-SALOON LEAGUE

The Anti-Saloon League was the main pressure group advocating the prohibition of alcohol. It began life as a state society, founded in 1893 at Oberlin College, Ohio. The idea was taken up in other states and it became a national society in 1895. It was organized along business lines, and took a sophisticated approach to public relations, publishing its own newspapers to persuade the public of the evils of alcohol.

Backed by ministers and congregations of various Protestant denominations, particularly the Methodists, the League aimed to achieve temperance through legislation, and gained considerable political influence through its backing of 'dry' candidates – those who were prepared to vote for prohibition, regardless of whether they themselves were teetotal – in local and state elections. It began its successful campaign for national prohibition in 1913.

Above: Leaders of the Anti-Saloon League fought for an alcohol-free society. They argued for temperance and campaigned for the constitutional amendment which banned the production, sale and transportation of alcohol throughout the United States.

Below: Illegal distilleries proliferated on the streets to serve the trade of the speakeasies.

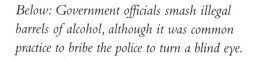

Below: Government officials smash illegal barrels of alcohol, although it was common practice to bribe the police to turn a blind eye.

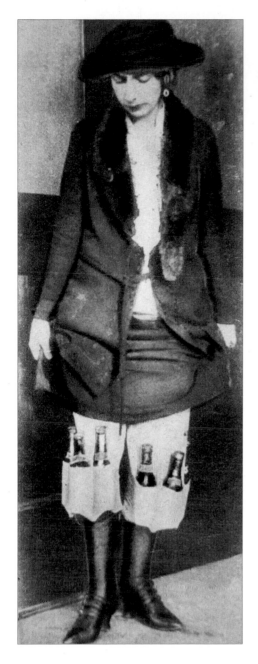

Above: Methods of transporting illegal alcohol from rural distilleries to the towns were ingenious: the activity became almost unstoppable.

stop Americans consuming alcohol. When he left the White House in 1921, Wilson took his private stock of Scotch whiskey and fine wine with him.

Some of those prepared to become bootleggers, to open speakeasies, to make moonshine or to risk smuggling alcohol between states became rich and famous. In Chicago, there were few who believed that Al Capone made his living, as he claimed on his business card, from dealing in furniture.

Above: Speakeasies were illegal drinking dens that operated and flourished during the era of prohibition.

Joseph P. Kennedy, the son of a former Boston saloon-keeper, amassed a large fortune during the 1920s and among his business connections were those who were profiting from the opportunities that prohibition created.

Henry Ford was prominent among those business leaders who supported prohibition: he claimed that he would rather close down his production line than see the legislation repealed. Others, such as Henry Joy, president of the Packard Motor Car Company, who had been active in the Anti-Saloon League, eventually admitted that they had made a mistake. In 1925 Joy wrote: "I was stupidly wrong. America must open its eyes and recognize that human nature cannot be changed by legal enactment."

Eight years later, Congress and the president came to agree with him. Although legislation forbidding alcohol would remain in force in a number of states, in 1933 Franklin Roosevelt signed the Twenty-first Amendment, bringing national prohibition to an end.

Right: The Eighteenth Amendment did not make it illegal to drink spirits; it was the manufacture, sale and distribution that the law disallowed.

BOOTLEGGERS, SPEAKEASIES AND MOONSHINE

Prohibition produced its own industrial language. Bootleggers (named after smugglers who carried contraband in the legs of their boots) acted as suppliers, carrying alcohol from rural distilleries to urban centres, or importing it from abroad. Liquor was retailed in speakeasies: illicit bars where it was still possible to enjoy a drink. The substitute for whiskey as the drink of choice was moonshine, which home-made stills produced in quantities to supply a thirsty nation. Problems of quality control were ignored by its makers, distributors, retailers and consumers alike.

Below: Producing alcohol for a thirsty nation was big business, and encouraged criminal activity.

CHAPTER SEVEN

WARREN HARDING TO FRANKLIN D. ROOSEVELT

1921–1945

BETWEEN THE TWO WORLD WARS, THREE DIFFERENT REPUBLICANS WON A PRESIDENTIAL ELECTION EACH. FROM 1932–44 ONE DEMOCRAT WON FOUR: FRANKLIN DELANO ROOSEVELT, THE MASTER POLITICIAN OF 'THE AMERICAN CENTURY'. THE OPTIMISM AND ENERGY OF THE 'ROARING TWENTIES' CAME TO A SHATTERING END AS THE STOCK MARKET IMPLODED, LOSING $30 BILLION IN VALUE IN THE WALL STREET CRASH, AND BOOM BECAME BUST. THE UNITED STATES STRUGGLED THROUGH THE DEPRESSION OF THE 1930S, DESPITE THE OPTIMISM SURROUNDING THE NATIONAL RECOVERY PROGRAMME OF ROOSEVELT'S 'NEW DEAL'.

BY THE END OF WORLD WAR II, THE USA'S POSITION OF INTERNATIONAL PRE-EMINENCE WAS CONFIRMED. THE INVENTION OF NUCLEAR WEAPONS DIRECTED THE WAY TO A HIGH-RISK FUTURE. PRESIDENTS KNEW THAT ORDERING THEIR USE COULD MEAN THE END OF THE WORLD. AT THE SAME TIME, THE IDEALISM OF WOODROW WILSON WAS SEEN AGAIN IN THE CREATION OF THE UNITED NATIONS.

Left: The Wall Street Crash of 1928 is remembered as one of the most infamous days in the history of share trading.

WARREN HARDING
1921–1923

President Warren Harding felt that "normalcy" was what the country needed after the energy of progressivism and the trauma of war. In his inaugural address he suggested that Americans "must strive for normalcy to achieve stability". Harding then settled into a leadership style that allowed him time to indulge his habitual leisure pursuits: golf, poker and extra-marital affairs.

Born in 1865, a few months after the end of the Civil War, Harding graduated from Ohio Central College at the age of 17. He had been editor of the campus newspaper, and in 1884, with the help of a couple of friends, he bought the *Marion Star* newspaper, which became the platform for his subsequent political career. In 1891, Harding married Florence Kling De Wolfe, a wealthy divorcée. They had children, but not with each other: hers was a son by her former husband; his would be a daughter by Nan Britton, one of his long-term mistresses. In 1899

Above: Warren Harding was the first 20th-century chief executive to die from natural causes while in office.

Harding entered the Ohio State Senate as a Republican, beginning a career in public life that spluttered along until his election to the federal Senate in 1914 and to the White House six years later.

Some of his Cabinet choices – Charles Hughes as secretary of state, Andrew Mellon as treasury secretary and Herbert Hoover as secretary of commerce – were very good. On the other hand, his crony Harry Daugherty, who became attorney general, was comprehensively dishonest, and Albert Fall, the secretary for the interior, took bribes in return for allowing oil companies to exploit the government's oil reserve in Teapot Dome, Wyoming. "Normalcy" seemed to mean a return to the widespread corruption of the Grant administration.

In 1923, and in failing health, Harding set out on a 'Voyage of Understanding' across the USA, intended to deflect the mounting criticism of his presidency as it creaked under the weight of scandal. On 2 August, aged 57, he died from natural causes in a San Francisco hotel, although unsubstantiated rumours claimed he had been poisoned. Warren Harding was simply unsuited to the office he held with such lack of distinction. It was, as he once said, "a hell of a job".

FLORENCE HARDING

Born in Ohio in 1860, Florence Kling eloped at 19 with her first husband, Henry De Wolfe, who was an alcoholic. They had one son and divorced in 1886. By then she had met Warren Harding, whom she married five years later. She helped make his newspaper profitable and supported his political career, campaigning indefatigably when he ran for president. As first lady, her common touch made her popular. She died in 1924, a year after her husband's death in office.

Below: The Harding administration began cutting income tax to boost the post-war economy.

Born: 2 November 1865, Corsica, Ohio

Parents: George (1844–1928) and Phoebe (1843–1910)

Family background: Medicine

Education: Ohio Central College (1882)

Religion: Baptist

Occupation: Newspaper editor and publisher

Military service: None

Political career: Ohio State Senate, 1900–4

Lieutenant governor of Ohio, 1904–6

US Senate, 1915–21

Presidential annual salary: $75,000

Political party: Republican

Died: 2 August 1923, San Francisco, California

VOTES FOR WOMEN

They protested, they picketed and they petitioned. During the 19th century, many who supported the cause of abolitionism and the demand for civil rights connected the case for racial equality with the call for women's rights. In 1848, at Seneca Falls, Elizabeth Cady Stanton argued for women's suffrage. After the Civil War, she found a formidable ally in Susan B. Anthony, who in 1872 managed to vote in the presidential election before being arrested and fined. She refused to pay and remained an indefatigable campaigner until her death at the age of 86 in 1906.

By the end of the 19th century women had gained the right to vote in several of the new western states, including Colorado, Idaho, Wyoming and Utah. As the progressive era took shape, the campaign gained momentum. Alice Paul and Lucy Burns adopted the more militant tactics they had witnessed while visiting the United Kingdom. Mass demonstrations and organized picketing, including a daily protest outside the White House, made sure that the issue remained high on the political agenda. Paul and Burns were arrested. After going on hunger strikes, they were force-fed.

In 1915, Carrie Chapman Catt began a second term as president of the National American Woman Suffrage Association. She campaigned to force reform at state and federal level. In 1917, New York became the first East Coast state to give women the vote. Two years later Congress finally passed the Nineteenth Amendment to the

Above: Alice Paul unfurls a banner from the balcony of the National Women's Party headquarters, showing a star for each state that has ratified the Nineteenth Amendment giving women the right to vote.

Constitution, introduced in 1878, which declared: "The right of citizens of the United States to vote shall not be denied or abridged by the United States or by any State on account of sex."

Ratification was achieved in time for women to cast their ballots in the 1920 presidential election. One who did so was Charlotte Woodward, aged 81, who was by then the sole survivor of the Seneca Falls Convention. As Carrie Chapman Catt put it in 1924, the women's suffrage movement had been "an effort to bring men to feel less superior and women to feel less inferior". Much had been achieved: more was left to do.

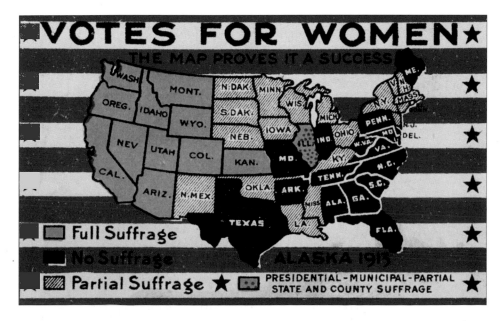

Left: A map of the USA indicating each state's position on women's suffrage in 1913.

THE DEVELOPMENT OF RADIO

In April 1922, the magazine *Telephony* informed its readers that: "President Harding has become one of the most enthusiastic radio telephone fans in Washington. Scarcely a day goes by that he does not 'listen-in' on the receiving set specially installed for him a short time ago by the wireless experts of the Navy Department." The previous month a pioneering radio station, KDKA in Pittsburgh, had broadcast the president's inaugural address, read simultaneously on air while he delivered the speech in Washington. Radio, as a medium of political communication and popular entertainment, seized the American imagination.

During World War I all US patents connected with the development of radio had been consolidated to help the war effort, and equipment was produced solely for the military. The Radio Corporation of America (RCA) was

Below: The first president to make use of radio, Roosevelt's 'fireside chats' were broadcast to millions.

established at the end of the war under the direction of David Sarnoff. In 1921, it allowed listeners to witness the world heavyweight boxing championship fight between Jack Dempsey and Georges Carpentier. Three years later, there were radios in more than 2.5 million US homes. By the end of the decade, the National Broadcasting Corporation (NBC) had been created as a subsidiary of RCA and William Paley had established the rival Columbia Broadcasting System (CBS).

The networks of radio stations affiliated to NBC and CBS provided a way for politicians to speak directly to the whole nation, rather than having their words transcribed, with editorial comments added, and read in newspapers. Franklin Roosevelt broadcast a long series of 'fireside chats', which served to shrink the distance between the president and the people. His first broadcast was made in March 1933, just over a week after he had taken office, and he continued the practice throughout his presidency: the last 'fireside chat'

Above: Radio, developed for the armed services in times of war, quickly became a source of popular entertainment.

took place in June 1944. During these talks he became a temporary guest in US homes.

Roosevelt used radio to reassure the nation in the depths of the Depression. Later he used it again to explain the need for America to go to war once more. He demonstrated that a president could achieve better ratings than many contemporary entertainment shows.

Radio audiences trusted what they heard. On 31 October 1938, the actor Orson Welles spooked the USA, broadcasting a live adaptation of H. G. Wells's story *The War of the Worlds* on CBS. Presenting the first part of the drama as a series of news bulletins, Welles convinced his audience that the United States was in the throes of an invasion from Mars. The reaction of the listeners dramatized the power of the medium, and showed how those adept at using it could influence their audience. As Roosevelt reportedly told Welles, there were two great actors in the USA at that time. Welles was the other one.

CALVIN COOLIDGE
1923–1929

When the writer Dorothy Parker was told that President Calvin Coolidge had died, she famously asked. "How could they tell?" Coolidge would have appreciated her witticism. He liked people to laugh. He allowed himself to be photographed in relaxed poses and in a variety of costumes that his advisors warned might make him look ridiculous. Coolidge knew better. His lack of affectation was a political asset; so too was his transparent integrity as he inherited the White House after the scandal-mired years of his predecessor Harding's administration.

Born in Vermont on Independence Day in 1872, Coolidge graduated from Amherst College in Massachusetts and became a lawyer, opening a practice in

Above: Coolidge's honesty restored public faith in the presidency, but his leadership remained uninspiring.

nearby Northampton in 1897. In 1905 he married Grace Goodhue, and they had two sons. Two years later, as a Republican, he was elected to the State Legislature. In 1910 he returned to Northampton as mayor. Having served in the state Senate, and as both lieutenant governor and governor of Massachusetts, he entered national politics as Harding's vice president. It was just before midnight on 2 August that he received the news of the president's sudden death. His father, a justice of the peace, with whom he was staying at the time, administered the oath of office and Coolidge went back to bed.

He remained untainted by the scandals that had emerged during Harding's administration and which eventually ended the career of Harry Daugherty as attorney general, though his image of absolute integrity could not disguise his limitations as a leader. With the economy buoyant and his party rallying behind him, Coolidge

won the Republican nomination in 1924 and was elected president in his own right.

Thereafter he did little to impress, introducing no domestic legislation of significance and issuing no public statements to indicate his views on the major political questions of the day. Coolidge presided over the rapid economic growth that characterized the 'Roaring Twenties'. He and his treasury secretary, Andrew Mellon, believed in reducing the tax burden and minimizing federal expenditure, leaving such issues as employment legislation and economic controls to state governments. He was even reluctant to spend federal funds on flood control after the Mississippi flood of 1927.

His major achievement was to restore public confidence in the presidency. By avoiding giving offence to anyone Coolidge tried to remain popular with everyone. It came as a surprise when he announced in 1927 that he would not run for re-election. Unlike Theodore Roosevelt, he meant it. Honest but uninspiring, 'Silent Cal' left the White House and retired to his adopted state of Massachusetts where he died in 1933 at the age of 60.

Born: 4 July 1872, Plymouth, Vermont

Parents: John (1845–1926) and Victoria (1846–85)

Family background: Farming, storekeeping

Education: Amherst College (1895)

Religion: Congregationalist

Occupation: Lawyer

Military service: None

Political career: Northampton Ma. City Council, 1899
City solicitor, 1900–1
Clerk of courts, 1904
Massachusetts Legislature, 1907–8 and 1912–15
Mayor of Northampton, 1910–11,
Lieutenant governor of Massachusetts, 1916–18
Governor of Massachusetts, 1919–20
Vice president, 1921–3

Presidential annual salary: $75,000

Political party: Republican

Died: 5 January 1933, Northampton, Massachusetts

GRACE COOLIDGE

From Vermont, Grace Goodhue was born in 1879 and married Calvin Coolidge in 1905. She had two sons, the eldest of whom died at the age of 16 while the family was living in the White House. Her charm and vivacity compensated for her husband's dour demeanour. She helped raise $2 million for the Clarke School for the Deaf in her adopted home town of Northampton in Massachusetts. After her husband died, she lived on for 24 years, dying in 1957 at the age of 78.

THE SCOPES TRIAL

1925

If a more modern, secular US society seemed to be in the making, it was not without its opponents. In July 1925, God went on trial in a courtroom in a small town in Tennessee. The three-time losing Democrat candidate for the presidency, William Jennings Bryan, argued with one of the most famous trial lawyers of the day, Clarence Darrow. Should the theory of evolution be taught as fact, challenging the biblical account of creation? John Scopes, a Dayton high school science teacher, was prosecuted for telling his students, in the words of one of them, "all about monkeys and things".

Scopes was found guilty and fined. That was no surprise: he had freely admitted his action in order to allow the proceedings to take place. In due course an appeal court overturned the verdict and dismissed "this bizarre case", which had seized the national imagination. The real issue was a profound and enduring clash of two cultures: scientific rationalism and religious conviction.

Charles Darwin's publication of *The Origin of Species* in 1859 and *The Descent of Man* in 1871 had introduced a scientific explanation for what had always been a matter of faith. The theory of evolution rippled outwards, and was applied to economic life as well as the natural world. 'Social Darwinism' with its accompanying mantra – 'the survival of the fittest' – justified the competitive capitalism of the Gilded Age, in which the strong prospered and the weakest were left behind. The process of natural selection was thought to ensure a healthier and wealthier society.

William Jennings Bryan had opposed such ideas throughout his political career. Championing the poor and the dispossessed, he had argued eloquently for economic and social reform. He agreed with those who accepted the Bible as literal truth and whose beliefs had coined a term: fundamentalism.

The Scopes trial allowed Americans to debate the place of religion in a modern secular society. The high point of the trial came when Darrow cross-examined Bryan, forcing him to admit that biblical stories were open to interpretation. Taking no comfort from the verdict, fundamentalists withdrew from the political arena for the next half century and appeared to be in retreat, only to re-emerge at the end of the 20th century as a formidable force in US presidential politics.

Below: The Scopes trial was a landmark case, but the teaching of evolution in US classrooms remains controversial.

MOUNT RUSHMORE
1927

On Mount Rushmore in South Dakota the heads of four presidents are carved from stone. It is, as President Calvin Coolidge said at the dedication ceremony on 10 August 1927, "decidedly American in conception, in its magnitude, in its meaning and altogether worthy of our Country". Theodore Roosevelt, the most contentious choice, appears between Thomas Jefferson and Abraham Lincoln. George Washington is more prominent.

The original idea had been more modest: a mountain sculpture of figures from the history of the West – Lewis and Clark, George Armstrong Custer, Buffalo Bill and the Native Americans they encountered there – designed to encourage tourism. But when the sculptor Gutzon Borglum was enlisted to work on the project, he had something far greater in mind. As the nation approached the 150th anniversary of the Philadelphia Convention, the memorial would symbolize the

Right: Gutzon Borglum working on the first model of the gigantic memorial.

contributions of four presidents to the establishment, growth, preservation and greatness of the United States.

For Coolidge, Washington "represents our independence, our Constitution, our liberty". Jefferson "embodied the spirit of expansion" and Lincoln had championed "the principle of freedom to all inhabitants of our land". Why should Theodore Roosevelt, Coolidge's fellow Republican, but a far more controversial and contemporary figure – he had died only eight years previously – share such company? According to Coolidge, Roosevelt had championed economic freedom as well as political liberty,

Above: An enduring icon, the carved stone masterpiece in the side of a mountain has immortalized four of the United States most respected presidents for ever. From left to right: Washington, Jefferson, Theodore Roosevelt and Lincoln.

and in the construction of the Panama Canal he had "realized the vision that inspired Columbus in his search for a new passage to the orient".

In the depths of the Depression, funding the work was a problem. By 1941 it was almost complete. Borglum died on 6 March and his son Lincoln, named for the Great Emancipator, spent the next seven months adding the finishing touches: carving was completed on 31 October.

Mount Rushmore endures as a monument not only to the presidents whose achievements it celebrates, but also to the ambition of those whose vision and persistence transformed the landscape of the Black Hills of South Dakota forever. Their enduring legacy was the creation of what remains, quite simply, the largest work of art on earth.

J. EDGAR HOOVER AND THE FBI

In 1924 J. Edgar Hoover (who was no relation to President Herbert Hoover) was appointed as the sixth director of the Federal Bureau of Investigation, which had been set up in 1908. He was to remain in the post for nearly 50 years. Knowing that information brought job security as well as power, he was rumoured to keep files of incriminating information on the eight presidents at whose pleasure – more often displeasure – he served, ensuring that he remained politically untouchable until he died, still in office, in 1972.

ORIGINS OF THE FBI

In 1803, the same year that his eldest brother, Napoleon, sold the Louisiana Territory to Thomas Jefferson, Jerome Bonaparte, on a visit to the United States, married an American, Elizabeth Patterson. Napoleon refused to agree to the match. Having accompanied her husband to Europe, Elizabeth returned without him to her home in Baltimore with their infant son, named for his father. Just over a century later, her grandson, Charles, would become attorney general in the administration of Theodore Roosevelt. He was the

Below: Fear of communism was rife in 1919. This cartoon depicts Bolshevism and anarchy creeping under the flag.

driving force behind the creation of the organization that became the Federal Bureau of Investigation.

Charles Bonaparte identified a problem. The Justice Department had "no … permanent detective force under its immediate control". He therefore set one up, and at the end of his term in office he suggested the creation of a permanent team of investigators attached to the department. Under his successor, George Wickersham, the team became known as the Bureau of Investigation. In its early days, there was little to investigate, because most crimes violated state rather than federal laws. Gradually, however, the Bureau's sphere of activity broadened: during World War I it was involved in cases of espionage, draft evasion, sabotage and the activities of those classed as 'enemy aliens'. Prohibition boosted not only the level of criminal activity, but also the opportunities for the Bureau to involve itself in more high-profile cases, particularly under its new director, J. Edgar Hoover.

Above: Hoover became synonymous with the government department he led. No president dared to fire him.

THE PALMER RAIDS

John Edgar Hoover was born on New Year's Day, 1895, in Washington DC. After graduating from George Washington University with a law degree, he began his government career in the Department of Justice in 1917. By the following year, he was an assistant to the attorney general, A. Mitchell Palmer.

Palmer's reaction to the wave of bombings that took place across the United States in 1919, in which, along with his family, he escaped injury as one of the explosions damaged his own house in Washington, produced a campaign against those who were allegedly planning a socialist revolution in the USA: the 'Red Scare'.

With Hoover as an enthusiastic accomplice directing operations, the attorney general launched a series of raids to round up suspected radicals and foreigners with scant regard for their civil rights. At first Palmer had the support of the public, but his credibility was undermined when the excesses of his actions were exposed. Nevertheless, in 1921 Hoover, who had benefited from the nationwide attention given to the raids, became assistant director of the Bureau of Investigation.

DIRECTOR OF THE FBI

Three years later, after a few months as acting director, Hoover was appointed to the position that he would hold for almost 48 years. At the time the Bureau employed about 450 special agents. In 1935, having been briefly renamed the Department of Investigation, it was formally given the title by which it has since been known: the Federal Bureau of Investigation. Hoover had already put his personal stamp on it, introducing new selection and training procedures. He carefully crafted the image of his special agents, or 'G-Men', as the resourceful crime-fighters of popular

Below: The Wall Street bombing in September 1920 killed 40 people and injured hundreds more.

G-MEN

George 'Machine Gun' Kelly, one of the most notorious prohibition gangsters, reputedly first used the term. In 1933, as FBI agents burst into a Memphis house to arrest him, he implored the 'G-Men' – government men – not to shoot. It became the stuff of legend and was popularized by Hollywood, notably in the James Cagney film *G Men* (1935), one of the gangster movies in which the Bureau's crime-fighting heroics were dramatized.

Right: G-Men came to prominence in the 1930s when the Bureau took on many high-profile federal cases.

myth, their exploits dramatized by Hollywood as they took on the gangsters and organized crime that thrived during the prohibition era.

Under Hoover's direction the FBI helped to shape the federal government's national security policies before, during and after World War II. The attitudes he had adopted as Palmer's assistant were the foundation for his own anti-communist crusade during the Cold War. For Hoover, fighting domestic subversion became an obsession. Anyone he saw as a radical was a threat. Those involved in the campaign for civil rights and the opponents of US military action overseas – notably during the Vietnam War – he deemed to be engaging in 'un-American activities'. Hoover identified them as legitimate targets of investigations that in many cases opened the FBI to charges of ignoring the civil liberties that were enshrined in the Bill of Rights.

Hoover was peerless as a bureaucratic survivor. His assumed knowledge of the potential embarrassments that littered the lives of prominent politicians and public officials, including successive presidents, none of whom dared to confront him, allowed him to remain the FBI's longest serving director.

When Hoover died in May 1972, his body lay in state in the Capitol building in Washington: an honour accorded to few Americans. His own private life, which had been the object of gossip and speculation while he lived, was soon investigated and exposed in lurid detail, overshadowing his long career as the nation's most famous G-Man.

HERBERT HOOVER
1929–1933

When the US stock market crashed in 1929, the president, along with many Americans, could not have realized either the depth or the length of the economic slump that would follow changing the landscape of US politics. Nevertheless, it was Herbert Hoover's inability to provide workable solutions to the problem as well as political leadership as the Depression took hold that led to him losing the presidency.

Hoover was the first 20th-century incumbent not to be re-elected, and the Republican party would not regain the White House for another 20 years. As president, he would be forever eclipsed by his successor, Franklin D. Roosevelt. Hoover, the former engineer and self-made millionaire, had encountered a problem he could not fix.

Born in Iowa in 1874 to Quaker parents, Hoover was an orphan by the age of nine. He travelled west to live with relatives in Oregon, and later went to Stanford University in San Francisco, where he was a member of the newly established college's first cohort of

Born: 10 August 1874, West Branch, Iowa

Parents: Jesse (1847–80) and Hulda (1848–83)

Family background: Orphaned aged nine; raised by uncle in Oregon

Education: Stanford University (1895)

Religion: Quaker

Occupation: Mining engineer

Military service: None

Political career: Secretary of commerce, 1921–8

Presidential annual salary: $75,000

Political party: Republican

Died: 20 October 1964, New York, New York

students. He graduated in 1895. His degree in geology opened the way to a career as a mining engineer, and he became an internationally renowned expert in his field. In 1899 he married Lou Henry, a fellow Stanford student. They had two children. The family travelled widely as Hoover's career took him to live and work in a number of countries, including Australia and China. By the age of 40 he had become rich through his consultancy work and ownership of profitable silver mines in Burma. He and his wife published their own translation of Georgius Agricola's

Above: A successful businessman turned politician, Hoover had his presidency wrecked by the USA's economic collapse.

classic 16th-century treatise on mining and metallurgy, *De Re Metallica*, which remains in print today.

Hoover was a progressive Republican and supported Theodore Roosevelt's bid to return to the White House in 1912. During World War I he took on a number of high-profile administrative tasks and relief work: he had been raised as a Quaker, and having achieved success in his career he wanted to focus on

Above: Dining on the edge of the abyss. Unable to prevent the USA toppling into the depression, Hoover, like many others, lost his job.

public service. He organized the evacuation from Europe of US civilians caught up in the conflict, oversaw the provision of humanitarian aid to Belgium and directed the US Food Administration, set up to supply the US army and its allies as well as domestic needs. His campaign for voluntary rationing in American households became known as 'Hooverizing'. After the war he co-ordinated US relief efforts aimed at rebuilding war-torn Europe, and he was with Woodrow Wilson as he negotiated the League of Nations and Peace Treaty at Versailles.

Hoover became secretary of commerce in Warren Harding's Cabinet, and is acknowledged to have been one of the president's few competent appointees. He remained in that position throughout Coolidge's administration, although their relationship was less than cordial. Hoover's popularity among Republicans and in the country at large enabled him to win the party's presidential nomination and the 1928 election. His opponent, Al Smith, was a Catholic and this caused the Democrats to lose the support of the 'solid South' for the first time since the end of reconstruction.

STOCK EXCHANGE CRISIS

Hoover had been in office a little over six months before 'Black Thursday'. On 24 October 1929, the New York Stock Exchange was jolted by a major fall in share prices. Five days later it was 'Black Tuesday' as the value of shares once more spiralled downwards, confirming the trend of the previous week. Wall Street had crashed, and the economic recession had arrived.

Hoover understood what had happened and coined the term 'Depression' to describe it. But he did not know how to deal with it, as the aftershocks of the USA's sudden plunge into economic reverse were felt around the world.

The banking system, never particularly robust, collapsed as banks failed across the nation. The downward spiral was aggravated by a severe drought in the summer of 1930, which hit the country's agricultural heartland and led to further defaulting on mortgages as well as food shortages.

Unemployment soared, reaching over 11 million in 1931. Hoover tried to stem the tide by pressing Congress

Below: Queues for work and for dole became a common sight as desperate people sought to keep home and family together.

to increase public expenditure to create jobs, with little success. With no federal system of welfare relief in place, poverty became widespread. In 1932, an army of unemployed veterans of World War I congregated in Washington to pressure Congress for advance payment of their war bonuses, which were not due for another 13 years. After scenes of rioting in the capital, General Douglas MacArthur defied the president's orders and used troops to clear the makeshift camps that the protesters had set up in Virginia, across the Potomac River from the White House – they were known as 'Hoovervilles'. Predictably, this move was a public relations disaster.

The United States' power to influence the course of international events was also diminished. In 1932, Japan invaded China and annexed Manchuria. Meanwhile, a state of political turmoil in Spain, Italy and Germany was paving the way for the emerging dictatorships in Europe.

Hoover ran for re-election more out of faith than conviction and was defeated comprehensively. An engineer who had more than demonstrated his humanitarian compassion when first he entered public life now left it because of his inability to show a common touch when confronted with an economic catastrophe that he, like many of his contemporaries, failed fully to understand. Herbert Hoover died in 1964 at the age of 90.

LOU HOOVER

Born in Iowa in 1874, she met her husband while both were geology students at Stanford. Lou Henry married Hoover in 1899 and they had two sons. They travelled extensively, and she became a proficient linguist. As first lady, she made regular radio broadcasts and speeches in support of her husband's policies. She died in 1944 at the age of 69.

CHARLES LINDBERGH
AND THE *SPIRIT OF ST LOUIS*

Charles Lindbergh was the first – and last – person to travel from New York to Paris in 33.5 hours sitting on a wicker chair. In May 1927, he flew across the Atlantic Ocean alone. His specially designed plane, the single-engine *Spirit of St Louis*, was made as light as possible to increase its flying range. His achievement made him a hero in Europe and in the United States, opening new horizons in the development of flight.

Born in Michigan in 1902, Lindbergh grew up in Minnesota. In 1920 he enrolled as an engineering student at the University of Wisconsin.

He dropped out, becoming a 'barn-stormer' or stunt pilot under the name 'Daredevil Lindbergh' and entertaining crowds by flying at fairs and airshows across America.

Following pilot training in the Army Air Service Reserve, he flew the mail between St Louis and Chicago. Attracted by the $25,000 prize offered for the first successful non-stop flight between New York and Paris, Lindbergh

Below: Just 20 years after flight was pioneered, Lindbergh made his ground-breaking record attempt to fly from New York to Paris in a single journey.

persuaded nine St Louis businessmen to invest in a plane that was capable of covering the distance. Named for its sponsors' home town, it was built in San Diego by the Ryan Aeronautical Company. When it was ready, Lindbergh flew it from California to New York, where he would take off on his transatlantic flight from Roosevelt Field. With an overnight stop in St Louis, he set a new record of 20 hours 21 minutes for the coast-to-coast journey.

THE RECORD FLIGHT

On 20 May at eight minutes before eight in the morning, Lindbergh left New York. Overcoming fog, ice, lack of sleep and hunger – he took only five sandwiches with him – he flew all day, through the night, and for most of the following day. Later he would recall at times almost skimming the ocean and, as he approached the Irish coast, shouting at a fisherman for directions, to no avail. Having found his way to Paris and circled the Eiffel Tower, he finally landed at the nearby Le Bourget airfield at 10.20 in the evening, local time, on 21 May. A large crowd had gathered to greet his arrival. The *New York Times* reported the historic event: "'Well, I made it,' smiled Lindbergh, as the little white monoplane came to a halt in the middle of the field." He became an instant international celebrity.

Lindbergh did not fly back. Returning on the USS *Memphis*, he travelled to Washington, where President Coolidge presented him with the Distinguished Flying Cross. A ticker-tape parade of unprecedented proportions greeted him in New York. Piloting the *Spirit of St Louis*, he embarked on a three-month nationwide tour. In March 1929, the president gave him the Congressional Medal of Honour. Two months later, Lindbergh married Anne Morrow, whom he had met when

day President Roosevelt ordered all government investigative agencies to co-operate with the New Jersey authorities in solving the crime. Two years later, Bruno Hauptmann, a German carpenter, was tried and executed for kidnap and murder, although controversy surrounded the conviction.

In 1935, the Lindberghs moved to Europe to escape incessant media attention. While there they made several trips to Germany, meeting members of its Nazi government, including Hermann Goering, from whom Lindbergh accepted a medal. In 1939, after his return to the United States, he became involved in the 'America First' movement, arguing against US involvement in World War II. Remarks suggestive of antisemitism and accusations of pro-Nazi sympathies damaged his credibility. Pearl Harbor undermined his argument. Lindbergh later served as a civilian advisor to American forces in the Pacific and flew around 50 combat missions. After the war he withdrew from public life. In 1974, he died at his home in Hawaii.

Below: The Nazi official Hermann Goering (centre) presented Lindbergh with a medal for his contribution to aviation.

Above: The success of the flight helped promote national pride, and Lindbergh received a hero's welcome on his return.

he had made a goodwill visit to Mexico, where her father was then the US ambassador.

KIDNAPPING AND AFTER

The fame Lindbergh had found as a solo pilot led to the defining moment of his family life. On 1 March 1932, the Lindberghs' eldest son, named for his father and then aged 20 months, was taken from their home in New Jersey. A number of ransom notes were received. J. Edgar Hoover offered his Bureau's assistance. On 12 May the baby's body was found. The following

THE WALL STREET CRASH
THE GREAT DEPRESSION, 1929

The stock market staggered, it tried to recover, then it collapsed. In the space of a week in October 1929, millions of US investors panicked. Economic confidence was shattered. The value of shares fell dramatically as sellers tried to stem their losses at any price. Those who had had the foresight to stop speculating before the crash – Joseph Kennedy was one of them – escaped with their fortunes intact. Many others lost everything.

On 31 December 1928, the Dow Jones Industrial Average, the index of the value of shares in leading industrial companies, had reached another all-time high, closing the day at 300 exactly. For many Americans, investing in the stock market seemed a one-way bet: a way of sharing in the economic wealth that the nation had generated throughout the decade of expansion and optimism that became known as the 'Roaring Twenties'. Hundreds of thousands of small investors took part, many borrowing more than half the value of the shares they were buying, accruing total loans of over $8.5 billion.

Three weeks after President Hoover's inauguration, on 25 March 1929, there was an ominous sign of what was

to come. The stock market tumbled in what the *New York Daily News* called a "selling avalanche". It rallied only after the banks intervened to provide cheaper credit for those who had borrowed to invest. By the summer it was business as usual again: the market reached record highs month after month.

Yet confidence proved to be brittle. In September, after the economist, Roger Babson, warned that, "Sooner or later, a crash is coming, and it may be terrific," Wall Street began to experience turbulence; in the following weeks the

Above: Americans took desperate measures when the value of their investments plummeted in the stock market crash.

market spiralled out of control. On 24 October – 'Black Thursday' – a wave of selling saw 13 million shares traded. Banks intervened, buying stocks in the hope of restoring equilibrium, and a late rally continued the following day. It was a short respite. Frenzied activity on 28 and 29 October – 'Black Monday' and 'Black Tuesday' – began a week in which the market lost $30 billion of its value, ten times the federal budget, and more than the United States had spent on its involvement in World War I. The Wall Street Crash became the defining event that marked the end of an era. It may not have caused the Depression, but it was a sign of the economic downturn that led to it.

Two months later the United States lurched into the 1930s, the decade of the Depression, the 'New Deal' and the leadership of one of its greatest presidents: Franklin Delano Roosevelt.

Left: The Wall Street Crash led to a nationwide run on the banks as widespread panic ensued.

FRANKLIN D. ROOSEVELT

1933–1945

When in his inaugural address in 1933 Roosevelt told Americans of his "firm belief that the only thing we have to fear is fear itself – nameless, unreasoning, unjustified terror which paralyzes needed efforts to convert retreat into advance," he was talking from experience. He spoke with the conviction that resulted from his long battle against the debilitating illness that had threatened his life. In 1921, at the age of 39, he contracted poliomyelitis. The disease was incurable, and – before the invention of the iron lung – if it caused paralysis of the chest it was fatal. He lost the use of his legs. His wife Eleanor said of him: "I know that he had real fear when he was first taken ill, but he learned to surmount it. After that I never heard him say he was afraid of anything." Franklin Roosevelt survived.

Born in 1882 at Hyde Park, the long-established family estate north of New York City, he was the only child of James Roosevelt and his second wife, Sara Delano. He spent his teenage years

Above: For just over 12 years, Franklin Roosevelt rewrote the political rule book. His unique achievement was not only his longevity in office; he was the architect of the modern presidency and his legacy has yet to be surpassed.

admiring the political career of his distant cousin, Theodore, but unlike the Republican Oyster Bay Roosevelts, the Hyde Park branch of the family were Democrats. Educated at Groton, an exclusive private school, he went on to Harvard. He dropped out of Columbia Law School, like Theodore before him, preferring to pursue a political career.

In 1905 he married Eleanor, Theodore Roosevelt's niece. They had six children, one of whom, a son named for his father, died in infancy. It was a turbulent relationship, but his wife would become one of Roosevelt's greatest political assets as well as an influential voice in US society in her own right.

Roosevelt was elected as a state senator in 1910, and three years later, following once more in his cousin's footsteps, he became assistant secretary to the navy in Woodrow Wilson's administration. In 1920, as a rising star

among Democrats, he was selected as the party's vice-presidential candidate. The example set by Theodore occurred to New York's party bosses, as the nomination for vice president would effectively remove a Roosevelt who had antagonized Tammany Hall from meddling in state politics. Defeated at the polls, he was temporarily out of the political limelight when, a year later, he was struck down with polio.

It was a long and painful recovery. Roosevelt regained partial use of his legs, but was largely confined to a wheelchair. The extent of his disability was kept from public knowledge in case it damaged his chances of returning to public office. In 1924, at the Democrat National Convention in Madison Square Garden, he gave the presidential nomination speech for the New York state governor, Al Smith. More relevant than his failure to influence the delegates, who selected John Davis from West Virginia instead, was the fact that he was able to walk a few steps to the podium, appearing his usual relaxed and confident self.

In 1928, Smith invited Roosevelt to give the nomination speech again, and as the party's presidential candidate he persuaded his fellow New Yorker to run for office as the state's governor. Smith lost to Hoover in the presidential election, but Roosevelt won an upset victory in New York. Four years later he became president and the Democrats gained control of Congress. He was 51 years old when he entered the White House: it was to be his home for the rest of his life.

THE NEW DEAL

Roosevelt was the outstanding politician of his generation. He understood that radio let him talk directly with the people. Moreover by making news he controlled the political agenda. Hoover

Born: 30 January 1882, Hyde Park, New York

Parents: James (1828–1900) and Sara (1854–1941)

Family background: Business, landowning

Education: Harvard College (1903)

Religion: Episcopalian

Occupation: Public service

Military service: None

Political career: New York State Legislature, 1911–13

Assistant secretary of the navy, 1913–20

Governor of New York, 1929–33

Presidential annual salary: $75,000

Political party: Democrat

Died: 12 April 1945, Warm Springs, Georgia

had held one press conference a month during his last 12 months in office; Roosevelt averaged one a week during his 12 years in the presidency. He was aware of the importance of symbolic gestures: flying to the Democrat convention to make a speech accepting his nomination in 1932 was news because it was new. So too was his programme to aid national recovery, its name partly borrowed from his cousin's political lexicon: the New Deal.

Roosevelt's New Deal was introduced in a whirlwind of legislation during the frenzied activity of his first hundred days in office. It was initially aimed at bringing stability to the nation's financial system, devising a system of federal relief and job creation for the unemployed and reviving US capitalism. It was less a coherent plan than a way of giving effect to what he had referred to in a speech before he became president as "bold, persistent experimentation" to cure the ills of the Depression. He had back-up. His 'Brains Trust' was a group of intellectuals and

Below: Roosevelt convinced Americans that it was safe to reinvest their money in the nation's banks.

academic advisors who helped formulate the major legislative initiatives of the New Deal.

To stabilize the banking system, Roosevelt moved swiftly. After declaring a four-day bank holiday, he persuaded Congress to pass emergency legislation allowing them to open for business again only after their financial probity had been checked. His first 'fireside chat' on 12 March 1933 explained in simple terms the principles of banking to

Above: The construction of the Grand Coulee Dam was instigated under the presidency of Roosevelt, in a drive to end the Depression and provide employment.

his audience and persuaded them that it was safer to keep their money in a "reopened bank than under the mattress". The following day, queues formed outside banks to put back the cash that had been taken out in a panic. Roosevelt's was the voice of reassurance. Later in the year the Federal Reserve Board brought the banking system under tighter control.

The most controversial part of the New Deal, passed during the first hundred days, was the National Industrial Recovery Act. It established the Public Works Administration, a job creation agency, and the National Recovery Agency, which aimed to place the relationship between employers and their workforces on a more equitable basis. Unsurprisingly this generated opposition among industrial and business leaders. In 1935 the Supreme Court declared it unconstitutional.

Government involvement was seen as the key to economic regeneration, nowhere more so than in the Tennessee Valley Authority (TVA), set up in 1933. Roosevelt envisaged it as "a corporation

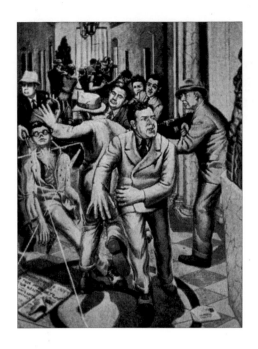

Above: Huey Long, US Senator, was a popular and charismatic radical who promoted the redistribution of wealth. He was assassinated in 1935.

clothed with the power of government but possessed of the flexibility and initiative of a private enterprise". Through major public works projects that provided employment in an area badly affected by the Depression, the TVA brought electricity to rural areas, encouraged new industries to come to the region and also worked to revive agricultural production.

As the economic recession in Europe deepened, demagogues assumed dictatorial power. In January 1933, a few weeks before Roosevelt was inaugurated, Adolf Hitler became chancellor of Germany. In Italy, Benito Mussolini had held office for a decade. The former governor of Louisiana, senator Huey Long, appealed to Americans with his radical populism and his call for a redistribution of the USA's wealth from rich to poor. Initially Long supported Roosevelt but the success of his 'Share our Wealth' organization, established in 1934, made him potentially a power-broker in national politics and fed his own presidential ambitions. In September 1935, Long was assassinated in the state capitol in Baton Rouge.

Re-elected in a landslide victory, Roosevelt's second administration was dominated by his attempt to 'pack' a recalcitrant Supreme Court with his supporters. The president proposed new legislation that would allow him to nominate an additional member for each justice over the age of 70, but the move was defeated in the Senate. It was a major political humiliation but it also left a lasting impression on the Supreme Court, which never again struck down New Deal legislation.

Roosevelt started to reform the executive branch of government to create 'the modern Presidency' with access to sources of information and power independent of the major departments of state represented in the Cabinet. The economy spluttered along. A civil war was fought in Spain. War broke out in Europe. The president ran for an unprecedented third term and once more won an easy victory.

AFTER PEARL HARBOR

World War II brought the Depression to an end. It revitalized the US economy as the United States became, in Roosevelt's words, "the great arsenal of democracy". After the Japanese attacked Pearl Harbor in 1941, US troops crossed the Atlantic to join the conflict in Europe and at the same time fought their way across the Pacific against Japan.

Their commander-in-chief, by now exhausted and ill, was re-elected for a fourth term in 1944. On 12 April 1945, a little over a month after his inauguration, Franklin Roosevelt, whose place among the greatest of American presidents was assured, died in Warm Springs, Georgia, where more than 30 years previously he had convalesced from polio. He was 63 years old.

ELEANOR ROOSEVELT

Eleanor Roosevelt was born in New York City in 1884. She married Franklin Roosevelt at the age of 20, and they had six children. Eleanor was the most high-profile first lady up to that time, and she became a political figure in her own right, speaking out on a variety of issues and travelling widely within the United States as well as overseas. After her husband died, she continued to be active in public life, at one time as a member of the USA's delegation to the United Nations. She died in 1962, aged 78.

Left: Eleanor Roosevelt proved to be a formidable first lady.

HOLLYWOOD
IN THE 1930s

The Jazz Singer (1927) revolutionized the film industry: it was the first feature-length movie to have synchronized sound. Movies now talked and their accent was American.

The 1930s were Hollywood's 'Golden Age': by the end of the decade, more than 500 films were being made each year. Numerous films that are still regarded as classics were produced and the studios created a host of enduring stars. As the USA's economic depression deepened, the Hollywood studios provided glamour and escapist entertainment for audiences who faced mounting challenges in their drab daily lives.

The five major studios – Warner Brothers, MGM, Paramount, RKO and 20th Century Fox – all used the so-called 'studio system'. This determined how the industry was organized: studios produced movies primarily on their own film-making lots, owned the distribution rights and even the theatres

Below: The epic production Gone With the Wind *remains the highest grossing film of all time.*

in which their films were shown. At the same time, under the star system, the studios controlled the lives of the actors and actresses they placed under contract. Names were changed, biographies were re-written, and the stars reflected the image that the studio wanted to project. The contracts gave the actors little or no say in the choice of parts they played, and often included 'morality clauses' in an attempt to guard against adverse publicity.

Irving Thalberg, vice president of production at MGM, used the star system with outstanding success, fostering the careers of Greta Garbo, Joan Crawford, Jean Harlow, Clark Gable and Spencer Tracy among others. At other studios Katherine Hepburn, Marlene Dietrich, Cary Grant and Gary Cooper also became major stars.

The early 1930s produced classics of the gangster genre, such as *Little Caesar* (1930), *The Public Enemy* (1931) and *Scarface* (1932), with stars such as Edward G. Robinson and James Cagney. The Marx Brothers made comedies, and Charlie Chaplin directed the satire *Modern Times* in 1936. Fred Astaire had a screen test at RKO. His report read, "Losing hair. Can't sing. Balding. Can dance a little" – which he

Above: Shirley Temple presented a special Academy Award to Walt Disney for Snow White and the Seven Dwarfs *in 1939; it was one of the biggest ever box office hits.*

proceeded to do with Ginger Rogers throughout the decade. Other notable movies included Frank Capra's *It Happened One Night* (1934), which won five Oscars, and Walt Disney's first feature-length cartoon, *Snow White and the Seven Dwarfs* (1937). In 1939 *Stagecoach*, John Ford's revival of the Western with John Wayne as the Ringo Kid, was released, and Clark Gable starred with Vivien Leigh in *Gone with the Wind*.

Hollywood avoided the harsher realities of contemporary life. Out of the thousands of films made during the New Deal years, very few touched upon the Depression, or such contemporary European events as the Spanish Civil War and the advance of fascism in Italy and Germany.

In 1937 Warner Brothers gave an acting contract to a radio announcer from Illinois. Forty-three years later, Ronald Reagan, who believed in happy endings, landed his most important role: president of the United States.

PEARL HARBOR
1941

"Yesterday, December 7, 1941, a date which will live in infamy, the United States of America was suddenly and deliberately attacked by naval and air forces of the Empire of Japan." In response, President Roosevelt asked Congress to declare war.

Pearl Harbor on the Hawaiian island of O'ahu was then the headquarters of the US Pacific fleet, which in May 1940 had moved there from its San Diego base. By the time the Japanese air strikes had ended, eight of its ships had been crippled or sunk, three others were damaged, almost 200 aircraft had been destroyed, and close to 2,500 personnel had been killed. Bombers flying from

Below: During the Japanese attack, a small boat attempts to rescue survivors from the USS West Virginia.

Japanese aircraft carriers 320km (200 miles) away had taken the US forces by surprise.

JAPAN ATTACKS
It was Admiral Isoroku Yamamoto's idea. If the USA's naval presence in the Pacific could be neutralized by this one bold attack, Japan could launch an offensive against Hong Kong, Malaya, the Philippines and Guam, bringing it new bases and access to raw materials. Defences could be prepared against the inevitable counterattack. It was a high stakes gamble. The Japanese prime minister, General Hideki Tojo, observed: "Our Empire stands at the threshold of glory or oblivion."

On Sunday 7 December, the first wave of attacks came at just before eight in the morning, local time; 183 bombers

Above: More than half of those who died in the raid were on board the USS Arizona.

took part. The Japanese commander Mitsuo Fuchida's message back to the fleet – "Tora! Tora! Tora!" – signalled that the surprise was complete. The greatest explosion came as the forward magazine of the USS *Arizona* was hit. Almost one thousand members of its crew died. The raid took a little more than half an hour. There was a lull; then, 25 minutes later, the second wave of 167 bombers arrived. The major damage to the fleet had been done, but Pearl Harbor continued to be pounded for another hour before the Japanese broke off their attack. Even so, they left important potential targets, including fuel storage tanks, intact.

The Japanese had achieved a short-term tactical victory. Its strategic significance was predictable: the United States fought back. The attack turned public opinion from a position of isolationism to a recognition that the United States should enter the war. As Yamamoto later came to realize: "We have awakened a sleeping giant and have instilled in him a terrible resolve."

WORLD WAR II
1939–1945

On 11 December 1941, four days after Pearl Harbor, in accordance with the terms of their Axis pact with Japan, Germany and Italy declared war on the United States. Within two weeks, Winston Churchill, the British prime minister, had arrived in Washington. He urged Roosevelt to stand by the strategy agreed to earlier in the event that the United States was drawn into conflict with the Axis powers. Japan could wait. The war in Europe was the priority.

In January 1942, Roosevelt and Churchill settled on an Anglo-American invasion of Axis-held territory in North Africa. 'Operation Torch' began in November. Allied troops landed in

Above: Europe on the eve of World War II in 1939. War broke out when Germany invaded Poland.

THE AXIS PACT

In September 1940, Hitler, Mussolini and Saburo Kurusu, the Japanese ambassador in Berlin, signed the Axis pact, a tri-partite pact formalizing the military alliance between their three countries. It committed them "to assist one another if one of the Contracting Powers is attacked by a Power at present not involved in the European War or in the Japanese–Chinese conflict". In December 1941, Kurusu was in Washington when the Axis powers declared war on America.

Below: Mussolini and Hitler, the two European members of the Axis pact.

Morocco and Algeria and fought their way towards Tunisia. They met with some resistance from forces loyal to the Vichy government in France. German reinforcements fought to prevent the Allies linking up with the British Eighth Army, under the command of General Bernard Montgomery, which was moved east from Egypt after its victory at the Battle of El Alamein. Seven months later, Axis troops surrendered and the North African campaign came to an end.

On the eastern front, the year began with the Soviet forces lifting the German Siege of Leningrad, and ended with the Battle for Stalingrad. In December, Nazi atrocities against the Jews were denounced by the governments in Washington, London and Moscow. The perpetrators would be tried as war criminals.

Roosevelt became the first president to travel overseas during wartime, as well as the first to visit Africa, when he

met Churchill at the Casablanca Conference in January 1943. Joseph Stalin had been invited, but his concerns about the situation in Russia and misgivings over Allied strategy kept him at home. Roosevelt and Churchill agreed that the war would be fought until Germany surrendered unconditionally. They also planned the next invasion: Sicily. It took place on 10 July 1943. By September, Italy had surrendered. Earlier that year, Soviet troops had retaken Stalingrad and the tide of war on the eastern front began running against Germany. At the end of November, Roosevelt, Churchill and Stalin, the 'Big Three', met in Tehran and committed the Allies to the invasion of France.

Under General Eisenhower's command, 'Operation Overlord', also known as the Normandy landings, began on

6 June 1944. Two weeks later, there were more than half a million Allied troops in France. By August, Paris had been liberated. Allied armies fought their way towards Berlin. In February 1945, the 'Big Three' conferred at Yalta in the Crimea. With his armies advancing towards Germany, Stalin forced Churchill and Roosevelt, whose health was in terminal decline, to agree that Soviet troops would remain in occupied territory in Eastern Europe. When Roosevelt reported their discussions to Congress on 2 March, he remained seated: it was the first public acknowledgement of his disability. The following month he died, just 18 days before Hitler's suicide in Berlin. On 7 May Germany surrendered.

WAR IN THE PACIFIC

In the Pacific, the attack on Pearl Harbor had signalled the start of an offensive that, by the end of May 1942, had brought Japan territorial gains including the Philippines, Malaya, Burma, French Indo-China, the Dutch East Indies, Hong Kong and Singapore. On 4 June the Japanese and US navies faced each other at the Battle of Midway. America's decisive victory marked the beginning of the end. In August, the Allies started their first major offensive at Guadalcanal in the

THE VICHY GOVERNMENT

After Germany invaded France, Henri-Philippe Pétain's government, based in Vichy, controlled that part of it that remained unoccupied. Charles de Gaulle, leader of the Free French forces in exile, challenged its legitimacy. German troops marched into Vichy after the Allied invasion of North Africa. Following France's liberation, its leaders were tried as collaborators. Some were executed, though Pétain escaped that fate. De Gaulle commuted his sentence to life imprisonment. Pétain died in 1951.

Above: The largest seaborne invasion during World War II took place in Normandy in 1944 as the Allies invaded France.

Below: Roosevelt meets Churchill and Stalin at Yalta in the Crimea in February 1945; he died two months later.

Above: The iconic image of the Pacific War: Marines raise the US flag on Mount Suribachi, Iwo Jima.

Solomon Islands. It would be six more months before the Japanese withdrew from the island.

During 1943, a grim war of attrition took shape, forcing Japan gradually to relinquish control of its newly acquired territories. In June, Allied forces began the campaign to recover the islands in the Pacific. The Battle of Iwo Jima in February 1945 produced the most famous image of the Pacific War when, after fierce fighting, marines raised the US flag on Mount Suribachi. By the time war in Europe ended in May, the Japanese faced defeat. On 6 August an atomic bomb was dropped on Hiroshima, followed by another, three days later, on Nagasaki. The broadcast by the Japanese emperor on 15 August, the first time his voice had been heard in public, announced the surrender. It was over.

Below: The War in the Pacific continued after the conflict in Europe ended.

Below: The Battle of Midway significantly weakened Japan's military capacity.

AMERICAN CAMPAIGNS OF WORLD WAR II

1942

7 May: Battle of the Coral Sea

3 June: Battle of Midway

7 August: Guadalcanal

17 August: First USAAF raid in Europe

15 September: Papua New Guinea campaign

8 November: Operation Torch

1943

4 January: Tunisian campaign

2 March: Battle of the Bismarck Sea

30 June: South Pacific offensive

15 August: Aleutians retaken

17 August: Patton conquers Sicily

9 September: US army lands at Salerno, Italy

9 October: Schweinfurt raid

20 November: Central Pacific campaign begins

1944

22 January: Allies land at Anzio, Italy

7 February: Marshall Islands taken

4 June: Rome liberated

6 June: D–Day (Operation Overlord begins in Europe)

19 June: Battle of the Philippine Sea

15 August: Allied invasion of France

10 September: France liberated

11 September: Invasion of Germany

23 October: Battle of Leyte Gulf

24 November: Bombing of Japan begins

16 December: Battle of the Bulge

1945

9 January: Philippines Luzon campaign

8 February: Rhineland campaign

23 February: Battle of Iwo Jima

9 March: USAAF Tokyo raid

1 April: Okinawa campaign

2 May: Fall of Berlin

8 May: VE Day (Germany surrenders)

6 August: Atomic bomb dropped on Hiroshima

2 September: VJ Day (Japan surrenders)

THE INVENTION OF THE ATOMIC BOMB
1941–1945

Albert Einstein wrote to Franklin Roosevelt on 2 August 1939. The most famous physicist in the world, who had escaped from Nazi antisemitism to come to Princeton University, had a warning for the president: "It may become possible to set up a nuclear chain reaction in a large mass of uranium." If this happened, he said, "extremely powerful bombs of a new type may thus be constructed". German scientists might already be working on such a device. Roosevelt ordered a programme of research and development that would culminate in the 'Manhattan Project'.

It was Robert Oppenheimer who took charge of the bomb's design at a laboratory at Los Alamos in the remote mountains of New Mexico. Enriched uranium was produced at Oak Ridge in Tennessee. In 1943, work began at Hanford in Washington State to construct a facility to make plutonium. By early 1945, scientists had enough enriched uranium and plutonium for their purposes.

Above: Almost a quarter of a million people perished immediately or in the aftermath of the explosions.

Below: Truman's decision to drop atomic bombs on Japan ended the war, heralding the dawn of the nuclear age.

On 16 July a plutonium bomb was tested. It worked. As the mushroom cloud rose over the New Mexico desert, Oppenheimer recalled that the explosion brought to his mind a line from the *Bhagavad-Gita*, the Hindu scripture: "Now I am become Death, the destroyer of worlds."

LITTLE BOY AND FAT MAN

The decision to use the bomb was President Truman's. He had been unaware of the Manhattan Project's progress until he took office in April 1945. On 25 July, after informing Stalin of the successful test, news of which spies had already reported to the Soviet leader, Truman authorized its use against the Japanese.

Hiroshima was first. The *Enola Gay*, the bomber piloted by Colonel Paul Tibbets, dropped a uranium bomb, 'Little Boy', obliterating the city. 'Fat Man', the plutonium bomb, which exploded over Nagasaki, brought similar destruction. Those closest to the detonations were incinerated. Others who survived the initial blast died later from the effects of radiation.

Many scientists who worked on the Manhattan Project regretted developing a weapon of mass destruction. Politicians – none more so than the president of the United States, whose finger has hovered over the nuclear button at times of extreme international tension – have had to have the calm judgement and self-restraint not to use it again.

THE UNITED NATIONS

1944–1945

Even before the United States entered the war, its president looked forward to the peace. In August 1941, Roosevelt and Churchill met on ships of their respective navies in Placentia Bay, Newfoundland. One outcome of their discussions was the Atlantic Charter, issued on 14 August, establishing "certain common principles in the national policies of their respective countries on which they base their hopes for a better future for the world". These included an end to imperial ambitions, international economic co-operation and a "permanent system of general security" based on disarmament.

On 1 January 1942, 24 countries joined the United States and Britain in agreeing to subscribe to the Charter's provisions. They were convinced "that complete victory over their enemies is essential to defend life, liberty, independence and religious freedom, and to preserve human rights and justice in their own lands as well as in other lands". Roosevelt had proposed the collective term embodied in the statement's title and used for the first time: it was a "Declaration by the United Nations".

In November 1943, a Senate resolution, introduced by Tom Connally, chair of its Foreign Relations Committee, which had been framed in the office of the then junior senator from Missouri, Harry Truman, was approved. It recognized "the necessity of there being established at the earliest practicable date a general international organization, based on the principle of the sovereign equality of all peace-loving states, and open to membership by all such states, large and small, for the maintenance of international peace and security". The United States was thus committed to play a leading role in creating the United Nations.

A NEW CHARTER

Representatives from America, Britain, the Soviet Union and China met at Dumbarton Oaks, a mansion in Washington, from August to October 1944 and drew up proposals for "an international organization under the title of The United Nations", the membership of which was "open to all

Below: Fifty-one countries signed up to the charter to become the original members of the United Nations.

Above: The United Nations works to resolve international confrontations and to promote peace.

peace-loving states". The following year, 50 countries sent delegations to San Francisco to draw up its charter at a conference that opened on 25 April. The proceedings attracted media interest from around the world. One correspondent from Hearst's *Chicago World Herald and Tribune* observed them and became pessimistic about the organization's chances of success: his name was John F. Kennedy.

A COALITION FOR PEACE

The principal purpose, it was agreed, was "to maintain international peace and security". Unlike the League of Nations, the United Nations would be able to call on member states to give military support to its peacekeeping efforts. Through its General Assembly and Security Council it provided the mechanisms for the potential arbitration and resolution of international conflicts, although agreement would prove difficult as the post-war world became divided along the ideological fault lines of the Cold War.

Right: Though the United Nations building is situated in New York, the land it stands on is considered international territory.

On 26 June 1945, China became the first country to sign the Charter of the United Nations, followed by representatives from the other 49 nations. A State Department official, Alger Hiss, flew to Washington the next day and delivered the Charter to the White House. It was to come into force once it had been ratified by the governments of the nations comprising the permanent members of the Security Council – the United States, Britain, France, China and Russia – together with a majority of the other signatories. While this process took place, Poland also signed, to join as an original member of the organization. On 24 October, just over two months after the war ended, the United Nations was established. In December, Congress unanimously invited it to base its headquarters in the United States, and the following February the General Assembly agreed on New York as its permanent home.

ISRAEL AND PALESTINE

In 1947 the United Nations inherited one of its most intractable issues. Britain announced that it would terminate the mandate under which it had administered Palestine and asked the United Nations to decide the future government of that country. On 29 November the recommendations of the Special Committee on Palestine were accepted and the UN proposed the partition of the area into a Jewish state and an Arab state, with Jerusalem becoming an international zone. The compromise proved to be unworkable.

On 14 May the British mandate was relinquished, the State of Israel was proclaimed and fighting broke out. The Palestinian question, and the broader issues of Middle Eastern politics, would become continuing preoccupations not only for the United Nations but also for successive presidents of the United States government.

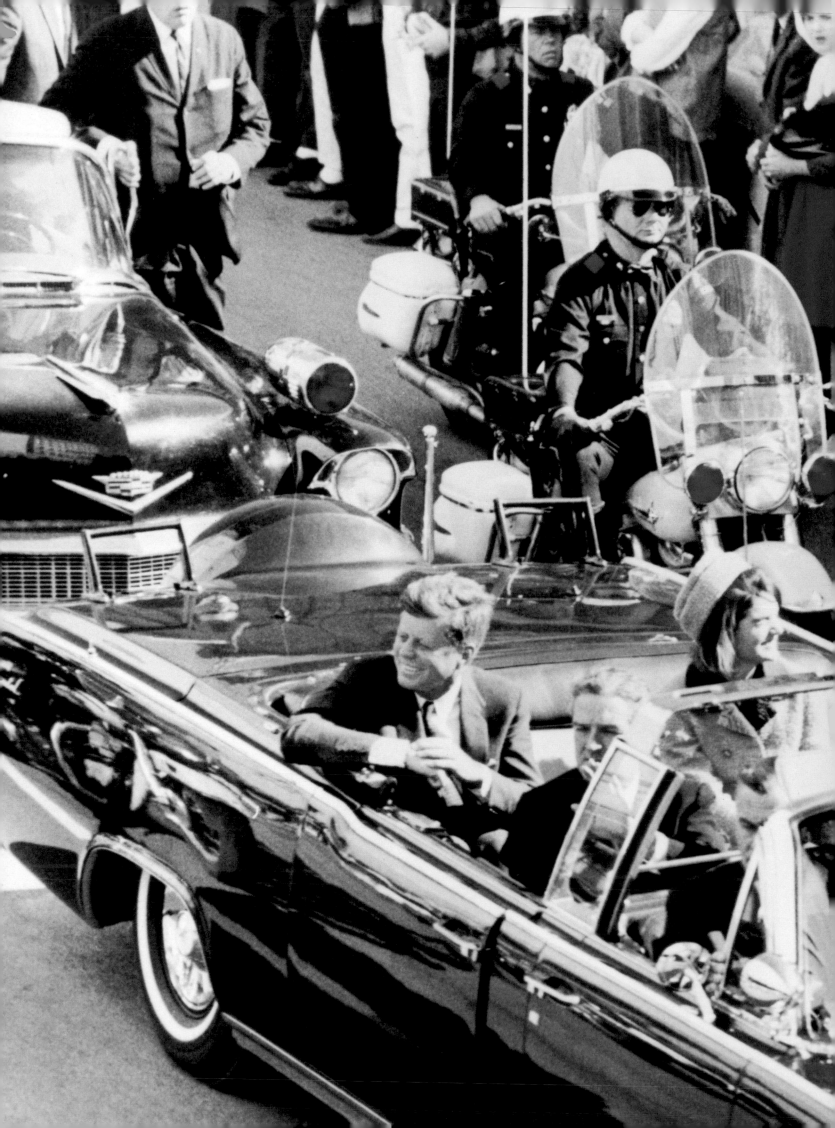

CHAPTER EIGHT

HARRY TRUMAN TO JOHN F. KENNEDY

1945–1963

AMERICANS HATED COMMUNISM AND FEARED
NUCLEAR WAR. THEIR REACTION TO THE
KNOWLEDGE THAT COMMUNISTS HAD ATOMIC
WEAPONS WAS PREDICTABLE. SOON AFTER
WORLD WAR II ENDED, THE FORMER ALLIES
BECAME IDEOLOGICAL ENEMIES. IN 1947, A
FORMER PRESIDENTIAL ADVISOR, BERNARD
BARUCH, OBSERVED THAT: "WE ARE TODAY IN THE
MIDST OF A COLD WAR." THE PHRASE STUCK.
THE BATTLE LINES IN A NEW CONFLICT OF IDEAS,
COMPETING ECONOMIC SYSTEMS AND POLITICAL
ORGANIZATION WERE DRAWN. IN AUGUST 1949
THE SOVIET UNION TESTED AN ATOMIC BOMB.
DURING THE FOLLOWING YEAR COMMUNISTS
TOOK CONTROL IN CHINA. WITH ITS ENEMIES
NOW LED BY DICTATORS SUCH AS JOSEPH STALIN
AND MAO TSE TUNG, HOW MIGHT THE UNITED
STATES RESPOND? ANXIOUS AMERICANS LOOKED
TO THEIR PRESIDENT FOR LEADERSHIP. THE COLD
WAR BROKE OUT INTO OPEN CONFLICT IN
KOREA, AND THE UNITED STATES BEGAN ITS
INVOLVEMENT IN THE QUAGMIRE OF VIETNAM.

*Left: John F. Kennedy's open-top presidential limousine nears
the Book Depository in Dallas, Texas.*

HARRY TRUMAN
1945–1953

The sign on his desk said 'The buck stops here', a saying borrowed from his favourite pastime: poker. Harry Truman dealt the cards and played the USA's hand in the high-stakes game of post-war international politics. The only commander-in-chief to have seen active service in World War I, as president he fought once more for his belief that the United States should keep the world safe for democracy in its confrontation with communism. Stepping from the shadow of Roosevelt was a challenge in itself, but Truman understood the meaning of presidential power and accepted its responsibilities.

He was born in 1884 in Missouri. A protective mother, weak eyesight and studious inclinations set him apart from his contemporaries in the town of Independence. His one-time inclination to become a concert pianist was replaced by an ambition to have a military

Above: Truman's presidency encompassed the end of World War II and the beginning of the Cold War as the United States became a 'superpower'.

career, but he ended up working on the family farm. In 1905 he joined the National Guard. He went to France in World War I, becoming a captain in the artillery. In 1919 he married Bess Wallace, and their only daughter, Margaret, was born in 1924.

Politics provided an escape route for Truman from his failed haberdashery

business. In 1922, supported by Tom Pendergast's Kansas City Democrat machine, Truman was elected as a district judge. He remained a local politician until in 1934 he was elected to the federal Senate. When the United States entered the war, Truman headed a committee investigating waste in defence appropriations and spending. In 1944 he emerged as the compromise candidate for the vice presidency. He had been in his job for only 82 days when Roosevelt died.

ATOMIC BOMB

"We have discovered the most terrible bomb in the history of the world," Truman confided to his diary on 25 July 1945. That day, at the Potsdam conference, he had told Stalin the news. On 1 August the Potsdam Declaration made it clear that the Allied leaders expected the Japanese to agree to an unconditional surrender or else "the alternative for Japan is prompt and utter

Below: Truman's first administration was marked by industrial unrest in part due to Congress's anti-union legislation.

Born: 8 May 1884, Lamar, Missouri
Parents: John (1851–1914) and Martha (1852–1947)
Family background: Farming
Education: University of Kansas City Law School (did not graduate)
Religion: Baptist
Occupation: Farmer, public service
Military service: Colonel, US Army, World War I
Political career: Judge: Jackson County Court, 1922–4
Presiding judge: Jackson County Court, 1926–34
US Senate, 1935–45
Vice president, 1945
Presidential annual salary: $75,000, increased to $100,000 + $50,000 expenses (1949)
Political party: Democrat
Died: 26 December 1972, Kansas City, Missouri

THE MARSHALL PLAN

On 5 June 1947, a speech given at Harvard University by George C. Marshall, Truman's secretary of state, invited European governments to co-operate in planning the distribution of $20 billion of US aid. The Marshall Plan was eagerly embraced in western Europe, but rejected by the Soviet Union and the countries it dominated in the east. Congress approved the plan the following year and US dollars began to flow across the Atlantic, laying the foundations for the creation of the European Economic Community.

destruction". Atomic explosions ended the war and detonated the way to a high-risk future in the nuclear age.

At home, the transition to a peace-time economy took place against a background of industrial unrest. Truman asked Congress for powers to draft striking workers into the military in an emergency. It cost him electoral support. In 1946, the Democrats lost control of Congress. The following year, the legislature, overturning Truman's veto, passed the Taft-Hartley Act, restricting the activity of the unions.

Abroad, the Truman Doctrine (see next page) saw a world divided into those prepared to defend democracy and those who sought to undermine it.

BESS TRUMAN

Elizabeth 'Bess' Wallace was born in Independence, Missouri, in 1885. She went to school with Harry Truman. In 1919, she married him. Five years later, their daughter, Mary Margaret, was born. After the high-profile public life of her predecessor, Eleanor Roosevelt, Bess Truman was a more traditional first lady, leaving politics to her husband while she pursued charity work. She died in 1982 at the age of 97: the longest-living first lady.

On 26 July 1947, Congress, which shared the president's concern about the threat from communism, passed the National Security Act, establishing the National Security Council, the Central Intelligence Agency and re-naming the Department of War the Department of Defense. The following year, it approved the European Recovery Programme – the Marshall Plan – to provide aid to that part of Europe that had not disappeared behind the 'Iron Curtain'.

On election night 1948, the *Chicago Herald Tribune* had as its front page headline "Dewey Defeats Truman". He did not. In an upset victory, Truman was re-elected and the Democrats regained control of Congress. In his inaugural address in 1949, the president suggested that it was "the beginning not only of a new administration, but of a period that will be eventful for us and for the world". So it proved.

The Soviet Union acquired nuclear weapons. The communist People's Republic of China was proclaimed. The United States began to develop the hydrogen bomb. Senator Joseph McCarthy embarked on his crusade against communism within the United States. Mao and Stalin became allies. In June 1950, North Korea invaded South Korea. US forces, under the auspices of

Above: The United States provided most of the troops from 16 member countries sent to fight in Korea under a United Nations Joint Command.

the United Nations, fought an increasingly unpopular war in South-east Asia. In 1952, when a strike threatened steel production for the war effort, the president ordered the federal government to take over the mills, an action later declared unconstitutional.

Truman retired to Independence, his home town in Missouri, to write his memoirs. He was resigned, he said, to his administration being "cussed and discussed for years to come". Harry Truman died on 26 December 1972.

THE 'IRON CURTAIN'

Winston Churchill coined the vivid expression that described the post-war ideological division in Europe: "From Stettin in the Baltic to Trieste in the Adriatic, an iron curtain has descended across the Continent." He called on the western democracies to unite in the face of the communist challenge, emphasizing the 'special relationship' between Britain and the United States: the cornerstone of contemporary British foreign policy.

THE TRUMAN DOCTRINE

1947

After World War II, the British Empire was bankrupt. It could not maintain its military presence overseas, even close to home. In February 1947, its Labour government, having already retreated from India, Burma and the Middle East, decided to withdraw its forces from Greece and Turkey. Would Americans be persuaded to fill the international power vacuum? If they did not, what would be the outcome?

The previous year, George Kennan, then a senior US diplomat in Moscow, had sent his 'long telegram' to the State Department outlining what he saw as the Soviet Union's intentions. Once it was decided on a course of action the Soviet government was "like a persistent toy automobile wound up and headed in a given direction, stopping only when it meets with some unanswerable force. In these circumstances it is clear that the main element of any United States policy toward the Soviet Union

Above: Harry Truman and Joseph Stalin at the Potsdam conference. Soon after, wartime allies became ideological enemies and the Cold War began.

Below: During the Cold War, the Pentagon, built in 1941, became the command centre of the American military.

must be that of long-term, patient but firm and vigilant containment of Russian expansive tendencies." The United States had to stand up and be counted. There could be no retreat into isolationism.

This was the president's message to Congress on 12 March 1947, requesting $400 million for aid to Greece and Turkey, which became known as the 'Truman Doctrine'. Like President Monroe's Doctrine, adopted over a century earlier, it defined the terms of

US foreign policy. It aimed to contain what it saw as an aggressively expansionist ideology. Nations had to "choose between alternative ways of life": either democracy or a system that "relies upon terror and oppression, a controlled press and radio; fixed elections and the suppression of personal freedom".

Truman argued that "it must be the policy of the United States to support free peoples who are resisting attempted subjugation by armed minorities or by outside pressures". Congress agreed. In 1950, a National Security Council Report (NSC 68) recommended the development of "a level of military readiness which can be maintained as long as necessary as a deterrent to Soviet aggression" and that "the internal security of the United States against dangers of sabotage, subversion and espionage" be assured.

The Cold War was "a real war in which the survival of the free world is at stake". Its architecture had been constructed within three years of the meeting between Truman and Stalin as wartime allies in Potsdam.

THE POWER OF TELEVISION

On 4 September 1951, President Truman was in San Francisco. His speech opening the conference that concluded the Peace Treaty with Japan was seen on television, in the first nationwide broadcast in US history. Truman was already familiar with the new medium. In October 1947 he had made the first televised address from the White House. By the time of his West Coast broadcast, there were 13 million television sets in the United States. Two years later, half the nation's population had a set.

In 1952, Dwight Eisenhower's presidential campaign televised a series of political advertisements. They were called 'Eisenhower Answers America'. However, the most famous broadcast of the campaign came from his vice-presidential candidate, Richard Nixon, who had been accused by the press of having a 'secret fund' donated by wealthy backers. Before an audience estimated at 60 million people, he revealed details of his financial affairs and told the tale of a gift his family had received: "A little cocker spaniel dog, and our little girl Tricia, the six-year-old, named it Checkers. And you know, the kid, like all kids, loved the dog, and regardless of what they say about it, we are going to keep it." The overwhelmingly positive public reaction to the 'Checkers Speech' meant that Nixon kept his place on the ticket as well. The response also convinced him of the value of appealing directly to the people. He believed he could use television to his advantage, until he came up against an even better performer: John F. Kennedy.

Television's power to influence its audience was confirmed when Edward R. Murrow, the highly respected CBS correspondent, made a documentary about the 'Red Scare' that helped to turn public opinion against Senator

Joseph McCarthy's anti-communist witch-hunt. In 1957, Murrow observed that in the television age, neither Jefferson nor Lincoln could have become president: "Jefferson had a most abrasive voice and did not suffer fools gladly. Mr Lincoln did not move gracefully, was not a handsome man, had a wife who was not a political asset and was a solitary man." From the 1950s onwards, Americans who had previously only heard their presidents on radio now became used to seeing them on television. This brought a new style to presidential politics, placing a premium

Above: President Truman quickly became aware of the persuasive power of television. From this time on image became all-important.

on both appearance and performance. It was John F. Kennedy who symbolized the change. He looked good on television and this was believed to have given him the decisive edge when he debated with Nixon during the 1960 campaign. Television became the dominant medium of political communication as the drama of the presidency was played out in homes across the United States.

Left: California senator Richard M. Nixon speaks to the nation on a coast-to-coast radio-television hook-up. The senator, who was at the time the Republican vice-presidential candidate, addressed the American people from Los Angeles in an attempt to explain fully his controversial $18,000 expense fund. His political future was expected to hang on the reception of this one dramatic speech.

THE KOREAN WAR
1950–1953

Korea had been occupied by Japan during World War II, and after the war it was left a divided country. Following the Japanese surrender, the Soviet Union took control of the north of the country and the United States the south, with the border fixed along the 38th parallel. Despite the promise of reunification, by 1948 two separate states were established: the Northern Democratic People's Republic of Korea, headed by Kim Il-sung, and the Southern Republic of Korea, led by Syngman Rhee. The north was under the protection of Soviet Russia and the south by the United States. On 25 June 1950, North Korea invaded the South in an attempt to re-unify the country by military force. The south were caught off guard, despite rumours of impending North Korean action.

The United Nations immediately called for North Korea to withdraw its forces. Four days later, the South Korean capital of Seoul had been occupied. On 30 June President Truman committed

Below: The Korean peninsula was divided between the communist North and the non-communist South.

US troops to intervene to enforce the United Nations resolution demanding a cessation of hostilities. The president chose not to ask Congress for a declaration of war because technically he was acting to fulfil the USA's obligation to assist in a United Nations mission to restore peace.

The United Nations command was established under General Douglas MacArthur. Its troops were initially forced into retreat, but on 15 September they mounted a successful counter-attack with an amphibious landing at Inchon, behind North Korean lines, fighting their way back up the Korean peninsula. By the end of the month, they had recaptured the territory up to the 38th parallel.

Truman then agreed to MacArthur's proposal to invade the North, potentially transforming the United Nations 'police action' into what could be seen as a war of national liberation. He did so on the understanding that should the Soviet Union or China intervene on

Below: Despite advances in battle tactics gained in World War II, the Korean War battles were based on trench warfare.

Above: United Nations forces parachute into the Korean War. The USA supplied the greatest number of combat troops.

North Korea's side, risking escalation to a wider – and possibly a nuclear – war, then the Americans should stop their advance. MacArthur ignored Truman's proviso. Despite a warning from the Chinese foreign minister Chou En-Lai that his country would intervene if United States forces crossed the 38th parallel, he started moving US troops to the Yalu River.

The Chinese remained true to their word. In November, the Chinese People's Volunteer Army, with some military aid from the Soviets, entered the war, forcing the Americans into a hasty retreat from the Chosin Reservoir.

In early January 1951 Seoul was abandoned once more, and by the end of the month China's forces had advanced further south before being once again pushed back. By March, Seoul was once more under the control of the United Nations, but the conflict had developed into a stalemate that, despite diplomatic efforts, seemed incapable of resolution.

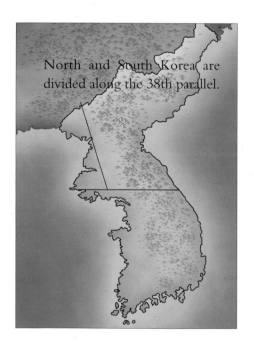

North and South Korea are divided along the 38th parallel.

Above: The 38th parallel became the line marking the demilitarized zone and the border between North and South Korea.

In the fevered atmosphere that accompanied the Chinese intervention, Truman's remarks at a press conference had been interpreted to suggest that the United States was contemplating using atomic bombs to end the conflict. It was not the case, but General MacArthur would have been happy to exercise the nuclear option. The morale of the retreating US forces was low, and a war of containment was indecisive: for MacArthur there was "no substitute for victory". His campaign against Truman's conduct of the Korean conflict, fought in private and in public, amounted to insubordination: challenging a basic principle of the USA's republican government, that a civilian commander-in-chief – the president – should control the military. On 12 April 1951, Truman fired him.

There was a public outcry in support of MacArthur. On his triumphant return to the United States (for the first time in 20 years), he was welcomed with a ticker-tape parade in New York

that was twice the size of that which had greeted Eisenhower when he had arrived back from Europe in 1945, demonstrating that his celebrity could temporarily eclipse his lack of political judgement. However, there were few who supported his demand to escalate the war against China. Instead, lacking

an obvious exit strategy, the United States became resigned to a lengthy military commitment in Korea.

In 1952, Eisenhower was elected to the presidency not least because of his promise to end the war in Korea. In November, as president elect, he travelled to Korea to inject new life into the peace negotiations. An armistice was signed in July 1953. A demilitarized zone – which remains in place today – was established around the 38th parallel, and the two separate nations continued to maintain an uneasy peace.

Estimates of the human costs of the war vary: of 150,000 US casualties, approximately 34,000 were killed in action. The Chinese suffered in the region of 900,000 casualties and the Korean dead and wounded may have been as high as two million. The lessons from the Korean War had been all but forgotten when in the following decade the United States intervened militarily in another war in a divided country in South-east Asia: Vietnam.

Below: Truman sacked MacArthur, but he returned home from Korea to a hero's reception.

DWIGHT EISENHOWER

1953–1961

The first Republican president since Ulysses S. Grant to serve two full terms in the White House was Dwight Eisenhower, a trusted war hero. No 20th-century commander-in-chief had more military experience than the former supreme commander of Allied forces in Europe during World War II. The reassuring image projected by the president did much to shape nostalgic memories of his time in office. Americans elected Eisenhower to the White House because he made them feel safe.

Born in Texas in 1890, Eisenhower grew up in Kansas. Despite his mother's pacifism, in 1911 he entered the military academy at West Point, graduating in 1915 and marrying Mamie Doud the following year. During World War I he trained tank crews in Pennsylvania. Following studies at the army's Staff College at Fort Leavenworth in Kansas, he became an aide to General Pershing and then to General MacArthur. In Washington, shortly after the attack on Pearl Harbor, Eisenhower's capacity for

Born: 14 October 1890, Denison, Texas
Parents: David (1863–1942) and Ida (1862–1946)
Family background: Engineering
Education: US Military Academy, West Point (1915)
Religion: Presbyterian
Occupation: Soldier
Military service: Supreme Allied commander (Europe), World War II General of the army
Political career: None
Presidential annual salary: $100,000 + $50,000 expenses
Political party: Republican
Died: 28 March 1969, Washington DC

strategic thinking and military planning impressed the army chief of staff, George Marshall.

From 1942 onwards, as the United States entered World War II, Eisenhower took charge of the Allied invasions of North Africa, Sicily and Italy, followed in 1944 by the Normandy landings of Operation Overlord. He returned to the USA as army chief of staff.

In 1948 he left the military to become president of Columbia University in New York. He then spent another two years in Europe as supreme commander of the North Atlantic Treaty Organisation (NATO). Both Democrats and Republicans courted him as a potential presidential candidate. In 1952, he defeated Robert Taft,

Above: Eisenhower, already a military hero, regained the presidency for the Republicans after an interval of 20 years.

'Mr Republican' and son of the former president, to win the party's nomination and then the White House.

A NEW PHASE OF INTERNATIONAL RELATIONS

Less than two months after Eisenhower took office, Stalin died. US relations with the Soviet Union entered a new phase when Nikita Khrushchev established himself as its undisputed leader. The USA's fear of communism at home and abroad remained. In 1951, the atmosphere of the times was dramatized in the high-profile trial of Ethel and

Above: Eisenhower and Nikita Khrushchev in 1955 at the first Cold War summit meeting between US and Soviet leaders.

Below: The Rosenbergs, members of the American Communist party, were found guilty of treason and executed for passing state secrets to the Soviets.

Julius Rosenberg who were found guilty of passing atomic secrets to the Soviets. They received the death penalty but the trial and conviction caused controversy. In June 1953 Eisenhower

Below: Federal troops escort black pupils to school in Arkansas. The state refused to accept the Supreme Court's desegregation ruling.

refused Ethel's last-minute clemency plea and she was executed on the same day as her husband; they were the only two US civilians to be executed for espionage during the Cold War.

In October 1953, the president announced a 'New Look' defence and national security policy, which made it clear that, "In the event of hostilities, the United States will consider nuclear weapons to be as available for use as other munitions." The threat of massive

retaliation using atomic bombs would be the basis of Eisenhower's strategy to keep the peace.

When North Vietnamese communist forces won the battle of Dien Bien Phu in 1954, ending France's hope of re-establishing its empire in Indo-China, Eisenhower explained the implications of the defeat: "You have a row of dominoes set up, you knock over the first one, and what will happen to the last one is the certainty that it will go over very quickly." US aid to South Vietnam was increased to try to stop communist expansion and the toppling of more dominoes. Although Eisenhower did not commit US troops to Vietnam in any great numbers, his 'domino theory' became part of the strategic thinking that eventually drew the United States inexorably into the Vietnam War.

DEEPENING CRISES

In July 1955, Eisenhower had a meeting with Khrushchev in Geneva. As Cold War tensions temporarily eased, the president's prestige was high and he contemplated running for re-election. In September, he had a heart attack, but he recovered and went on to win a second term. In the midst of the election, British and French troops seized the Suez Canal after Egypt had nationalized and then closed it. Soviet

STATES ENTERING THE UNION DURING EISENHOWER'S PRESIDENCY:

ALASKA

Entered the Union: 1959
Pre-state history: Land bought from Russia (1867); organized as Alaska Territory (1912)
Total population in 1960 census: 223,866
Electoral College votes in 1960: 3

HAWAII

Entered the Union: 1959
Pre-state history: Republic of Hawaii (1894); annexed by US and organized as Hawaii Territory (1898)
Total population in 1960 census: 632,772
Electoral College votes in 1960: 3

tanks moved into Hungary and crushed the national uprising against the country's communist government. Eisenhower's refusal to support the USA's European allies forced them to withdraw from Suez, and his decision not to intervene behind the Iron Curtain meant that the Soviet Union remained in control of Hungary. After these two crises, and in response to the threat of the further expansion of Soviet influence, particularly in the Middle East, the 'Eisenhower Doctrine'

committed the United States military to protect that region against "overt aggression from International Communism".

His second term ended amid criticisms of complacency. When Russia launched Sputnik, the artificial satellite led to doubts about the USA's lead over the Soviet Union in missile technology. As well as rising international tensions, the Civil Rights movement gained momentum, increasing difficulties on the domestic front. The president had to send federal troops to Little Rock, Arkansas, to force its racially segregated high school to admit nine black students who had legally enrolled there in 1957. In 1960 his Paris summit with Khrushchev collapsed after revelations that an American U-2 spy plane had been shot down over the Soviet Union.

At the end of his term of office Eisenhower retired to his farm at Gettysburg. He died in 1969. His last words expressed a wish and a command: "I want to go; God take me."

Left: Eisenhower supported the construction of the interstate highway system leading to major improvements in the USA's transportation network.

BROWN v. BOARD OF EDUCATION
1954

Thurgood Marshall was an African-American descended from slaves, whose interest in the law derived from being made to read the Constitution as a school punishment. As chief counsel for the National Association for the Advancement of Colored People (NAACP) he argued a landmark case known as Brown v. Board of Education of Topeka before the Supreme Court.

In the class action the named plaintiff, Oliver Brown, was one of 13 parents who set out to challenge the 'separate but equal' policy under which schools in Southern states were segregated, arguing that the result was not equal but inferior education for black students. In 1954, the Supreme Court reached its decision, paving the way for desegregation in the South. Earl Warren, a former Republican governor of California, and appointed chief justice by President Eisenhower, made sure the Court's decision on the case was

Below: Thurgood Marshall (centre), with George Hayes (left) and James Nabrit (right), the lawyers who argued the case for school desegregation.

unanimous, and between them Marshall and Warren helped advance the cause of civil rights. The ruling was that the school system that had existed in the South since the end of the Civil War was unconstitutional, opening the way for the dismantling of 'Jim Crow' laws and the end of racial segregation.

After the end of World War II, despite violence and intimidation, Southern blacks began to take legal action against the self-evidently inferior facilities in which their children were educated. Overcrowded, poorly constructed, a long way from the neighbourhoods in which they lived, with no transportation to them, black schools did not compare to those that whites attended. In 1951, a South Carolina judge, Julius Waring, in a dissenting opinion in the case of Briggs v. Elliot, had argued that "segregation in education can never produce equality". It was this case and others like it that paved the way for the Supreme Court to make its ruling.

Marshall put the case against 'Jim Crow' laws. If individual states had the power to deny the Fourteenth Amendment, which prohibited them from

passing and enforcing "any law which shall abridge the privileges or immunities of citizens of the United States", then, as he pointed out, "like the old Confederation, the Union becomes a mere rope of sand".

Warren's opinion, given additional force by the Court's complete agreement with him, relied on psychological and social scientific research suggesting that segregated education in itself induced a feeling of inferiority among black children. The Court shaped the law by not relying on precedent or analysis of the historical intent behind the Fourteenth Amendment.

The decision was not universally accepted. In Virginia, for example, the 'Massive Resistance' campaign against integration had state support that had to be fought in the federal courts.

The Warren Supreme Court made several other important decisions advancing the cause of civil liberties. In 1967, Warren was still chief justice when the first black American was appointed to it: Thurgood Marshall.

THE THREAT OF COMMUNISM

In February 1950, during a speech in Wheeling, West Virginia, Senator Joseph McCarthy from Wisconsin confronted his audience with a list of 205 communists whom he alleged were "shaping the policy of the State Department". The previous month, a prominent State Department official, Alger Hiss, had been convicted of perjury. He was sentenced to five years in prison. In his appearance before the House Un-American Activities Committee (HUAC), he had denied allegations that he was a communist. The case had brought national attention to Richard Nixon, the Committee member who

Right: McCarthy's dramatic denunciations of communists created a climate of fear throughout the United States.

pursued the accusation most aggressively. Truman's secretary of state, Dean Acheson, refused to condemn Hiss, using a biblical analogy: this was the final straw for McCarthy. His speech reserved its greatest invective for Acheson: "When this pompous diplomat in striped pants, with a phoney British accent, proclaimed to the American people that Christ on the Mount endorsed communism, high treason, and betrayal of a sacred trust,

THE HOUSE UN-AMERICAN ACTIVITIES COMMITTEE (HUAC)

HUAC was established in 1937 to investigate subversive activities by American extremists at both ends of the ideological spectrum. After World War II it concentrated on the perceived communist threat, launching its investigation of Hollywood and pursuing the case against Alger Hiss. HUAC operated independently of McCarthy's Senate committee but was equally zealous in its pursuit of communists, either real or imagined.

Below: The House Un-American Activities Committee investigated communist infiltration into all areas of public life.

the blasphemy was so great that it awakened the dormant indignation of the American people." Joseph McCarthy's anti-communist crusade was up and running.

McCarthy launched his investigations as chair of the Senate Committee on Government Operations, whereas HUAC was a committee set up by the House of Representatives. Three years previously, it had investigated communist activity in Hollywood. Some of those it called to testify, who refused to answer the question: "Are you now or have you ever been a member of the Communist party?" had been jailed for contempt, despite the fact that their right to silence was enshrined in the Fifth Amendment to the Constitution. 'Friendly' witnesses such as Walt Disney, Gary Cooper and the then president of the Screen Actors Guild, Ronald Reagan, expressed their concerns about communist influence in the industry. In 1951, a second round of hearings, influenced by the hysteria whipped up by McCarthy, resulted in the 'naming of names'. Hollywood's blacklist of those found guilty or regarded as guilty by association was established.

Right: The playwright Arthur Miller, who was called before the House Un-American Activities Committee, wrote The Crucible *(1953), set in Puritan New England, as an allegory of McCarthy's witch-hunt.*

So great was its influence that its victims found themselves out of work and shunned by their former colleagues.

In the Senate, McCarthy, together with his aides, the lawyer Roy Cohn (who was instrumental in securing the conviction of Julius and Ethel Rosenberg) and the anti-communist propagandist David Schine, intimidated, abused and terrified witnesses, as bogus allegations were made in an attempt to undermine the reputations of their enemies in public life. Nobody was immune from accusations that could destroy careers and ruin lives. In 1953, Robert Kennedy, who had worked for McCarthy as an assistant counsel, resigned because he "disagreed with the

Below: The 'Hollywood Ten' (included here) were screenwriters accused of being communists and were blacklisted by the industry.

way that the Committee was being run". In the same year, McCarthy mixed his personal and political agendas: when Schine was drafted, Cohn tried to influence the army into giving him special privileges. When the army refused, the senator supported Cohn, his chief counsel, and made the army a target for his investigations. It proved to be a fatal error.

In March 1954 Ed Murrow's exposé on his CBS programme, *See It Now*, concluded that "the line between investigating and persecuting is a very fine

one", and that McCarthy had "stepped over it repeatedly". From 22 April to 17 June, Americans could watch him in action. The Army–McCarthy hearings were broadcast to a nationwide audience on TV. As the hearings came to a close, Stuart Symington, the Democrat senator from Missouri, told McCarthy that his credibility had been destroyed: "The American people have had a look at you for six weeks. You are not fooling anyone." During almost 200 hours of broadcasting, the senator's methods had been held up to public scrutiny, and few liked what they saw. In December he was reprimanded by his peers for bringing the Senate into disrepute. The word 'censure' was excised from the final resolution. One of the senators who was absent from the vote was John F. Kennedy, who was then recovering from surgery on his back.

'McCarthyism' affected the lives of many Americans including a number of high-profile casualties, among them Charlie Chaplin, who in 1952 left the United States to travel to Europe. His right to re-enter the country was revoked. Meanwhile the prominent black actor and singer Paul Robeson was denied the right to leave the country when his passport was taken away. After the Senate reprimand, McCarthy went into terminal decline. Losing his battle with the bottle, he died from the effects of alcoholism in 1957.

ELVIS PRESLEY
AND THE NEW CULTURE OF YOUTH

In 1954, an unknown teenager walked into the studios of Sun Records in Memphis, Tennessee, and asked to make a recording. Known as the Hillbilly Cat, he sang locally with two backing guitarists and a drummer, who made up a band known as the Blue Moon Boys. A poor white boy from the South, who had grown up listening to black music – gospel and rhythm and blues – Elvis Presley was singing his way to fame. The following year, now managed by Colonel Tom Parker (the military title was strictly honorary) he signed with RCA Victor, who acquired his recording contract from Sun for an unprecedented $35,000. In 1956, 'Heartbreak Hotel' became his first chart-topping hit.

Presley represented one side of the 'generation gap' that was emerging in the 1950s – the decade that invented the 'teenager'. Increasingly, the musical taste of the new generation also defined their attitudes and lifestyle. Elvis combined black musical influences with

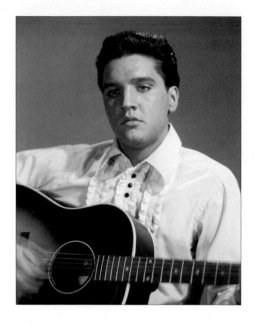

dance movements that some found suggestive and others thought provocative. He was 'Elvis the Pelvis'.

In June 1956, he sang his version of 'Hound Dog' on television, delighting the younger members of the studio audience but causing consternation among adults. His performance was condemned as vulgar and obscene in

Left: Elvis Presley changed the face of youth culture in the United States in the 1950s, and introduced rock stardom to the world.

the press, but the ratings were huge. When he next sang the song on television, Elvis appeared in a tuxedo and addressed the song to a live basset hound. It led to three appearances on *The Ed Sullivan Show*, during which the camera focused on him solely from the waist up and he earned an endorsement from the host: "This is a real decent, fine boy. You're thoroughly all right."

Through records, live concerts, further television appearances and Hollywood movies, Elvis Presley rapidly became an icon of contemporary US popular culture. In 1958, he embarked on two years of military service, earning promotion to sergeant just prior to being discharged in March 1960. His recording company had issued a succession of hit singles and albums during his absence, and he resumed his recording and movie career.

In December 1970, 'the King' met the president. Presley had written to Richard Nixon, offering to become a federal agent-at-large in the Bureau of Narcotics and Dangerous Drugs. He had made "an in-depth study of drug abuse and communist brainwashing techniques" and was well placed to help deal with the problems posed by the counterculture. At the White House, he presented Nixon with a World War II vintage Colt .45. In return, the president gave him a federal badge of office. The photograph of their meeting is the single most requested item in the US National Archives.

Seven years later, addicted to prescription drugs, Elvis Presley died at Graceland, his home in Tennessee.

Left: Elvis and President Nixon in the Oval Office at the White House.

JOHN F. KENNEDY
1961–1963

President for just over a thousand days, Kennedy's premature death made him a tragic hero whose potential to lead the United States during a troubled decade was unfulfilled. In the words of the title of a book by his close friends, *Johnny, We Hardly Knew Ye*.

John F. Kennedy was an outsider. He was born into a large Irish-American Catholic family in Massachusetts. His health was never robust but his family's wealth ensured a privileged upbringing. After graduating from Harvard in 1940, Kennedy joined the navy during World War II and commanded a motor torpedo boat – *PT 109* – in the South Pacific. It was sunk by a Japanese destroyer. Kennedy's actions in ensuring that he and his crew survived and were rescued became the stuff of heroic legend. His elder brother, Joe, was not so fortunate. He was killed flying a high-risk bombing mission in Europe, and John inherited his father Joseph's ambition for a son to become president.

Above: Kennedy's tragic death shaped the public's memory of his presidency and ensured his enduring popularity.

Born: 29 May 1917, Brookline, Massachusetts
Parents: Joseph (1888–1969) and Rose (1890–1995)
Family background: Business, public service
Education: Harvard College (1940)
Religion: Catholic
Occupation: Author, public service
Military service: Lieutenant, US navy, World War II
Political career: US House of Representatives, 1947–53
US Senate, 1953–61
Presidential annual salary: $100,000 + $50,000 expenses (refused by Kennedy)
Political party: Democrat
Died: 22 November 1963, Dallas, Texas

Elected to Congress in 1947, his political career progressed in the House of Representatives and then in the Senate. He married Jacqueline Bouvier in 1953. Kennedy's health problems – malaria, Addison's disease and chronic back pain – meant that he attended Congress infrequently. In 1956 he was recovering from life-threatening back surgery when he published the Pulitzer Prize-winning *Profiles in Courage*, an examination of key moments in the Senate's history. In the same year he tried unsuccessfully to become the Democrats' vice-presidential candidate.

His 1960 campaign for the presidency, managed by his brother Robert, was an insurgency, capturing the nomination through accumulating support in the primary elections. Kennedy's charismatic appeal helped defuse the issue of his religion: no Catholic had

JACQUELINE KENNEDY

The youngest first lady of the 20th century, Jacqueline Bouvier was 24 when she married John F. Kennedy in 1953. They had three children, only two of whom, Caroline and John, survived to adulthood. As first lady she added glamour and sophistication to the Kennedy White House, and supervised its restoration, appearing on television to give Americans a guided tour of her achievement. Five years after Kennedy's assassination, she shocked many Americans when she married Aristotle Onassis, the Greek shipping magnate, who was 23 years her senior. Widowed again in 1975, she lived the remainder of her life in New York, where she worked in publishing. She died in 1994.

Below: Jacqueline Kennedy was one of the youngest ever first ladies.

ever been elected to the White House in what remained a predominantly Protestant nation. His father's money helped his cause. He won the closest presidential election of the 20th century by just over 100,000 votes. He was 43 years old.

Above: The Kennedy family in 1934, with John F. Kennedy pictured third from right.

THE CHALLENGES OF OFFICE

In his speech accepting the Democrat nomination, Kennedy had talked of the United States being on the edge of a 'New Frontier' of "unfulfilled hopes and dreams". This campaign slogan summed up the feeling of optimism surrounding his administration as he took office. The challenges of political reality rapidly became apparent.

Kennedy inherited from Eisenhower the plan to invade Cuba. In April he took action, and the Bay of Pigs was a disaster. Two months later, the president met Khrushchev face to face for talks in Vienna, to try to defuse international tensions. Kennedy felt that the summit had not gone well: he had not convinced the Soviet leader of the USA's intent to stand firm against communist expansion. South-east Asia was a potential testing ground for US resolve. The president reportedly

Below: Kennedy's campaign for the White House was groundbreaking: he was the first Catholic to be elected president.

admitted: "Now we have the problem of making our power credible and Vietnam looks like the place." The former capital of what was now a divided Germany was another Cold War flashpoint. In August 1961, the Soviets built the Berlin Wall.

Lacking support in Congress, Kennedy did not achieve as much as he anticipated in terms of domestic legislation. He faced increasingly difficult confrontations, particularly in the South, where segregation was still rife, though under siege. The Civil Rights movement worked to overcome the 'Jim Crow' laws in education and transportation. The Kennedy administration, and notably Robert Kennedy as

attorney general, supported the protesters against intransigent Southern governors and violent racist reactions.

There were some lighter times. With the Kennedys as popular hosts, the White House became the social, cultural and intellectual centre of the New Frontier. In April 1962, at a dinner honouring 49 Nobel Prize-winners, Kennedy famously observed that it was

Below: The Cuban Missile Crisis could have ended in nuclear war: its peaceful resolution was Kennedy's greatest triumph.

MARILYN MONROE

"I can now retire from politics after having had 'Happy Birthday' sung to me in such a sweet, wholesome way." It was 19 May 1962. John Kennedy had almost turned 45 and the party was at Madison Square Garden, New York. The performer was Marilyn Monroe. Just under three months later, she was dead.

Born in 1926, Marilyn Monroe was the iconic blonde of the age: the perfect blend of glamour and Hollywood stardom in the post-war era of US celebrity. After a brief first marriage that ended as her career took off, in 1954 she married the legendary baseball player, Joe Di Maggio. A year later they divorced.

Her relationship with the playwright Arthur Miller lasted longer: their marriage endured for five years, ending in 1961. During that time Arthur Miller wrote the screenplay for *The Misfits*, the last film she would complete. During filming she had a nervous breakdown.

By the time she sang at Madison Square Garden, she knew both Jack and Bobby Kennedy well, having been introduced to them by their brother-in-law, Peter Lawford. She allegedly had affairs with both of them.

Her premature death at 36 from barbiturate poisoning, officially recorded as "probable suicide", unleashed a torrent of speculation in which the mystery surrounding her last hours, together with the potent mix of celebrity, sex and politics, led conspiracy theorists to argue that it was the Kennedys who were responsible for her murder. She remains an American icon, preserved in the memory of generations of fans and of those who knew her.

It was Joe Di Maggio who continued to leave flowers at Marilyn's grave.

Above: Marilyn Monroe's death and her relationship with the Kennedys remains the subject of popular debate.

probably the greatest concentration of genius that had been present in the White House, with the possible exception of when "Thomas Jefferson dined alone".

The defining moments of Kennedy's presidency came during 13 days in October 1962. He negotiated his way through the Cuban Missile Crisis, triggered by the discovery that the Soviets were placing missiles in Cuba and bringing the world to the brink of nuclear war. His reputation soared in the United States and overseas. In June 1963, he travelled to Berlin. Standing in front of the Wall, he proclaimed his support for the city: "*Ich bin ein Berliner*" ("I am a citizen of Berlin").

Throughout his presidency, the situation in South-east Asia had been volatile. Kennedy sent US military advisors to South Vietnam while the regime of its leader, Ngo Dinh Diem, crumbled in the face of increasing internal opposition to his authoritarian rule. On 1 November 1963, Diem died in a coup.

Three weeks later, Kennedy travelled to Dallas, Texas. On 22 November, as his motorcade left the airport for the city, he told Jacqueline, who was accompanying him on the visit, that they were heading into "nut country". As the presidential limousine slowly travelled along Elm Street, Nellie, wife of the Texas governor John Connally, said to him,

"You can't say Dallas doesn't love you, Mr President". Moments later he was assassinated. After a state funeral in Washington DC, John F. Kennedy was buried in Arlington National Cemetery.

Below: John F. Kennedy and Nikita Khrushchev met for the first time at the Vienna summit, in 1961.

THE BERLIN WALL
1961

Berlin was a divided city. The Allied occupation after World War II established the US, British and French zones in its western part, and the Soviet sector in the east. An isolated outpost, West Berlin became the scene of tense confrontation and dramatic events as the Cold War played out in Europe. In June 1948, it was blockaded. Only daily supplies delivered by Allied planes until September 1949 prevented it from being starved into submission.

In 1952, following the establishment of the Federal Republic of Germany in the west and the German Democratic Republic in the east, the border between the two states was closed. Berlin remained a chink in the 'Iron Curtain': until 1957, when it was forbidden, it was still possible to travel from the eastern to the western zones, either with permission or, at greater risk, without it. Many East Germans took advantage of this to trade a life under communism for one in West Germany.

Below: A worker builds the Berlin Wall.

Above: The Brandenburg Gate, which was designed as a symbol of peace. It became a symbol of German power.

By the time Kennedy and Khrushchev met in Vienna in 1961, the Soviet leader wanted control of the city. Kennedy stood firm and the war of words threatened to end in military action. The crisis was defused. The president recognized the Soviet leader's problem, telling Walt Rostow, one of his security advisors: "East Germany is haemorrhaging to death ... He has to do something to stop this. Perhaps a wall." By signalling his concern to protect West Berlin rather than the entire city, Kennedy gave Khrushchev an exit strategy. On 13 August 1961 the first rudimentary structure was built. The following day, the Brandenburg Gate in the city was closed, but the route from West Berlin to the Federal Republic stayed open. It signalled a compromise. As Kennedy put it: "A wall is a hell of a lot better than a war."

Kennedy was not the only US president to visit Berlin. In 1987, Ronald Reagan stood in front of the Brandenburg Gate and famously invited his Soviet counterpart, Mikhail Gorbachev, to "Tear down this Wall." On 9 November 1989, it came down, symbolizing the end of the Cold War and paving the way for Germany's reunification the following year.

Below: The Wall came down in 1989 as communist regimes throughout Eastern Europe lost power or were overthrown.

THE CUBAN MISSILE CRISIS
1962

The Soviet Union had placed missiles in Cuba that were capable, as Khrushchev later recalled, of devastating "New York, Chicago, and the other huge industrial cities, not to mention a little village like Washington". President Kennedy now faced the most serious confrontation of the Cold War. During the crisis, he walked the tightrope across the abyss of nuclear war, and after 13 days of intense debate, public action and secret diplomacy, he made it safely to the other side.

On 14 October 1962 a United States U-2 surveillance flight over Cuba confirmed the presence of missile bases there. Although there was no evidence that nuclear warheads were also on the island, with Soviet ships on the way, the United States feared that it was only a matter of time before they arrived. Kennedy brought together a group of advisors from the National Security Council, dubbed 'ExCom', to determine what should be done.

One option was a high-risk pre-emptive strike to destroy the missiles on Cuba, but Kennedy was concerned that such a move would provoke Soviet retaliation and a reciprocal attack on Berlin. The president's brother Robert Kennedy, who emerged as a key member of ExCom, together with Robert McNamara, the secretary of defense, argued in favour of the more prudent course of action that was eventually taken: the setting up of a naval blockade to prevent the Soviets from delivering more missiles or warheads to Cuba.

After it had been given a less aggressive title, the president announced the "quarantine" in a nationwide television address on Monday 22 October. Two days later it went into effect. On Wednesday 24 October, Russian ships approached the quarantine zone, which was patrolled by US forces. They stopped,

Above: The Cuban Missile Crisis saw the world teeter on the brink of escalation to nuclear war.

then turned away. The secretary of state, Dean Rusk, famously observed: "We're eyeball to eyeball and I think the other fellow just blinked."

With the missiles still in place, Kennedy's military advisors pressed for an invasion of the island. On Friday 26 October, the president received a letter from Khrushchev, proposing that if the United States pledged not to take military action in Cuba, then the missiles would be dismantled and removed. The following day, the Soviet leader, under pressure from his own military, sent another, less conciliatory message: it demanded that as part of any

resolution to the crisis the United States should remove the nuclear weapons it had stationed in Turkey.

ROBERT KENNEDY

It was Robert Kennedy who found a way out of the confusion caused by the contradictory statements made by the Soviet leader: they should ignore the second letter and proceed on the basis of what had first been suggested. He had good reason to believe that this tactic would work. Throughout the crisis, he had been meeting secretly with the Soviet ambassador, Anatoly Dobrynin. He had already hinted that the president might find a missile trade acceptable. Late at night on Saturday 27 October, after his brother had made a public pledge not to invade Cuba, Robert Kennedy met once more with Dobrynin and gave him private assurances that the United States would remove its nuclear capability from Turkey. There was also an ultimatum: the Soviet Union must agree to this secret compromise within 24 hours, or the United States would take military action against Cuba. Earlier that day, a U-2 plane photographing sites for an

Left: Castro's militiamen train for conflict in the mountains of Cuba.

invasion had been shot down over the island and its pilot had been killed.

Khrushchev ended the crisis. The following morning, on Radio Moscow, it was announced to a somewhat bewildered Russian audience, who had not known about the existence of the missiles on Cuba, that they would be dismantled and taken away. By April the following year, the USA's missiles in Turkey were quietly scrapped.

As a result of the missile crisis, the 'hot line' was set up allowing rapid and

direct communication between leaders in Washington and Moscow. Cold War rhetoric softened. As Kennedy put it in a speech on 10 June 1963: "In the final analysis, our most basic common link is that we all inhabit this small planet. We all breathe the same air. We all cherish our children's future. And we are all mortal."

Below: Reconnaisance flights by the US military showed a Russian attack submarine close to Cuba.

Above: While war seemed imminent, a resolution to the crisis was negotiated away from the public gaze.

THE HOT LINE

During the tense negotiations of the Cuban Missile Crisis, it had taken nearly 12 hours to receive and decode a 3,000-word letter from Khrushchev, showing the value of a reliable, fast and easy method of communication between the presidents of the United States and the Soviet Union. The hot line, or 'red telephone' between the White House and the Kremlin was set up by an agreement signed in Geneva on 20 June 1963. It was first used during the Six Day War between Egypt and Israel in 1967, during which the superpowers kept each other informed of naval movements in the area that might otherwise have appeared provocative.

THE ASSASSINATION OF KENNEDY
1963

At lunchtime in Dallas on Friday 22 November 1963, John F. Kennedy was on his way to the city's Trade Mart to deliver a speech in which he planned to talk about peace. He was travelling in a presidential motorcade, in an open-top car so that everyone could see him. Among the spectators was Emile Zapruder, who had with him his home movie camera. He would capture the moment that an assassin's bullet would once again claim the life of a United States president.

He was an easy target. As the motorcade passed the Texas School Book Depository building, President John F. Kennedy was shot and fatally wounded. More than 40 years later, there is much about his assassination that remains controversial. The story of his presidency is sometimes over-whelmed by the desire to speculate on the drama of his death.

Kennedy was rushed to Parkland Hospital, but he had already succumbed to his traumatic injuries: no recovery was possible from the bullet that had hit him in the head. On television, the CBS newscaster, Walter Cronkite, made the announcement: "From Dallas, Texas, the flash, apparently official. President Kennedy died at 1 p.m. Central Standard Time, two o'clock Eastern Standard Time." Cronkite, 'the most trusted man in America', removed his glasses and appeared to shed a tear.

MURDER OF THE MURDERER

Within 90 minutes of the assassination, Lee Harvey Oswald, a former marine who had spent time in the Soviet Union, was apprehended on suspicion of the murder of J. D. Tippit, a Dallas police officer, who had tried to arrest him. Oswald worked at the Book Depository, had been witnessed leaving the building shortly after the shooting and was the owner of the mail-order rifle found at the scene. He was charged with the president's assassination. Two days later, while being transferred to the county jail, in front of a watching tele-vision audience, Lee Oswald was shot dead by Jack Ruby, a Dallas strip-club owner. Initially found guilty and sentenced to death, Ruby's conviction was subsequently overturned. He died in 1967 while awaiting a new trial for Oswald's murder.

The Warren Commission, set up by President Lyndon Johnson, sat for ten months and concluded that Oswald had acted alone. It was one of several gov-ernment investigations, all of which have returned the same verdict. None has done anything to undermine

Above: Kennedy's state funeral was attended by dignitaries from more than 90 countries.

popular belief that the assassination was a conspiracy, and it is still the subject of widespread speculation.

On 17 March 1964, St Patrick's Day, in his first major speech after his brother's death, Robert Kennedy quoted from a poem written for the Irish hero Owen Roe O'Neill:

We're sheep without a shepherd,
When the snow shuts out the sky —
Oh! Why did you leave us, Owen?
Why did you die?

Left: The moment the bullet hit Kennedy in his open-top cavalcade as it travelled past the Book Depository.

CHAPTER NINE

LYNDON B. JOHNSON TO JIMMY CARTER

1963–1981

BETWEEN 1963 AND 1981 THE PRESIDENCY
EXPERIENCED POLITICAL TURBULENCE
UNPARALLELED IN ITS 20TH-CENTURY HISTORY.
PUBLIC CONFIDENCE IN THE INSTITUTION
COLLAPSED. THOSE WHO HELD THE OFFICE HAD
THEIR CREDIBILITY, PERSONAL INTEGRITY AND
CAPACITY TO PROVIDE NATIONAL LEADERSHIP
DOUBTED, QUESTIONED AND FOUND WANTING.
IN THE LIGHT OF THE ASSASSINATION OF JOHN F.
KENNEDY, WHOSE STATURE WAS IMMEDIATELY
ASSURED, OTHER PRESIDENTS FAILED TO MEASURE
UP. ONE WAS A CASUALTY OF WAR, ANOTHER AN
HEROIC FAILURE; THEIR TWO SUCCESSORS PROVED
UNABLE TO RESTORE THE PRESIDENCY TO ITS
FORMER POSITION AS THE LYNCHPIN OF THE
US POLITICAL SYSTEM. LYNDON B. JOHNSON,
RICHARD NIXON, GERALD FORD AND
JIMMY CARTER ALL LEFT OFFICE WITH A
SENSE OF PROMISE UNFULFILLED.

*Left: The hostage crisis in Tehran finally ended on the day that
Jimmy Carter left office.*

LYNDON B. JOHNSON
1963–1969

Lyndon Johnson's presidency was a political watershed: he was the first candidate from a former Confederate state to be elected. His support of civil rights ushered in the end of the Democrats' domination of Southern politics, which had endured since reconstruction, and re-established the region as a place from which presidents might be elected.

Johnson was born in Texas in 1908, into a family whose roots went deep into the history of the Lone Star State. He left high school at the age of 15 and drifted to California, before returning to enrol at Southwest Texas State Teachers College in 1927. After graduating he taught briefly before going to Washington in 1931 as secretary to Congressman Richard Kleberg. He was elected to the House of Representatives in 1936, but failed

Above: Johnson was never able to escape from the shadow that memories of John F. Kennedy cast over his presidency.

in his first attempt to become a senator four years later. He served briefly in the navy during World War II. In 1948 he finally reached the Senate amid charges of ballot-rigging in a disputed election. Seven years later, Johnson was its youngest ever majority leader.

He recovered from a heart attack to become the most effective political operator the Senate had ever seen, relentlessly gathering information to help to win over fellow senators.

Kennedy thwarted his presidential ambitions in 1960, but Johnson accepted his rival's invitation to become his running mate. Marginalized as vice president in Kennedy's administration, he moved to centre stage on 22 November 1963, as president of a nation traumatized by the shock of the events in Dallas.

A DIFFICULT TASK

Johnson negotiated his first difficult days in the White House with sensitivity and skill. Though he came from the South, he championed civil rights, responding to the movement led by Martin Luther King Jr. Knowing the value of the

Below: Johnson takes the oath of office on Air Force One – the presidential plane – at Love Field in Dallas, Texas, witnessed by his predecessor's widow, still wearing the coat spattered with her husband's blood.

Born: 27 August 1908, near Johnson City, Texas

Parents: Samuel (1877–1937) and Rebecca (1881–1988)

Family background: Farming, public service

Education: Southwest Texas State Teachers College (1930)

Religion: Disciples of Christ

Occupation: Teacher, public service

Military service: Commander, US naval reserve, World War II

Political career: Congressional secretary, 1931–7

US House of Representatives, 1937–49

US Senate, 1949–61

Vice president, 1961–3

Presidential annual salary: $100,000 + $50,000 expenses

Political party: Democrat

Died: 22 January 1973, near Johnson City, Texas

political capital invested in the reputation of his assassinated predecessor, he exploited it, cajoling Congress to pass landmark legislation advancing the cause of racial equality as a tribute to Kennedy's memory. The legislation paved the way for women to press their case for equal rights as well. In January 1964, he announced his intention to declare "war on poverty" and in May he outlined his vision of the "Great Society" based upon "abundance and liberty for all" and demanding "an end to poverty and racial injustice". The Civil Rights Act, which he signed in July, was the most radical since reconstruction, and its architect was a president who came from a former Confederate state. The 'Great Society'

'LADY BIRD' JOHNSON

Above: Claudia Johnson's childhood nurse gave her charge the pet name 'Lady Bird'.

Claudia Taylor was born in Texas in 1912. Less than three months after graduating from the University of Texas she met Lyndon Johnson. They married in 1934 and had two daughters, Lynda Bird and Luci Baines. As first lady, she was a staunch advocate of civil rights and also campaigned for the conservation and enhancement of America's natural environment. She died on 11 July 2007, at the age of 94.

Above: In 1968 President Johnson signed the Civil Rights Act, also known as the Fair Housing Act, which prohibited discrimination in the sale, financing and rental of housing on the basis of race, religion and national origin. It has been updated twice to disallow discrimination on the basis of sex or disability.

Below: A contemporary cartoon depicts Johnson as a Texan cowboy, more at home with domestic than foreign policy.

was built in a flurry of legislation unmatched since Franklin Roosevelt's 'New Deal'. In 1965, Congress enacted its twin centrepieces, Medicare and Medicaid, extending health insurance provision for the elderly and those on low incomes.

FAILING FOREIGN POLICY

Johnson's substantial domestic achievements contrasted with his disastrous military intervention abroad. At the same time as radical domestic changes were being implemented, the question of involvement in Vietnam began to consume Johnson's attention.

The political situation in Vietnam had deteriorated quickly in the aftermath of Diem's assassination. "I knew from the start that I was bound to be crucified either way I moved," he said in an interview in 1970. "If I left the woman I really loved – the Great Society – in order to get involved in that bitch of a war on the other side of the world, then I would lose everything at home. But if I left that war and let the Communists take over South Vietnam, then I would be seen as a coward and my nation

Above: Johnson's presidency was characterized by widespread civil unrest. Race issues continued. Martin Luther King was assassinated and the war in Vietnam escalated intensifying the anti-war protests.

would be seen as an appeaser and we would both find it impossible to accomplish anything for anybody anywhere on the entire globe."

Johnson took a decision, and it proved to be a disastrous mistake. In August 1964, in response to alleged North Vietnamese attacks on US naval vessels, he asked Congress to approve the 'Tonkin Gulf' Resolution, authorizing the president to use military force there should it prove necessary. It was a 'blank cheque for war'.

Johnson did not cash his cheque immediately. During the campaign leading up to the presidential election in September that year he had pledged not "to send American boys nine or ten thousand miles away from home to do what Asian boys ought to be doing for themselves". Portraying his Republican opponent, Senator Barry Goldwater, as dangerously right wing in a world in

which China had just acquired nuclear weapons and Khrushchev had been ousted in the Kremlin had won Johnson a convincing victory.

As more and more troops were drafted to fight in Vietnam, opposition to the war escalated. At last, on 31 March 1968, increasingly beleaguered, Johnson effectively resigned from the presidency, announcing that he would not seek his party's nomination for a further term in office.

Johnson's presidency was further undermined by the enduring power of the myth of John F. Kennedy. His assassination had robbed the United States of a leader whose stature was assured the moment he was shot, and whose reputation was steadily embellished by a nation whose memories and perceptions were shaped by the events that had followed his death. If Kennedy had lived, would the United States have had to suffer the trauma of Vietnam?

As the nation's involvement in the conflict in South-east Asia grew, those who protested against Lyndon Johnson's war looked to Robert Kennedy to end it. He emerged from a period of introspection after his brother's death to

begin a political journey that led him to speak for the USA's dispossessed and to condemn the Vietnam War. But minutes after he had given his victory speech on winning the California primary, an assassin's bullet once more left the promise unfulfilled.

Johnson retired to his Texas ranch. He left office with his 'Great Society' rioting in the streets, protesting against the war he had made it fight. As a consequence, Lyndon Johnson's ambition to be regarded as the greatest president since Franklin Roosevelt was crushed by the USA's war in Vietnam. In 1973, his successor, Richard Nixon, told him privately that negotiations with the Vietnamese had been concluded in Paris. On 23 January 1974, Nixon announced that "peace with honor" had been achieved. But Lyndon Johnson had died the previous day.

TONKIN GULF

In August 1964, North Vietnamese torpedo boats were reported to have attacked US naval vessels off its coast in the Gulf of Tonkin. President Johnson ordered retaliatory air strikes and asked Congress to approve a resolution giving him the power to take further military action. Only later was it revealed that the incidents had been fabricated. In 1965, Johnson admitted: "For all I know, our Navy was shooting at whales out there." By then he had his pretext for war.

Below: The Tonkin Gulf resolution gave Johnson the authority to fight the Vietnam War.

ROBERT KENNEDY
ATTORNEY GENERAL AND NEW YORK SENATOR

Mount Kennedy, overlooking the Lowell Glacier in Canada close to the border with Alaska, was the highest unclimbed mountain in North America. In 1965 it was named in memory of Robert Kennedy's brother and in the same year, although he suffered from a fear of heights, Robert Kennedy made the first ascent of it. For him, courage was, as Ernest Hemingway defined it, 'grace under pressure'.

Robert Kennedy was born on 20 November 1925. He grew up in the shadow of his elder brothers, Joe and John, physically smaller but no less competitive. He was the seventh of nine children and, as he later recalled, "when you come from that far down you have to struggle to survive".

After graduating from Harvard in 1950, he married Edith Skakel. They had 11 children. He managed John F. Kennedy's 1952 Senate campaign and

Below: Robert Kennedy survived the initial shooting, but died later in hospital. Five others were also wounded.

the following year joined the staff of McCarthy's investigative committee. He did not stay long. Later he worked for the Senate committee investigating corruption in organized labour, gaining a national reputation for relentlessly pursuing the Teamsters' Union leader, Jimmy Hoffa. As his brother's campaign manager in the 1960 election, suspicion

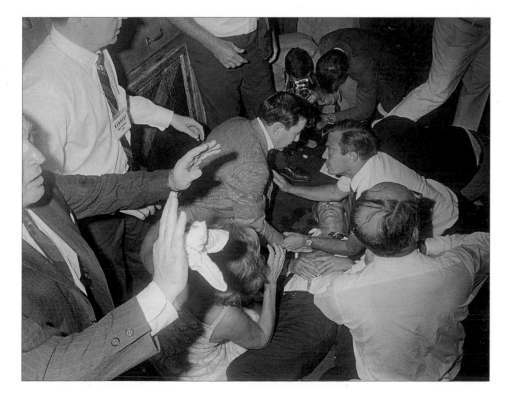

Above: Sirhan Sirhan (beneath the raised arm) is held tight after his fatal attack upon Robert Kennedy.

that he opposed offering Lyndon Johnson the vice-presidential nomination led to their mutual hatred. When, after the assassination in Dallas, Johnson needed to know the exact wording of the oath of office, he telephoned the attorney general: Robert Kennedy. It was, as Lady Bird Johnson remembered, "an excruciating call".

ASSASSINATION

In 1964, Kennedy resigned as attorney general and was elected as a New York senator. Four years later, he ran for the presidency. He had been his brother's most trusted advisor, involved in key decisions, not least during the Cuban missile crisis. More radical, championing the dispossessed and aware of the limitations on the exercise of military power overseas, he had just won the California primary and seemed on course to secure his party's nomination when, on 6 June 1968, he was shot dead at the Ambassador Hotel in Los Angeles. He was 42 years old.

THE CIVIL RIGHTS MOVEMENT

The Civil Rights movement defined the domestic politics of the decade. It did not begin in the 1960s, but the accumulated grievances of a century's neglect meant that its pent-up political energy exploded during the Kennedy and Johnson administrations, as its supporters took their protest to the streets.

There was progress. The courts, the Congress and the president were forced to respond to the demand for racial equality. The campaign of civil disobedience aimed to achieve peaceful integration. For some it was not enough. A more radical movement, advocating 'black power', sought change through violent confrontations. Race remained a major fault line in US culture and society.

In Montgomery, Alabama, on 1 December 1955, Rosa Parks, a member of the NAACP, refused to give up her

Below: Civil rights protesters demonstrated to force the South to obey the Supreme Court ruling that segregation was unconstitutional.

seat on a bus to a white man, in defiance of the state's segregation laws. She was fined. In protest, blacks began a boycott of the city's public transportation system: their demonstration lasted for almost 13 months, until a Supreme Court decision forced an end to discrimination on the buses.

It was during the Montgomery bus boycott that a local Baptist minister emerged as an activist and civil rights leader: Martin Luther King Jr. In 1957, he became president of the Southern Christian Leadership Conference, which organized acts of non-violent civil disobedience, dramatizing the racial injustices that pervaded the South.

In 1960, four black students in Greensboro, North Carolina, staged a sit-in to draw attention to discrimination at a Woolworth's lunch counter. Similar protests took place elsewhere. Young blacks joined the Student Nonviolent Co-ordinating Committee (SNCC). Together with the Congress of Racial Equality (CORE) it organized a series of 'freedom rides': during the

BLACK PANTHER PARTY

The Black Panther party was founded in Oakland, California, in October 1966 to promote civil rights for African-Americans. Its militant and sometimes violent pursuit of black liberation led J. Edgar Hoover to describe it in 1969 as "the greatest threat to the internal security of the country". Its leaders were arrested and jailed. The party rejected the integrationist policy of Martin Luther King in favour of black nationalism. It espoused a radical socialist ideology and successfully organized welfare programmes among the poorest black communities.

spring and summer of that year groups of blacks and whites travelled together on buses throughout the South to see if laws banning segregation in interstate travel facilities were being observed. Their non-violent protests were met with violence as they were attacked by mobs of Southern whites.

CHANGING ATTITUDES

In October 1962, amid riots and with his safety in the hands of federal troops sent by President Kennedy, James Meredith became the first black student to enrol at the University of Mississippi. The following year, after Martin Luther King had been arrested and jailed in Birmingham, Alabama, more civil rights protests took place. Television audiences were able to watch the city's police chief, Eugene 'Bull' Connor, using dogs and fire hoses against those involved in the demonstrations. The Civil Rights movement gained support and momentum as a result. In August 1963, 200,000 people joined the 'March on Washington' and saw King give the speech that defined his image in the public's imagination.

Above: 'Freedom riders' travelling the South on interstate buses were met with hostility, not least from local police.

Black churches were bombed. Civil rights workers were murdered. The Ku Klux Klan gained fresh recruits in Southern states. Other black leaders, who were more militant than King, also gathered support. One was Malcolm X, then a spokesman for the Nation of Islam, who observed that, "The only people in this country who are asked to be non-violent are black people." He advocated black resistance to white intimidation and demanded more than the recognition of civil rights: "An integrated cup of coffee isn't sufficient pay for 400 years of slave labour." He maintained that the development of a distinctive black identity was necessary, based on a recognition of the reality of history: "We're not Americans, we're Africans who happen to be in America. We were kidnapped and brought here against our will from Africa. We didn't land on Plymouth Rock, that rock landed on us."

Malcolm X was assassinated in February 1965. The following year, Stokely Carmichael, leader of the SNCC, echoed his message and coined the expression 'Black Power', urging blacks "to unite, to recognize their heritage, and to build a sense of community action". Later he joined Bobby Seale and Huey Newton in the Black Panther party.

In 1968, Martin Luther King was assassinated and an increasingly fragmented Civil Rights movement seemed to lose some of its earlier momentum. But by then it had changed the landscape of American politics. The 'Jim Crow' laws constituting a system of legal apartheid in the South had been dismantled, and the racial hatred and moral hypocrisy of those who supported that system had been exposed. Attitudes would change only slowly but the movement had laid the foundations for the advance to a more racially tolerant US society.

Below: Rosa Parks' refusal to give up her seat to a white man sparked the Montgomery bus boycott.

MARTIN LUTHER KING JR
CIVIL RIGHTS ACTIVIST

On 3 April 1968 Martin Luther King Jr recalled the time a decade earlier, during a book signing in Harlem, when he had been stabbed by "a demented black woman". The *New York Times* reported that had he sneezed it would have been fatal. He was, he said, "so happy that I didn't sneeze". The following evening he was assassinated at a motel in Memphis. He was 39 years old.

Martin Luther King had been an ordained minister for 20 years. In 1954, he became pastor at the Dexter Avenue Baptist Church in Montgomery, Alabama. During the city-wide bus boycott, he was elected president of the Montgomery Improvement Association, which co-ordinated the protest, going on to help form the Southern Christian Leadership Conference to press for civil rights reform. He visited India in 1959, returning "more convinced than ever before" that Gandhi's philosophy of "non-violent resistance is the most potent weapon available to oppressed people in their struggle for justice and human dignity".

In 1960 King was arrested and jailed in Atlanta after a sit-in at a restaurant. John F. Kennedy, campaigning for the

presidency, phoned Coretta King in support of her husband's action. His brother Robert called Georgia's governor and King was freed.

Imprisoned again in April 1963, he wrote the 'Letter from a Birmingham Jail' in which he defended his actions against the charge that they were 'unwise and untimely'. The time was now. Three months later, King gave his most famous address to the crowds in front of the Lincoln Memorial after the 'March on Washington', sharing his

Above: King, leader of the Civil Rights movement, advocated peaceful protest.

dream that racial equality would be achieved. The following year he was awarded the Nobel Peace Prize.

In 1965, in Selma, Alabama, King led a campaign to register black voters and was arrested once more, along with many of his supporters. It dramatized the struggle for civil rights, as King was able to point out in a national newspaper advertisement that "there are more Negroes in jail with me than there are on the voting rolls." Towards the end of his life he became more radical. In 1967 he criticized the USA's involvement in Vietnam as "one of history's most cruel and senseless wars". His violent death sparked riots in cities across the United States.

In 1986, the third Monday in January was designated as a federal holiday, Martin Luther King Day. Only two other individuals have been honoured in this way: Christopher Columbus and George Washington.

Left: Thousands of people marched on Washington to hear King deliver his "I have a dream..." speech in 1963.

WOMEN'S RIGHTS

Just as women had taken up the cause of abolitionism in the 19th century, seeing affinities between their repressed position in society and the plight of black slaves in the South, so in the 20th century their demand for gender equality became part of the broader struggle for civil rights.

In 1961, President Kennedy appointed Eleanor Roosevelt to chair his Commission on the Status of Women. In order to highlight the contemporary problems of discrimination against women in the workplace, the commission would have needed to look no further than NASA. Although a number of women were selected as potential astronauts in the initial Mercury space programme, none of them had the opportunity to emulate the achievement of Valentina Tereshkova, who in 1963 became the Soviet Union's first female cosmonaut.

That same year, the writer and activist Betty Friedan published *The Feminine Mystique*. In it, she questioned the traditional stereotypes of women as mothers and homemakers: "We can no longer ignore that voice within women that says: 'I want something more than my husband and my children and my home.'" Three years later, Friedan was a founder member of the National Organization for Women (NOW), which aimed "to take action to bring women into full participation in the mainstream of American society now, exercising all the privileges and responsibilities thereof in truly equal partnership with men". It rapidly became the most powerful feminist lobbying group in the United States.

In 1973 the Supreme Court decided the case of Roe v. Wade, brought by a pregnant woman against the State of Texas. She contested the constitutionality of the Texas law restricting the legality of abortion to cases in which it

was medically prescribed in order to save the mother's life. The Court declared state anti-abortion laws unconstitutional, igniting a political firestorm that still rages in contemporary American political life. The 'right to choose' and the 'right to life' define alternative perspectives on what still remains, both for women and for men, a complex and difficult decision.

The women's movement failed to achieve its goal of adding an equal rights amendment to the Constitution, but more women were encouraged to participate in politics, running successfully for elective office at both state and national levels. Presidents responded to

Above: National Organization for Women president Betty Friedan and other feminists march in New York City on 26 August 1970, on the 50th anniversary of the passing of the Nineteenth Amendment, which granted American women full suffrage. The organization called upon women nationwide to strike for equality on that day.

the demand for gender equality by appointing women to the Supreme Court and to Cabinet offices including those of attorney general and secretary of state but throughout the 20th century some 'glass ceilings' remained firmly intact, not least that of the Oval Office itself.

THE VIETNAM WAR
CIRCA 1959–1975

In 1961, after his Vienna summit meeting with Khrushchev, President Kennedy met with President de Gaulle, who predicted that if Americans were to become involved in a war in Vietnam, "you will, step by step, be sucked into a bottomless military and political quagmire". He spoke from experience. In 1954 the French defeat at Dien Bien Phu had abruptly ended the French attempt to re-impose colonial control in South-east Asia.

Vietnam was divided, with Ho Chi Minh's nationalist government in the North and the US-backed regime of Ngo Dinh Diem in the South. Many Vietnamese regarded this settlement as temporary and awaited a reunification election. The problem was that Ho Chi Minh, who looked likely to win it, was a communist. The United States refused to hold the election; instead, Americans imagined an independent democratic nation called South Vietnam. They tried to build it and were then forced to defend it. It was the biggest foreign policy debacle of the 'American Century'.

By the time Kennedy came to the White House, Diem's regime in South Vietnam was in serious trouble. The North Vietnamese Army (NVA) together with the guerrilla insurgents of the Viet Cong (VC) were fighting the army of the Republic of Vietnam (ARVN) in a civil war that became a war of national liberation. For the United States, it was always a military rather than a foreign policy problem: to oversee the administration's policy on

Above: As the Vietnam War escalated, more and more Americans were drafted to fight in a strange and unfamiliar land.

Vietnam, Kennedy chose Robert McNamara, his secretary of defense, rather than Dean Rusk, the secretary of state. Even before its troops were committed in numbers, it had become the USA's war as well.

In 1962, McNamara was confident. On a visit to South Vietnam he argued that "every quantitative measure …

KHE SANH AND TET
The siege of the isolated US base at Khe Sanh, near the North Vietnamese border, took place between January and March 1968. It became part of the Tet offensive – named for the Vietnamese New Year celebrations in which it started. Khe Sanh and Tet symbolized the tenacity of the Vietnamese in resisting the USA's military intervention.

VIETNAMIZATION
President Nixon's policy of Vietnamization was aimed at shifting the burden of fighting the Vietnam War from the US forces to the South Vietnamese army. The United States still provided the military hardware, but the policy, which was the basis of the 'Nixon Doctrine', allowed the progressive withdrawal of American troops from South-east Asia.

216

Above: The Vietnam Veterans Memorial in Washington DC is one of the most visited memorials in the nation's capital city.

Above: Despite the USA's overwhelming fire power, Vietnamese resistance broke its resolve.

shows that we are winning the war". The following year, in his State of the Union address, Kennedy claimed: "The spearpoint of aggression has been blunted in South Vietnam." Soon afterwards, the political situation spiralled out of control, culminating in a coup against Diem by officers of the South Vietnamese Army and his assassination. Three weeks later, Lyndon Johnson inherited the presidency with an avowed intention: "I am not going to lose Vietnam. I am not going to be the president who saw South-east Asia go the way China went."

McNamara later realized the reality: "We had no sooner begun to carry out the plan to increase dramatically US forces in Vietnam than it became clear that there was reason to question the strategy on which the plan was based." US technology, firepower and military resources were overwhelmingly superior to those of the North Vietnamese and Viet Cong. The United States controlled the battlefield in a war of attrition. What could not be won was the struggle for the 'hearts and minds' of the Vietnamese. When a US army officer admitted that "it was necessary to destroy the village in order to save it", the futility of the US enterprise became clear.

In 1967, the administration claimed that there was "light at the end of the tunnel". The following year, the 'credibility gap' was confirmed. The Siege of Khe Sanh was swiftly accompanied by the Tet offensive. Americans watched on television as their embassy in Saigon was besieged by enemy troops. Fierce fighting developed around the old imperial capital of Hue. The psychological impact in the United States during a presidential election year was profound. Walter Cronkite, reporting the news from Vietnam, saw no sign of victory: "To say that we are mired in a stalemate seems the only realistic, yet unsatisfactory, conclusion." On 31 March Johnson announced a bombing pause as a prelude to peace negotiations

Below: Helicopters were used extensively to move troops quickly during the Vietnam War.

and said that he would not seek another term in the White House.

Richard Nixon came to the presidency with a 'secret plan' to end the war. It involved one last effort to win it, expanding the conflict into the neighbouring countries of Laos and Cambodia. 'Vietnamization' allowed US forces to be withdrawn. In 1973, the president's claim of 'Peace with Honor' allowed Americans to avoid recognizing the painful reality of defeat. Two years later, the last US helicopters clattered away from Saigon as the North invaded the South and Vietnam was reunified. As the Vietnam veteran and poet W. D. Ehrhart observed: "Didn't we think we bestrode the world. Didn't we have a lot to learn."

THE COUNTERCULTURE

The 'credibility gap' between what the president said and what the people believed, which emerged during Lyndon Johnson's time in the White House, symbolized an increasingly divided society. The political energies of the 1960s produced radical change and a younger generation prepared to question authority. They discovered personal empowerment in ways that ran counter to the accepted political, economic and social structures of the Cold War United States. The counterculture thrived on public displays of opposition to what it identified as the conformist values constraining society. The contrast between the 1950s and the 1960s can be seen in the actions of two icons of their times. Whereas in 1958, Elvis Presley obeyed his summons to serve in the US military, eight years later Muhammad Ali refused to be drafted to fight in Vietnam.

The counterculture's questioning of US values, and its perceived threat to traditional morality, produced its own reaction. Evangelical religion sought a

Below: The Kent State University shootings during a protest against the Vietnam War punctured the idealism of the counterculture.

transformation of US society, placing its interpretation of faith at the centre of what became an influential political organization.

On 9 May 1970, before dawn, President Richard Nixon surprised a group of anti-war demonstrators gathered at the Lincoln Memorial. The meeting was reported in *Time* magazine: "Before he left, Nixon said: 'Just keep it peaceful. Have a good time in Washington, and don't go away bitter.' " He was speaking across a political and cultural divide. Opposing the war had become a principled commitment among those whose values the president did not share and could scarcely understand.

They were members of the counterculture. Belonging meant being young and adopting a lifestyle that revolved around sex, drugs and rock 'n' roll. Nixon's early morning encounter in Washington happened ten years to the day after the Food and Drug Administration had approved the contraceptive pill for marketing, ushering in the 'sexual revolution'.

EMERGING YOUTH CULTURE

San Francisco led the way. By the mid-1960s, youth culture had emerged and hippies were spreading a gospel of 'free love'. In 1967, thousands converged on the Haight-Ashbury district for the 'Summer of Love'. The previous year, Timothy Leary had popularized the use of LSD with the catchphrase: "Tune in, turn on and drop out." The soundtrack was the music played at iconic events such as the Woodstock Festival in August 1969.

The Vietnam War was the catalyst for political activism, and 'flower power' was the slogan of non-violence adopted by those who burned their draft cards and refused to serve overseas. Protest became street theatre. In October 1967, during

WOODSTOCK

For three days in August 1969, around 400,000 people gathered at a farm in New York State for the Woodstock Music & Art Fair. Members of the rock 'n' roll aristocracy, including Janis Joplin, The Who, The Grateful Dead, Canned Heat, Crosby, Stills, Nash and Young, Jimi Hendrix, Joan Baez and Ravi Shankar played at an event that, for the counterculture, encapsulated the spirit of the times.

Above: Woodstock remains a symbol of the liberalism of the age.

a demonstration in Washington, Abbie Hoffman and Jerry Rubin, leaders of the Youth International Party – 'Yippies' – announced that they would levitate the Pentagon to exorcise the 'evil spirits' within the building.

On 4 May 1970, students at Kent State University in Ohio placed flowers in the rifle barrels of National Guard troops during an anti-war demonstration on campus. Four were shot dead and nine were wounded. It was a symbolic moment: a shock of reality after a decade of idealistic dreams. Looking back, Abbie Hoffman would admit: "The 60s are gone, dope will never be as cheap, sex never as free, and the rock and roll never as great."

MUHAMMAD ALI

President Kennedy took an interest in boxing. In 1962, he invited Floyd Patterson to the White House. Patterson was a role model for the National Association for the Advancement of Colored People and was about to defend his world heavyweight title against Sonny Liston, an ex-streetfighter with a conviction for armed robbery. Kennedy told the champion he had to win for the sake of the Civil Rights movement. Patterson lost.

Two years later, Liston was beaten in turn by Cassius Clay, who would win the world heavyweight title twice more over the next 15 years, justifying his nickname, 'The Greatest'. A gold medallist at the 1960 Olympics in Rome, Clay was distinguished by his exceptional speed and style, and between 1960 and 1963 he was undefeated in 19 fights. Born in 1942 in Louisville, Kentucky, he was the son of a billboard painter and had been raised as a Baptist. But in 1964 at the time of the title fight with Liston he joined the Nation of Islam, renouncing his name (like Malcolm X, he rejected the names given to his slave ancestors) and becoming Muhammad Ali.

In 1965, Floyd Patterson fought him for the heavyweight title. Ali, he said, had "taken the championship and given it to the black Muslims". Beating him "would be my contribution to civil rights". Patterson lost again.

Patterson later confessed: "I came to love Ali. I came to see that I was a fighter and he was history." Ali's reputation rests not just on his unparalleled boxing ability, but also on his actions outside the ring. In 1967, he refused to be drafted to serve in Vietnam. He was stripped of his title, fined and sentenced to a five-year prison term; while free, pending his appeal, he was barred from the boxing ring. He could not fight, but he could still talk. Support for his stand against the draft grew as public opinion turned increasingly against the war, and Ali became a popular speaker on university campuses across the country.

Above: Muhammad Ali and Malcolm X in 1964.

In 1970, he regained his boxing licence. After winning two comeback fights, in 1971 he went into the ring with Joe Frazier. Once more cultural symbolism surrounded a title fight, pitting Frazier as the unwilling representative of the establishment against the insurgent Ali. Frazier won a unanimous points decision. It was Ali's first professional defeat. His reaction was simple: "I whupped him." Later that year, he won his own unanimous decision, when the Supreme Court overturned his conviction for draft evasion.

Ali regained his title, knocking out George Foreman, in 1974. It was as much a political statement as it was a sporting achievement. He had dramatized the struggle against the Vietnam War and for black civil rights. "Man, I ain't got no quarrel with them Viet Cong," he said. "No Viet Cong ever called me nigger."

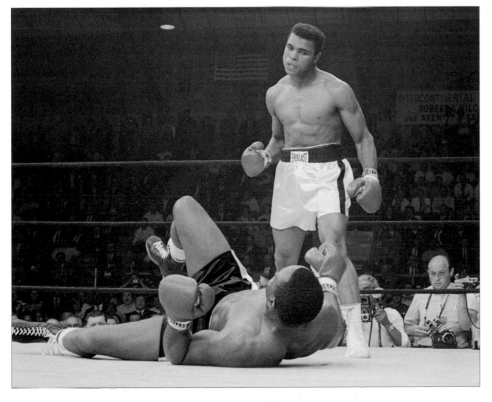

Left: Muhammad Ali became heavyweight champion by beating Sonny Liston. In the re-match in 1965, many at the ringside did not see his controversial 'phantom punch' which ended the fight.

SOCIAL UNREST
1968

"The spirit of resistance to government is so valuable on certain occasions, that I wish it to be always kept alive. It will often be exercised when wrong, but better so than not to be exercised at all. I like a little rebellion now and then. It is like a storm in the atmosphere." Thomas Jefferson had expressed this opinion in 1787. In 1968, protesters all over the world took him at his word. Sometimes the spirit was successful in bringing about change. On other occasions resistance was crushed.

In a decade of transformations, 1968 was a pivotal year. In January, Jeanette Rankin, who in 1916 had been the first woman to be elected to Congress and who had voted against the resolution supporting the USA's entry into World War I, led a march on Capitol Hill to demonstrate against the Vietnam War. With Rankin, then aged 87, were 5,000 women, including Coretta Scott King, the wife of Martin Luther King, and the folk singer and activist Judy Collins.

On 16 March US troops took part in the massacre of hundreds of South Vietnamese civilians at My Lai. In the United States the depth of anti-war sentiment was revealed in the same month when in the Democrat primary in New Hampshire, Eugene McCarthy, the 'peace candidate', did much better than expected.

In Europe, French universities closed amid a wave of strikes, as protest against the government peaked during the May 'events'. Students took to the streets and engaged in battles with the police, and the strikes spread until about ten million workers were involved. There was no revolution, as some had feared, but the protests brought down the Gaullist government and inspired similar student action all over Europe and in South America.

The 'Prague Spring', a liberalization of the communist regime orchestrated

by Alexander Dubček, ended in August when Warsaw Pact troops and tanks invaded Czechoslovakia. In the Middle East, a coup in Iraq brought the Baath party to power. One of its leaders was Saddam Hussein. The arab leader Yasser Arafat took control of the Palestine Liberation Organization.

During October, students led violent demonstrations in Mexico City. At the Olympic Games there, which had been boycotted by most African nations in protest at South Africa's apartheid regime, successful black US athletes gave

Left: American sprinters Tommie Smith and John Carlos raise their fists and give the black power salute at the 1968 Olympic Games in Mexico City. The move was a symbolic protest against racism in the United States. Smith, the gold medal winner, and Carlos, the bronze medal winner, were subsequently suspended from their team for their actions.

the black power salute while receiving their medals.

As television images recorded the tumult of events, 1968 became memorable as a year that symbolized a decade of dramatic political, social and cultural change across the United States and the world. In particular Americans witnessed not only death and destruction abroad, caused by their continued involvement in the Vietnam War, but also the assassinations of Martin Luther King Jr and Robert Kennedy at home.

There were riots on the streets of Chicago during the Democrats' national convention, which nominated Hubert Humphrey, Lyndon Johnson's vice president, as the party's candidate. In November the Republican party's candidate, Richard Nixon, defied political expectations after his defeat in 1960, and won the presidential election by a narrow margin. He would be the creative architect of a new foreign policy, heralding a shift in the USA's relations with China and the Soviet Union. As the year drew to a close, on 24 December, as Apollo 8 orbited the moon, in a live television broadcast, its crew read passages from the book of Genesis.

Left: The national guard were deployed during two days of rioting, arson and sniping that took place on the streets of Chicago during the Democrats' national convention in 1968. Police vehicles were covered in barbed wire.

RICHARD NIXON
1969–1974

He was a loner, an ardent American football fan and a successful poker player; he was an actor caught out in a lie. He changed the way the United States thought about the world, becoming the first president to visit communist China and building a new relationship with the Soviet Union based upon détente – reducing the international tension that had characterized the Cold War world.

Born in California in 1913 and brought up a Quaker, Nixon won a scholarship to Harvard, but his family could not afford the additional expense of an education so far from home. Instead, he attended the local Whittier College, where he played football with more enthusiasm than skill and continued to do well academically. He won a scholarship to Duke University law school in North Carolina.

Nixon spent World War II as a government lawyer in Washington and then in the navy in the Pacific, where he became the popular proprietor of a beer and hamburger stand, 'Nick's Snack Shack'. In 1946 he won election to the House of Representatives as a Republican with what became his trademark campaign style: the suggestion that his opponent had communist sympathies. He rapidly gained national attention by successfully revealing Alger Hiss as a former communist. In 1950,

Below: Spiro Agnew was Nixon's running mate in 1968 and 1972. In 1973 he resigned after a tax evasion scandal.

Above: Nixon set new directions for US foreign policy until the Watergate scandal destroyed his presidency.

Nixon was elected to the Senate and two years later, not yet 40, he became vice president elect.

During Eisenhower's administration, Nixon's high-profile anti-communist reputation was enhanced when he faced hostile demonstrations in Latin America and argued the merits of capitalism with Khrushchev in their impromptu 'kitchen debate' in an American showhouse at an exhibition in Moscow. After losing the 1960 presidential election, he stood for election as governor of California. He lost again. Even he appeared to believe his career was over, but he was bluffing. In 1968, a 'new Nixon' re-entered the political arena as president of the United States.

A NEW VISION

Nixon's interest was in foreign policy. With Henry Kissinger as his national security advisor, Nixon began to implement a vision that belied his earlier intransigent anti-communist

attitudes. His reputation as a hardline Cold Warrior gave him the political capital to spend on his innovative overtures to China and the Soviet Union without fear of being accused of being 'soft on communism'.

He was helped by the recognition of the cracks that had appeared in the apparent monolith of international communism. Nixon arrived in the White House two years after the Cultural Revolution in China, and while the Soviet Union was reinforcing its military on the border between the two nations.

In 1971, Henry Kissinger secretly visited China, paving the way for Nixon's historic meeting with Mao Zedong, chairman of the Communist party of China, in Beijing in February the following year. That May Nixon travelled to Moscow for a summit

Born: 9 January 1913, Yorba Linda, California
Parents: Frank (1878–1956) and Hannah (1885–1967)
Family background: Farming, store-keeping
Education: Whittier College (1934), Duke University Law School (1937)
Religion: Quaker
Occupation: Lawyer, public official
Military service: Commander, US naval reserve, World War II
Political career: Attorney, US Office of Emergency Management, 1942
US House of Representatives, 1947–51
US Senate, 1951–3
Vice president, 1953–61
Presidential annual salary: $200,000 + $50,000 expenses
Political party: Republican
Died: 22 April 1994, New York, New York

Above: Nixon with his secretary of state William Rogers (left) and Soviet leader Leonid Brezhnev (right) at the signing ceremony for the SALT treaty.

meeting with Leonid Brezhnev and to sign the treaty resulting from two and a half years of strategic arms limitation talks (SALT). In November, Nixon won re-election in a landslide.

In 1969 Nixon introduced a lottery: those, including a young Bill Clinton, whose birthdays were assigned high numbers in the draw, no longer faced the draft. Fewer troops were in Vietnam. Nevertheless opposition to the war continued. Peace negotiations dragged on in Paris.

In 1969, Nixon had authorized the covert invasion of Cambodia as part of his 'Vietnamization' policy, targeting Viet Cong bases and underlining US support for the South Vietnamese government. The *Pentagon Papers*, published in June 1971, revealed classified information about the history of United States intervention in South-east Asia and how the policies leading to the unwinnable war there had been made. It caused

political polarization, and domestic anti-war protests increased. Soon afterwards the White House recruited 'plumbers', so-called because they were to be responsible for stemming the flow of unauthorized leaks to the media.

During the 1972 election campaign, Nixon returned to his political roots, sanctioning a clandestine campaign of 'dirty tricks', in which members of the infamous Committee to Re-Elect the President (CREEP) solicited illegal

campaign contributions and identified their opponents as enemies who should be targeted with electronic surveillance. On 17 June 1972 burglars were arrested at the Democrat National Committee's offices in the Watergate building in Washington. They were there to plant bugging devices, but the significance of their actions lay not so much in the attempt itself as in the administration's actions immediately after the break-in. It was eventually revealed that a cover-up of the White House's involvement in the events at the Watergate building was orchestrated by Nixon's top advisors and the president himself. 'Watergate' became a shorthand expression for the corrupt practices that Nixon condoned in his pursuit of power.

Nixon's second term was overwhelmed by the scandal of Watergate. On 8 August 1974 he resigned rather than face impeachment. He spent the remainder of his life attempting to restore his political reputation by writing a series of books that drew on his experiences as an international statesman. He died in 1994. President Bill Clinton was among those who delivered eulogies at his funeral.

Left: Henry Kissinger being sworn in as secretary of state in September 1973. He was the first foreign-born citizen of the United States to become the nation's top diplomat.

WATERGATE

1974

The Watergate break-in was more than a burglary. The president had assumed he was above the law. It was one thing to exploit loopholes in the fabric of United States constitutionalism. It was another to abuse the Constitution itself.

When Richard Nixon ordered a cover-up of his administration's involvement in breaking and entering at the Watergate building, it was because he had other things to hide. Investigative reporters eventually lifted the curtain on a web of political corruption that had corroded his presidency, and Congress assumed its role in checking and balancing the executive. Public trust evaporated: the president was forced to resign. The aftershocks of Watergate continue to shape the limits of presidential power. Nixon's successors in the White House have had to beware of popular suspicions that they may be assuming more power than is granted to them by the Constitution.

"One of the five men arrested early Saturday in the attempt to bug the Democratic National Committee head-quarters is the salaried security co-ordinator for President Nixon's re-election committee." The lead paragraph in a story in the *Washington Post* on Monday 19 June 1972, two days after the break-in, appeared under the by-lines of Bob Woodward and Carl Bernstein. Once the link between the burglars and the White House had been established, the media had their story. It was Woodward and Bernstein who pursued it with remarkable tenacity.

They followed the trail of illegal campaign contributions and uncovered the plans for political espionage and sabotage that were part of the effort to guarantee that Nixon's bid for re-election would be successful. Guided by sources within the administration, Woodward and Bernstein were able to name those senior members of the Nixon administration involved in the scandal. Those sources included the infamous 'Deep Throat', named after a notorious pornographic movie of the time, who in 2005 was revealed as Mark Felt, then deputy director of the FBI.

In September 1972, Woodward and Bernstein wrote a story alleging that John Mitchell, who had resigned as director of the Committee to Re-Elect the President (CREEP) in the month following the break-in, had controlled a secret fund that had financed illegal political activities – including the electronic surveillance of the president's opponents in public life and the media – while he had been serving as Nixon's attorney general. Mitchell denied the charge. He was later sent to jail. By April 1973, two of the president's closest aides, John Ehrlichman and Bob Haldeman, had also been implicated in the scandal and were forced to resign, along with Mitchell's successor as attorney general, Richard Kleindienst. John Dean, the president's legal advisor, was fired. As Nixon put it, "there can be no white-wash at the White House".

Below: When the extent of his complicity in the Watergate scandal was revealed, Nixon resigned rather than face impeachment.

Above: Senator Sam Ervin (centre) whose congressional investigation into Watergate revealed that Nixon had bugged himself.

Dean appeared before the Senate Watergate Committee and in its televised hearings testified that he had met frequently with the president to discuss the Watergate cover-up. Senator Howard Baker asked what became a famous question: "What did the president know and when did he know it?" The answers came tantalizingly close when, in July 1973, Alexander Butterfield, a former White House aide, revealed that the president, who was accused of bugging others, had also bugged himself, routinely taping conversations and telephone calls in the White House.

There were more political casualties as Nixon fought to prevent the tapes being made public. When transcripts were released, they revealed a president who habitually used profanities – 'expletive deleted' became a refrain – and fulminated against those he thought were conspiring against him.

In November, he was still protesting his innocence. "People have got to know whether their President is a crook. Well, I'm not a crook." Few believed him. Congressional pressure increased. In July 1974, the House of Representatives approved the first of three articles of impeachment that charged the president with the obstruction of justice.

AN AUTHORIZED COVER-UP

On 5 August, the 'Smoking Gun', the incriminating evidence that confirmed the president's complicity in the attempt to subvert the course of justice in the aftermath of the Watergate burglary, was found. Taped conversations were released revealing that Nixon had authorized the cover-up and ordered the FBI not to proceed with its investigation of the break-in. Three days later, the president announced his resignation. He left office the following day.

Three years later, Nixon tried to justify his behaviour and explain his actions. In one of a series of televised interviews with David Frost, broadcast in May 1977, he argued that "When the president does it that means it is not illegal." With 45 million Americans among a worldwide audience, Nixon appealed to the precedent set by Abraham Lincoln during the Civil War. In a time of national emergency, Lincoln had claimed that, "Actions which otherwise would be unconstitutional, could become lawful if undertaken for the purpose of preserving the Constitution and the Nation."

The Vietnam War, like the Civil War, had divided the United States. During wartime, Nixon declared, "A president does have certain extraordinary powers which would make acts that would otherwise be unlawful, lawful." He was wrong. Richard Nixon's concern was self-preservation, rather than protecting the national interest.

Below: Carl Bernstein (left) and Bob Woodward (right) were the investigative journalists who pursued the cover-up all the way to the Oval Office.

GERALD FORD
1974–1977

Gerald Ford did not give an inaugural address. In his remarks on taking the oath of office he talked of "the lonely burdens of the White House". He could "only guess at those burdens" although he had "witnessed at first hand the tragedies that befell three presidents and the lesser trials of others".

Ford was a member of the Warren Commission, which had investigated Kennedy's assassination. He had been minority leader in the House of Representatives during Johnson's presidency and had become Nixon's unelected deputy as vice president. Now he was the USA's first unelected president. He inherited a White House that was suffering the effects of the aftershocks from the political upheavals of the previous decade. His transparent honesty was a refreshing change from his predecessor's secretiveness. Ford

Above: After 25 years in Congress, Gerald Ford was appointed vice president, inheriting the White House when Nixon resigned.

worked hard to restore public faith in the presidency, but it was difficult.

He was named for both his father and his stepfather. He was born Leslie King in 1913, but two years later his parents divorced. In 1916, his mother re-married and her son was brought up in Grand Rapids, Michigan, as Gerald Ford Jr. He won a sports scholarship to Michigan State University, then went to law school at Yale. He graduated in 1941. After war service in the navy, he returned to Grand Rapids where he practised law. In 1948, the year of his marriage to Betty Bloomer Warren, he was elected to Congress, and gradually rose through the ranks of the Republican party.

POLITICAL CAREER
While the Democrats remained the majority party in the House of Representatives, Ford became leader of the Republican minority in 1965. In 1973, after Spiro Agnew (Nixon's vice president) had been forced to resign amid charges of corruption, Ford, who had remained as minority leader in the House, succeeded him as vice president. Eight months later, Nixon resigned.

TWO YEARS IN OFFICE
Ford had been in office a month when he pardoned Nixon, believing it was necessary to move the country on and avoid the prospect of a former president facing criminal charges in court. His popularity plummeted. In 1975 Cambodia seized the *Mayaguez*, a US merchant ship that it claimed had strayed into its territorial waters. Ford authorized military action and the vessel was recaptured. The action gave a boost to national confidence in the aftermath of the Vietnam War.

Despite his efforts to restore public trust in the presidency, Ford could not escape the shadow of Watergate. In 1976, he lost his bid to be elected in his own right. His memoirs were called *A Time to Heal*. That challenge remained. Ford died in 2006 at the age of 93.

Born: 14 July 1913, Omaha, Nebraska
Parents: Leslie (King) (1881–1941) and Dorothy (1892–1967)
Stepfather: Gerald (Ford) (1890–1962)
Family background: Business (sales)
Education: University of Michigan (1935), Yale University Law School (1941)
Religion: Episcopalian
Occupation: Lawyer, public official
Military service: Lieutenant commander, US naval reserve, World War II
Political career: US House of Representatives, 1949–73
Vice president, 1973–4
Presidential annual salary: $200,000 + $50,000 expenses
Political party: Republican
Died: 26 December 2006, Rancho Mirage, California

BETTY FORD
Born Elizabeth Bloomer in Chicago in 1918, she married William Warren at 24, divorced in 1947, and married Gerald Ford the following year. They had four children. She was candid about her addictions to painkillers and alcohol, and open about her surgery and treatment for breast cancer, raising public awareness of these issues.

Below: In 1982 Betty Ford established the Betty Ford Center for the treatment of drug and alcohol dependency in California.

RELIGION AND POLITICS

The success of the Civil Rights movement, the failure of Vietnam and the revelations of the Watergate scandal meant that presidents now surveyed a new and often unfamiliar landscape of United States politics. Religion became more important in shaping political allegiances. The ideological consensus among liberals that the Cold War had to be fought aggressively to contain the threat of communist expansion fragmented. Some liberals, appalled by the outcome of the Vietnam War, opposed further military intervention overseas. Others, who became known as neo-conservatives, argued that the United States should still be able to project its military power overseas in support of its foreign policy ambition to remain the world's dominant superpower. Meanwhile, the 'Imperial Presidency' went into retreat. The USA's bicentennial celebrations in 1976 were edged with apprehension about its future.

During the 1960s the black churches of the American South had led the call for civil rights. In the following decade, white evangelists, particularly in the South, reacting against what they saw as the erosion of moral standards, entered the political arena. In 1979, Jerry Falwell co-founded the 'Moral Majority': it was

Above: Bicentennial celebrations took place throughout America in 1976, and helped bring closure to an era of discontent.

pro-life, anti-gay, in favour of strengthening US defence, against liberalism. Fundamentalist Christians found a political home within the Republican party and have since remained a force in national politics.

Senator 'Scoop' Jackson from Washington State supported Lyndon Johnson's policy on Vietnam. A staunch anti-communist, he tried for the Democrats' presidential nomination in 1972 and 1976, but his views were increasingly at odds with the outlook of his party. Two of his aides, Richard Perle and Paul Wolfowitz, like other Democrats who became concerned that the 'Vietnam Syndrome' was acting as a constraint on the president's power, joined the Republicans and became leading neo-conservative advocates of a more forceful foreign policy.

THE IMPORTANCE OF FAITH

In 1976, evangelical religion helped Jimmy Carter become the first former state governor since Franklin Roosevelt to become president. Carter was a Democrat whose Baptist faith was rooted in Christian tolerance. He disappointed many with fundamentalist convictions, who found political

sanctuary within the Republican party. The Imperial Presidency, the product of the ideological consensus established at the beginning of the Cold War, had crashed and burned in the political firestorms of Vietnam and Watergate. Presidents now faced the challenge of leading a more disunited USA as the nation's conflicting views on issues of moral concern, fuelled by a resurgence of religious activism, continued to rage.

THE IMPERIAL PRESIDENCY
Arguing that Johnson during Vietnam and Nixon during Watergate had ignored the principles of American constitutionalism, the historian Arthur Schlesinger Jr coined the term 'Imperial Presidency' to describe their abuses of executive power. As Congress reasserted its authority, it seemed that the presidency was more 'imperilled' than 'imperial' and the proper limits of presidential power have remained under constant debate.

THE VIETNAM SYNDROME
The public's reluctance to support US military intervention overseas after the debacle of Vietnam was seen initially by liberals as a useful restraint on the president's power. The so-called 'Vietnam Syndrome' later came to be viewed by neo-conservatives as an obstacle to be overcome, so that the use of military power could once more be an option should the USA's commander-in-chief deem it necessary to send troops to war.

JIMMY CARTER

1977–1981

Jimmy Carter, a born-again Christian from the former confederate South, campaigned better than he governed and once in power rapidly lost his electoral appeal. While Carter realized what was wrong with the United States, he could do little to put it right.

Carter was born in rural Georgia, growing up in a house that did not have electricity or indoor plumbing. His parents owned a peanut farm. In 1943 he entered the US Naval Academy in Annapolis, and three years later he married his sister's best friend, Rosalynn Smith. For the next seven years, he worked on the development of the USA's nuclear submarines, retiring from the navy in 1953 and returning to manage the family farm.

In 1958, Carter refused to join the White Citizens Council, which had been established to resist desegregation. As a result his business was temporarily boycotted. Four years later he embarked on a political career. In 1962 he won a seat in the State Senate after successfully contesting the electoral fraud that had occurred during the Democrat primary contest. In 1966 he was tempted to enter federal politics by running for Congress. Instead he chose to campaign to become governor of Georgia. He was comprehensively beaten in the

Below: Fuel shortages in the United States, caused partly by the Iranian revolution, resulted in panic buying.

Above: Little went right in Jimmy Carter's presidency, but he became a respected elder statesman of US politics.

primary election. Out of politics, and after a period of introspection, he became a 'born-again' Christian. Thereafter, religion became central to his life and public service. He stayed out of the political arena while the Vietnam War tore the Democrats apart, returning in 1970 to be elected as Georgia's governor. From his vantage point in Atlanta he watched Nixon entangle himself in the web of Watergate. When he ran for president in 1976, 'Jimmy Who?' was an outsider, distanced from the divisions of Vietnam and untainted by the corruption of the political establishment in Washington. He won a narrow victory.

DOMESTIC POLICY

Carter's first action was to declare a 'blanket pardon' for Vietnam draft resisters. The wording was important: an amnesty would have implied forgetting; a pardon symbolized forgiveness. Carter then confronted the realities of governing. He was unable to establish a

constructive relationship with Congress. The 'outsiders' who accompanied him to Washington, along with the president himself, were treated first with suspicion and then with outright hostility.

Carter's programme to conserve energy was the outcome of a growing realization that the USA's profligate consumption of natural resources was not only environmentally unsustainable but also made its economy vulnerable to fluctuations in the price of oil. He described his campaign to reduce energy consumption as one which would "test the character of the American people and the ability of the President and the Congress to govern". His policy did reduce US dependency on foreign oil but was complex and difficult to understand. As the economy worsened, the public simply saw longer lines at gas stations and paid higher prices for fuel.

CAMP DAVID

Carter attempted to shift US foreign policy towards a concern with human rights. In 1978, he brokered the Camp

Born: 1 October 1924, Plains, Georgia
Parents: James (1894–1953) and Lillian (1898–1983)
Family background: Peanut farming
Education: US Naval Academy, Annapolis (1946)
Religion: Baptist
Occupation: Farmer, public official
Military service: Lieutenant, US navy
Political career: Georgia State Senate, 1963–6
Governor of Georgia, 1971–5
Presidential annual salary: $200,000 + $50,000 expenses
Political party: Democrat

Above: Carter allowed the deposed Shah into the United States, unleashing a storm of anti-US protests in Iran.

David accords between Menachem Begin and Anwar Sadat, which led to the negotiation of a peace treaty between Israel and Egypt the following year. It was the high point of his presidency. By the following year, he was increasingly unpopular with the public at home. In July he gave what came to be known as his 'malaise' speech, although he never used that word to describe "a crisis that strikes at the very heart and soul and spirit of our national will". He identified its cause: "We were taught that our armies were always invincible and our causes always just, only to suffer the agony of Vietnam. We respected the Presidency as a place of honor until the shock of Watergate. These wounds are still very deep. They have never been healed." He could not supply the cure.

The Middle East, the backdrop for his greatest success, now damaged his presidency beyond repair. In November 1979, Islamic militants in Iran occupied the American embassy in Tehran, taking 52 hostages who were only released on the day Carter left office. It would not be the last time that political turmoil in the Middle East had an impact upon the reputation of a US president.

Carter's post-presidential career has been as illustrious as his presidency was disappointing. The Carter Center in Atlanta has advanced his human rights agenda. In his work for Christian aid organizations such as 'Habitat for Humanity', his involvement in monitoring worldwide democratic elections, his writings, and as recipient of the Nobel Peace Prize in 2002, Jimmy Carter has taken to heart the admonition of his favourite poet, Dylan Thomas: "Do not go gentle into that good night."

Below: Jimmy Carter, Anwar Sadat and Menachem Begin at Camp David.

ROSALYNN CARTER

Born Rosalynn Smith in Plains, Georgia, in 1927, she married Jimmy Carter at the age of 18. They had four children. A politically active first lady, she attended Cabinet meetings and National Security Council briefings. She chaired the Presidential Commission on Mental Health, and remains fully involved with the activities of the Carter Center in Atlanta.

THE IRANIAN HOSTAGE CRISIS

1979–1981

In 1953, President Eisenhower approved a CIA plan to stage a coup against Mohammad Mosaddeq, Iran's prime minister, whom the agency suspected had communist sympathies. Power was to be consolidated in the hands of the king, Reza Shah Pahlavi. US military equipment and Iranian oil money would support the Shah's regime. The coup was successful but the United States was now dependent on the Shah to keep Iran as an oil-rich pro-Western power in the Middle East.

In 1963, the Shah managed to quell growing religious protest against secularization and political unrest at the uneven distribution of wealth in the country. Iran's spiritual leader, the Ayatollah Khomeini, whose supporters had led the protests, was exiled. He eventually settled in France where he remained a focus of opposition to the Shah. Throughout his years in exile, he continued to influence Iranians who worked to undermine the Shah's hold on power. It was 16 years before they were successful.

In 1979, the United States was a bystander as a new round of protests escalated into a full-scale Islamic revolution, which forced the Shah to flee the country. Khomeini returned to Tehran as the popular leader of the revolution and the main influence shaping the future of Iranian politics. The revolutionaries abolished the monarchy and an Islamic Republic was established in its place.

Should the Shah of Iran, now travelling from country to country in exile and suffering from terminal cancer, come to the United States? Jimmy Carter asked his advisors. Later, his vice president, Walter Mondale, recalled that most of them favoured letting the Shah into the country. Carter then asked what action they would recommend should the Iranians react by taking the

staff in the USA's Tehran embassy hostage. In Mondale's words: "No one had an answer to that. Turns out, we never did." In October 1979 the Shah was allowed to come to the United States to receive medical treatment.

STORMING THE EMBASSY

The following month the Tehran embassy was occupied by Islamic militants who held 52 diplomats hostage, and the crisis dominated the remaining 14 months of Carter's presidency. His first response was to use economic

Below: US hostages being paraded by their militant captors on the first day of the crisis that ended Carter's presidency.

Above: Demonstrators storm the United States embassy in Tehran and set fire to the US flag.

sanctions and diplomacy to secure the hostages' release. Under domestic pressure for more dramatic action, on 11 April 1980 he tried a high-risk military rescue operation, but a desert sandstorm disrupted the mission and a helicopter crashed, causing eight US service personnel to lose their lives. The rescue attempt ended in failure and public humiliation for the United States and its president.

The crisis became a symbol of both the president's weakness and the USA's loss of international prestige in the post-Vietnam era. Carter persevered with frustrating negotiations that dragged on while his re-election campaign foundered: the lengthy crisis effectively ejected him from the White House.

The hostages were finally released minutes after his successor had taken the oath of office. It was as a private citizen and representative of President Reagan that Jimmy Carter flew to an emotional meeting with the released hostages in Germany on 21 January 1981.

CHAPTER TEN

RONALD REAGAN TO THE PRESENT DAY

1981–

ATTEMPTED ASSASSINATION, POLITICAL SCANDAL, MILITARY INTERVENTION IN THE MIDDLE EAST, IMPEACHMENT, A DISPUTED ELECTION AND THE 'WAR ON TERROR': AS THE 20TH CENTURY ENDED AND THE 21ST CENTURY BEGAN, THE US PRESIDENT CONTINUED TO BE AT THE EPICENTRE OF THE NATION'S POLITICAL LIFE. THREE FORMER STATE GOVERNORS, ONE FORMER VICE PRESIDENT AND ONE FORMER SENATOR WON THE EIGHT ELECTIONS HELD BETWEEN 1980 AND 2008. THREE WERE REPUBLICANS AND TWO WERE DEMOCRATS. ONE WAS THE OLDEST EVER TO OCCUPY THE WHITE HOUSE AND TWO WERE AMONG THE YOUNGEST TO BECOME CHIEF EXECUTIVE. THE OTHER TWO WERE FATHER AND SON. GEORGE W. BUSH'S LEGACY, THE CONTINUING WARS IN AFGHANISTAN AND IRAQ, REMAINED A CHALLENGING INHERITANCE FOR THE 44TH PRESIDENT OF THE UNITED STATES.

Left: From 1981 to 2009 every president since Reagan has authorized the use of the USA's military power, most controversially George W. Bush in his prosecution of the "war on terror".

RONALD REAGAN
1981–1989

Ronald Reagan was the first president since Eisenhower to complete two full terms in office. He was a politician who had once been a Hollywood star. He auditioned for the role of president, won election to the White House, and then turned in a performance that, if not flawless, was a tough act to follow. The oldest elected president defied conventional political stereotypes. Reagan's life spanned the 'American Century' and proved to him the limitless potential of the 'American Dream'.

He was born in Illinois in 1911. His family was of modest means, its resources further stretched when his father battled alcoholism. Ronald Reagan graduated from Eureka College in 1932, the same year that he first voted in a presidential election – as a Democrat supporting Roosevelt.

After working as a radio sports announcer in Iowa, in 1937 he was offered a contract in Hollywood by

Below: After the assassination attempt which almost killed Reagan, his press secretary James Brady (in the light blue suit) lies severely wounded.

Above: Ronald Reagan, 'The Great Communicator', left office as popular as when he entered it: a rare achievement.

Warner Brothers. In 1940, he married Jane Wyman. They had a daughter and adopted a son before divorcing nine years later. Reagan's film career, notable for an early role as football coach George Gipp in *Knute Rockne – All American* (1940) continued through the war years, during which he made

training films for the armed services. He won critical acclaim for his performance in *Kings Row* (1942). In 1947, he became president of the Screen Actors Guild and was active in its campaign against communism in Hollywood. He married Nancy Davis in 1952. As Reagan's movie career stalled, he found a new audience as the host of the Sunday evening television show *General Electric Theater*, touring the country as a speaker for its sponsor.

In 1962, he became a registered Republican. Four years later he was elected to the first of two terms as governor of California. After two unsuccessful bids for the Republican presidential nomination in 1968 and 1976, in 1980 he became its candidate, winning the White House in a landslide. A little under three weeks before his 70th birthday celebrations, he was inaugurated as the USA's 40th president.

A NEW ERA

Reagan did much to restore national self-confidence with his breezy optimism and infectious enthusiasm for the American Dream. His ability as the 'Great Communicator' was reminiscent of Franklin Roosevelt. At his best he was a visionary. At his worst, his lack of attention to the illicit activities of his subordinates ensnared him in the Iran–Contra scandal. It could have led to his impeachment. That it did not had much to do with Reagan's personality: even his opponents were charmed by his relaxed good humour.

Reagan was lucky to survive more than ten weeks: like James Garfield, he was the victim of an assassination attempt in Washington DC on 30 March 1981. Medical science had improved in the intervening century, and his life was saved. His remarks as he faced emergency surgery confirmed his strength of character. To Nancy it was:

Above: Over 3,000 people attended the rally in 1986 outside the American embassy in London to register 'disgust' at the United States' bombing of Libya. Reagan tried to reassert America's military power after the Vietnam War.

"Honey, I forgot to duck." To his surgeons it was: "I hope you're all Republicans." Within a month he had recovered sufficiently to seek support

Born: 6 February 1911, Tampico, Illinois
Parents: John (1883–1941) and Nelle (1883–1962)
Family background: Retail sales
Education: Eureka College (1932)
Religion: Disciples of Christ
Occupation: Film actor, public official
Military service: Captain, US army reserve and army air corps, World War II
Political career: Governor of California, 1967–75
Presidential annual salary: $200,000 + $50,000 expenses
Political party: Republican
Died: 5 June 2004, Los Angeles, California

Right: Colonel Oliver North was one of those responsible for involving Reagan in the Iran-Contra scandal. He became the star witness in congressional investigations into his plan to trade arms for hostages and fund the insurrection in Nicaragua. In later years he ran for the presidency.

from Congress for 'Reaganomics', his programme of tax cuts, reductions in social services and increased defence spending. The recession of the early 1980s was the worst since the 1930s, and the budget deficit rocketed before the economy began to recover in time for the president to benefit in his 1984 re-election campaign.

The realities of 'Vietnam Syndrome', the general reluctance of Americans to support US military interventions abroad, restricted Reagan's foreign policy ambition to aggressively confront communism, seeking to reduce its international influence, particularly in Latin America. This became evident in the case of Nicaragua. He could not persuade Congress to fund a US-backed military campaign against the left-wing Sandinista government there, and this led his administration into a labyrinth of illicit activity. Money to fund the Nicaraguan Contras – the insurgents who opposed the Sandinistas – was

channelled from the proceeds of arms sales to Iran, which were made in the hope of securing the release of US hostages held in the Middle East. It was as ingenious as it was illegal. Reagan, however, was not known as the 'Teflon President' – on whom no political mud would stick – without good cause. He emerged from the scandal with his reputation battered but intact and left the White House as popular as when he first arrived there.

In October 1983, during the Lebanese Civil War, US marines stationed in Beirut as part of an international

NANCY REAGAN

She was born Nancy Robbins in New York in July 1926. Her parents divorced when she was six and in 1929 her mother married Loyal Davis, who adopted Nancy and whose name she took. She became a Hollywood actress, under contract to MGM, and in 1952 married Ronald Reagan. They had two children.

Right: Nancy Reagan was devoted to her husband, and fiercely protective of him. She was an important influence during his presidency.

Left: Relations between Margaret Thatcher, prime minister of Great Britain, and President Reagan were particularly strong.

of his Strategic Defense Initiative (SDI), a missile defence system known popularly as 'Star Wars'. Critics dismissed it as fantasy or worried that it would destabilize the nuclear balance of power, by which both the United States and the Soviet Union were deterred from using nuclear weapons in the knowledge that the other side had the capacity to retaliate and destroy them. When, in 1985 and 1986, Reagan finally met Mikhail Gorbachev, the last leader of the Soviet Union, in Geneva and in Reykjavik, SDI framed their discussions, and progress was made towards reductions in the levels of nuclear arms. Reagan's early anti-communist rhetoric, condemning to the 'ash-heap of history' the 'evil empire', encountered the reality of Gorbachev's aim to restructure the Soviet Union, creating a more open society.

In his declining years Reagan bore his suffering from Alzheimer's disease with characteristic grace and fortitude. When he died in 2004 he could not recall having served as one of the USA's most popular 20th-century presidents.

Below: A 1987 treaty eliminated intermediate-range nuclear missiles.

PERESTROIKA AND GLASNOST

After Mikhail Gorbachev took over as Soviet leader in 1985, Americans became increasingly familiar with two Russian words: *perestroika* (restructuring) and *glasnost* (openness). The radical changes taking place in Soviet society altered President Reagan's perspective on the 'evil empire'. In his negotiations with Gorbachev, he became fond of quoting a Russian proverb: "*Doveriai, no proveriai*" ("Trust, but verify").

Below: Soviet troops prepare to return home at the end of the Cold War.

peacekeeping force were killed in a suicide bomb attack. Reagan withdrew US forces. In the same month, to show that the United States could still use its military power, he launched the invasion of Grenada, in response to political unrest caused by a coup that had brought a Marxist government allied to Cuba to power. It was a quick and easy victory.

Reagan believed it would be possible to make the United States immune to nuclear attack through the development

'STAR WARS'

Above: Reagan's vision, a defence system that could destroy missiles in space, alarmed those who thought it destabilized the nuclear balance of power. 'Star Wars' became a bargaining chip in negotiations between the superpowers. The Cold War came to an end after Reagan left office.

The president asked, "What if free people could live secure in the knowledge that their security did not rest upon the threat of instant US retaliation to deter a Soviet attack, that we could intercept and destroy strategic ballistic missiles before they reached our own soil or that of our allies?" In his address to the nation on defense and security on 23 March 1983, Ronald Reagan outlined his vision. An anti-ballistic missile shield would protect the United States from nuclear attack. Lasers and particle beams could be used to neutralize enemy missiles in space.

He challenged the scientific community "to turn their great talents now to the cause of mankind and world peace, to give us the means of rendering these nuclear weapons impotent and obsolete". The Strategic Defense Initiative Organization began to explore the problems associated with such a development. It remained a technological dream.

More significant than the practical issues was the fact that Reagan had shifted the strategic debate over nuclear weapons away from the theories of offensive deterrence, or 'mutually assured destruction', that had been developed during Eisenhower's administration. Negotiations with the Soviet Union aimed at limiting nuclear arms were now framed in a different context.

When Reagan finally talked about nuclear weapons with a communist face to face, in Geneva in November 1985, Mikhail Gorbachev came to appreciate that 'Star Wars' was based upon the US president's genuine desire to end the threat of nuclear war. In turn, Reagan saw Gorbachev's apprehension about the militarization of space – the development of weapons that could be deployed in space to be used against targets on Earth. The following year in Reykjavik, Iceland, President Reagan suggested that in both sides should eliminate nuclear weapons and jointly develop SDI to safeguard against the risk of their future redeployment. Gorbachev rejected the proposal, but was convinced that Reagan would not use nuclear weapons offensively. The Russian leader was able to move forward with the defence cuts that were essential to his plans for Soviet economic reform. Reagan deserved the credit for taking a political risk that encouraged Gorbachev to become his co-star in the drama that brought the Cold War to an end.

Below and right: Greenham Common, a US Air Force base in England became the headquarters of a women's peace movement in the 1980s. Anti-war protests became global.

THE IRAN–CONTRA AFFAIR

1986–1987

It was a 'neat idea' to use the proceeds of illegal arms sold to Iran, regarded by the US as a terrorist state, to fund an anti-communist insurgency in Nicaragua that Congress had refused to countenance. Colonel Oliver North, a member of President Reagan's National Security Council, did not appreciate that 'using the Ayatollah's money to support the Nicaraguan resistance' amounted to the privatization of US foreign policy. The Iran–Contra scandal broke the bounds of constitutional propriety, but Reagan survived the political firestorm when congressional committees called him to account for his actions.

In July 1985, Robert McFarlane, the national security advisor, told the president that Israel would act as an intermediary in selling arms to Iran; this would encourage Iranians who had contacts with Islamic extremist groups in Lebanon to influence the release of US hostages there. Reagan approved the plan. The first arms shipments resulted

Below: Anti-Sandinista rebels backed by the United States prepare for military action against the Nicaraguan government.

in freedom for a Presbyterian minister. The following year, North, who had been using private contributions to fund the Contras in Nicaragua, suggested to John Poindexter, McFarlane's successor, that proceeds from the arms sales could be diverted to help them in their campaign against the Nicaraguan government. In November 1986, his scheme unravelled. Justice Department investigators found the incriminating memo before his secretary, Fawn Hall, was able to shred it. Ed Meese, the attorney general, informed the

Above: A Sandinista war monument in Nicaragua commemorates the conflict and those who died.

president. Poindexter resigned. North was dismissed. In March 1987, Reagan admitted to a congressional committee: "I told the American people I did not trade arms for hostages. My heart and my best intentions still tell me that's true, but the facts and the evidence tell me it is not." The investigations concluded that he had not fulfilled his constitutional obligation to ensure "that the laws be faithfully executed".

Poindexter and North escaped jail. McFarlane, Casper Weinberger – the defense secretary later indicted for his part in the affair – and others involved received presidential pardons from George Bush, whose claim to have been "out of the loop" when arms for hostages had been discussed was later disputed. The conflict in Nicaragua continued until 1988. Violeta Chamorro, the United National Opposition candidate, defeated Daniel Ortega, the Sandinista leader, in the 1990 presidential election. In 1991, Terry Anderson, the last remaining US hostage in the Lebanon from the time of the scandal, was released.

GEORGE H. W. BUSH
1989–1993

George Bush is a member of an exclusive club: one of only four vice presidents to have been elected to succeed the presidents with whom they had served. Jefferson was re-elected but Bush, like Adams and Van Buren before him struggled to escape the shadow of a popular predecessor and failed to win a second term.

His father was Yale-educated, saw military service in World War I, was successful in business and became a Republican senator from Connecticut. Born in Massachusetts in 1924, George Bush followed in his father's footsteps: he graduated from Yale, became the youngest naval pilot in World War II and built a career in the oil industry before entering Republican politics.

Running for Congress from his adopted state of Texas, Bush served in the House of Representatives between 1967 and 1971, but lost two senate races in 1964 and 1970. President Nixon appointed him the USA's representative

Above: With the Cold War over, President Bush tried to shape a 'New World Order'.

in China, ambassador to the United Nations and chair of the Republican National Committee. He was head of the CIA during the Ford administration. Failing in his bid for the 1980 Republican presidential nomination, he became Reagan's understudy.

Famously described by *Newsweek* as a "wimp", Bush entered the 1988 presidential campaign more unpopular than any losing candidate for the previous 24 years. "Read my lips: no new taxes" was the pledge that would haunt him. He ran a negative campaign, vilifying his opponent, Michael Dukakis, and it worked. Bush won.

THE NEW WORLD ORDER

On 9 November 1989, a year and a day after George Bush had been elected president, the Berlin Wall was demolished: a symbolic event marking the end of the Cold War. Bush argued that the United States could now influence and shape a 'New World Order'. US power would guarantee international stability,

and US democracy would be an example to which other nations might aspire.

The following year the president of Iraq, Saddam Hussein, ignored Bush's message. In August, Iraq invaded Kuwait. On 11 September, addressing a joint session of Congress, Bush stated that it was his intent "to act to check that aggression". The president, who had used military force to remove Manuel Noriega from power in Panama the previous year, patiently built an international coalition with United Nations support and prepared the United States for its biggest military commitment overseas since Vietnam.

In the first test of the president's 'New World Order' US troops led a United Nations coalition in a war in the Middle East. Iraq's forces were ejected from Kuwait, which remained an independent state and a US ally in the volatile region of the Middle East. The Gulf crisis was also the president's chance to stage a final confrontation with the legacy of the nation's failure in South-east Asia. There would be, he pledged: "No more Vietnams". It was a swift and easy victory: a high-technology war with few US casualties. An exultant Bush immediately claimed that the United States had "kicked the Vietnam Syndrome once and for all". In a speech made soon after the war

---

Born: 12 June 1924, Milton, Massachusetts

Parents: Prescott (1895–1972) and Dorothy (1901–1992)

Family background: Business, public service

Education: Yale University (1948)

Religion: Episcopalian

Occupation: Businessman, public official

Military service: Lieutenant, US naval reserve, World War II

Political career: US House of Representatives, 1967–71
US ambassador to UN, 1971–2
Director of the CIA, 1976–7
Vice president, 1981–9

Presidential annual salary: $200,000 + $50,000 expenses

Political party: Republican

BARBARA BUSH

Barbara Pierce was born in 1925, in New York. She was 16 when she met George Bush. On his return from active service as a navy pilot during World War II, they married in 1945. They had six children. She was a popular first lady, and a political asset to her husband; her public approval ratings were often higher than his.

Above: George and Barbara Bush visit troops serving in the first Gulf War of 1990–1.

ended, however, the president was careful not to overreach himself and commit the United States to an overseas conflict of indeterminate length and uncertain outcome. America, he said, would not "risk being drawn into a Vietnam-style quagmire. ... Nor will we become an occupying power with US troops patrolling the streets

of Baghdad". To Bush's critics, not least among neo-conservatives, his reluctance to press home his advantage demonstrated that memories of Vietnam still shaped the nation's foreign policy. In Iraq, Saddam Hussein remained in power.

After his victory in the Gulf, Bush's approval ratings stood at an all-time

Below: George Bush campaigning for the presidency in 1980. Losing out to Reagan, Bush served eight years as vice president.

high. In March 1991, he had an 89 per cent approval rating. Leading Democrats were reluctant to confront an incumbent president who appeared destined to serve a second term.

Then his popularity plummeted. As the 1992 presidential election season started, Bush began to lose the political traction he had acquired from his successful foreign policy. At home, the economy worsened and memories of his broken promise not to raise taxes damaged his campaign.

The Republican party was disunited. The religious right mistrusted him. Others deserted him to support his fellow Texan, the maverick candidate Ross Perot. Bill Clinton, realizing that it was "the economy, stupid" that would decide the result, portrayed Bush as a patrician, out of touch with the concerns of ordinary Americans. The electorate agreed with him. Bush lost.

George Bush retired to the sidelines, cheering for his sons, George W., as governor of Texas, and Jeb, as governor of Florida. In 2000, he became a member of an even more exclusive club, joining John Adams as the only other former president to witness his son's election to the White House.

THE COLLAPSE OF COMMUNISM

The 'Iron Curtain' rusted from within. The Soviet Union and its various satellite governments in Eastern Europe faced an increasingly hard struggle to maintain the political disciplines of communism as their economies stumbled into stagnation. Further corrosion was caused by the tantalizing prospects of prosperity that lay just beyond the communist veil: the attractions of liberal democracy and capitalist consumerism in the West were self-evident. The dissident energy that provoked political and economic change had still to confront the state-controlled apparatus of potential repression, but in 1989, the Soviet bloc of countries began to disintegrate.

The end came quickly. On 4 June in Poland, Solidarity, the anti-communist party led by Lech Walesa, won a landslide election victory. Soviet tanks, however, remained at home. In August a human chain stretched across the Baltic States of Estonia, Latvia and Lithuania, highlighting the solidarity

Below: Crowds gather in Red Square to celebrate the failure of the attempted coup by Soviet hard-liners.

of those three nations in their call for independence. In October, the Communist party in Hungary surrendered its monopoly on power. Later that same month, Erich Honecker, increasingly unpopular as East Germany's leader, was forced to resign. In Bulgaria on 11 November, the same day that the Berlin Wall was torn down, the communist leader Todor Zhivkov left office after 35 years in power. Less than two weeks later, the leadership of the Communist party in Czechoslovakia relinquished

Above: Boris Yeltsin, the first president of Russia, with Mikhail Gorbachev, the last president of the Soviet Union.

power voluntarily. In December, Václav Havel, the dissident dramatist, became its president. In the same month, a popular revolt in Romania deposed and executed the communist dictator Nicolae Ceauşescu.

With its satellites spiralling out of its orbit, the Soviet Union now followed a similar political trajectory. In February 1990, the Communist party agreed to competitive elections taking place in each of its constituent republics. On 10 July, Boris Yeltsin took office as president of Russia. A month later he became the focus of opposition to the attempted coup against the Soviet government. Although the coup failed, it fatally undermined the political authority of Mikhail Gorbachev.

On 25 December 1991, Gorbachev resigned as president of the Soviet Union. By the end of the year, the Soviet Union itself had ceased to exist. From across the Atlantic, President George Bush and his fellow Americans watched as these last dramatic acts of the Cold War played out across Europe.

THE GULF WAR

1990–1991

On 2 August 1990, Saddam Hussein sent Iraqi forces to invade the neighbouring state of Kuwait, annexing what he claimed was Iraqi provincial territory. Others disagreed. Addressing the United Nations on 1 October 1990, President Bush compared Iraq's military aggression with the outbreak of World War I, speaking of the "still beauty of the peaceful Kuwaiti desert" being "fouled by the stench of diesel and the roar of steel tanks" as "once again ... the world awoke to face the guns of August". At other times, the president likened Saddam Hussein to Hitler and Iraq's action to Germany's invasion of Poland, which provoked World War II.

After six months during which an extensive military deployment took place and efforts, encouraged by the United Nations, were made to find a diplomatic solution, US air attacks started on 16 January 1991. By then Bush was reassuring Americans that there was one war to which the conflict in the Gulf would not be comparable.

Below: On the Iraqi-Jordanian border, hundreds of displaced refugees wait in long lines for food and water from relief workers.

Announcing the commencement of 'Operation Desert Storm' he pledged that "this will not be another Vietnam".

Following five weeks of intensive air bombing, the ground war was launched on 24 February. General Norman Schwarzkopf, the US commander, borrowed a tactical manoeuvre used by Ulysses Grant at the Battle of Vicksburg. Coalition forces unleashed a 'left hook' aimed at encircling the Iraqi forces in Kuwait. Many gave up without a fight. Within four days it was over. On 28 February a ceasefire went into effect.

Above: Iraqi soldiers waving white flags surrender to coalition forces.

SADDAM REMAINS IN POWER

The objective of ejecting Iraqi forces from Kuwait had been achieved, but Saddam Hussein remained in power. Bush did not intervene militarily when the Iraqi dictator crushed the political opposition of the Kurds, concentrated in the north of the country, who sought to capitalize on Saddam's defeat by rising up against his dictatorial regime. Instead there were United Nations sanctions and the imposition of 'no-fly zones' aimed at containing Saddam's potential military threat in the region. Meanwhile inspection teams were sent to verify that Iraqi chemical, biological and nuclear weapons, which it was thought were being developed to threaten neighbouring states in the Middle East including Israel, were dismantled.

US troops remained in Saudi Arabia, offending the sensibilities of militant Islamic fundamentalists everywhere. George Bush's involvement in the turbulent world of Middle Eastern politics helped shape attitudes both within and towards the region, with repercussions that would be felt most directly after his son became president.

BILL CLINTON
1993–2001

William Blythe III was born in Hope, Arkansas, in 1946, a few months after William Jefferson Blythe, his father, died in a car accident. When he was four, his mother married Roger Clinton. While his home life was fractious because of his stepfather's alcoholism, the young Bill Clinton established a reputation as an outstanding student, a talented musician and a gregarious personality. In 1963 he shook hands with President Kennedy at the White House. A political career beckoned. In 1964 he returned to Washington to attend Georgetown University. As a student, he worked for the Senate Foreign Relations Committee, chaired by the Arkansas senator William Fulbright, by then a leading critic of the Vietnam War.

In 1965 Bill Clinton was drafted into military service. Opposed to the war, he gave up the deferment he had gained by enrolling at the University of Arkansas

Above: Bill Clinton's achievements were overshadowed by his impeachment trial following an affair with a White House intern.

Law School, gambling instead on drawing a high number in the newly introduced draft lottery, which would enable him to escape military service in Vietnam. He did. In 1970, having given up his place at Arkansas, he went to Yale Law School to complete his education. There he met Hillary Rodham.

After graduating, Clinton returned to Arkansas. He married Hillary in 1975 and their daughter, Chelsea, was born in 1980. By then, Clinton, still in his early 30s, had served as attorney general and governor of Arkansas. He failed to be re-elected at the end of his first term, but returned to office in 1982, remaining as governor for the following decade.

Presenting himself as a 'New Democrat', in 1992 Clinton won the party's presidential nomination despite being buffeted by accusations of marijuana use ("I didn't inhale"), allegations of extra-marital relationships, and suggestions that he had been a 'draft dodger'. In the presidential election he was helped by a weakened economy, divisions among Republicans, and the

quixotic campaign of the wealthy Texan, Ross Perot, which siphoned support from the Republicans, taking almost 20 per cent of the popular vote. Bill Clinton defeated Bush to become the first president of the 'baby boomer' generation. He was the youngest president to take office since John F. Kennedy.

SCANDALS AND SUCCESSES
Clinton's first two years in office mirrored his first term as state governor in being marked by political miscalculations. A campaign commitment to end discrimination against gays in the armed forces provoked a firestorm of opposition from the military. His plan for health care reform, designed by a task force chaired by Hillary (an unprecedented political role for a first lady) was complex and confusing and was rejected by Congress.

Clinton's critics were convinced that he was politically and morally corrupt. Suspicion that the Clintons had been involved in shady real-estate dealing in

Below: Bill Clinton meets John F. Kennedy at the White House in July 1963. The 16-year-old Clinton was part of the Arkansas Delegation to the American Legion Boys Nation.

Born: 19 August 1946, Hope, Arkansas
Parents: William (Blythe) (1918–1946) and Virginia (1923–1994)
Stepfather: Roger (Clinton) (1909–67)
Family background: Mother a nurse; stepfather a car dealer
Education: Georgetown University (1968), Oxford University (Rhodes Scholar 1968–70), Yale University Law School (1973)
Religion: Baptist
Occupation: Public service
Military service: None
Political career: Arkansas attorney general, 1976–8
Governor of Arkansas, 1978–80 and 1982–92
Presidential annual salary: $200,000 + $50,000 expenses
Political party: Democrat

Above: The Oklahoma bombing was the most shocking act of terrorism on US soil before the events of 11 September 2001.

Arkansas, involving the Whitewater Development Corporation which bought land to develop for vacation homes, was compounded after Clinton's personal lawyer, Vince Foster, committed suicide. In January 1994 Robert Fiske was appointed as a 'special prosecutor' to investigate.

In the 1994 mid-term elections, the Republicans won control of both houses of Congress. The new Speaker, Newt Gingrich, rapidly established

HILLARY CLINTON

Born in Chicago in October 1947, Hillary Rodham graduated from Wellesley College, then went to Yale Law School, where she met Bill Clinton. They married in 1975. She stood by her husband during the scandals that rocked his presidency. In January 2007 she announced her candidacy for the 2008 Democrat presidential nomination, in a bid to return to the White House as the first woman to be elected president of the United States.

himself as the focus of opposition to the president. The following year Congress and the president battled over plans to balance the federal budget, and their refusal to compromise led to a delay in agreeing the level of federal expenditure in time to prevent a partial shutdown of the government, which could no longer pay its employees. Among those who continued to work in the White House were the unpaid political interns, one of whom was Monica Lewinsky.

Showing his trademark resilience, Clinton recovered from political setbacks to become the first Democrat to be re-elected president since Franklin Roosevelt. Clinton's political abilities were matched by his lack of moral sensibility. During his second term, rumours about Clinton and Lewinsky first appeared on the internet. It was Republican outrage at his personal behaviour in prevaricating about their affair, and subsequently being forced to acknowledge it, that led to an unsuccessful attempt to impeach him.

He extended free trade through the North American Free Trade Agreement (NAFTA), the economy hummed along and the federal budget deficit diminished. Abroad, Clinton extended

NAFTA

The North American Free Trade Agreement (NAFTA) came into effect on 1 January 1994. It aimed to eliminate obstacles to trade and investment between the United States, Canada and Mexico. While its American critics remain suspicious of its impact upon employment, particularly in manufacturing industries, its supporters point to the economic growth and rising living standards that have resulted from the free-market economy in North America.

diplomatic recognition to Vietnam. He was instrumental in developing Northern Ireland's peace process, and after sanctioning military intervention in the Balkans he brokered a peace accord between Bosnia, Serbia and Croatia. Iraq continued to be a problem, and terrorism, notably the 1995 bombing in Oklahoma City, remained a threat.

Below: A politically committed first lady, in November 2000, Hillary Clinton was elected to the Senate from New York.

THE IMPEACHMENT TRIAL

When radical Republicans focused their attention on holding the president to account for his standards of behaviour in the White House, and when Hillary Clinton suggested there was a vast right-wing conspiracy against her husband, they defined a contemporary fault line in US political debate. Since Nixon's conduct during Watergate, the issue of morality in US public life had been a consistent concern. Throughout his presidency, Clinton's moral and political integrity had been under attack, particularly from those who drew support from the increasingly vocal fundamentalist wing of the Republican party.

In August 1994, special prosecutor Robert Fiske was replaced by Kenneth Starr, a Republican. Meanwhile, an Arkansas state employee, Paula Jones, brought a lawsuit against Clinton, alleging that he had sexually harassed her while he was governor. The stage was set for the drama of impeachment. All that remained was to cast the starring role of a White House intern who had had an affair with the president: Monica Lewinsky.

By the time of Clinton's re-election in 1996, Starr had not been able to find significant evidence of misconduct in

Above: Senate Republicans could not muster enough votes for the impeachment of Clinton to be successful.

the Whitewater affair, the original remit of his investigation. The following year, Lewinsky revealed details of her relationship with Clinton to Linda Tripp, a former White House employee then working at the Pentagon. After Lewinsky denied the affair in an affidavit given to Paula Jones's lawyers, Tripp contacted Starr, who was then able to pursue a new line of enquiry: possible obstruction of justice and perjury orchestrated by the president.

When the House Judiciary Committee received his report it gave them the ammunition they needed to detonate the impeachment process.

The mathematics were simple. A two-thirds majority in the Senate was required to vote in favour of the charges brought by the House of Representatives. There were 45 Democrat senators. Whereas the impeachment trial of President Andrew Johnson had hung in the balance, it was widely acknowledged that Bill Clinton's opponents did not have the necessary support to convict him. The proceedings that took place in Congress during 1998 were a political entertainment in which the eventual outcome was predictable. Clinton survived with his reputation tarnished but his popularity undimmed.

Clinton's election had symbolized a generational change in US politics. Reactions to his personal conduct demonstrated that the nation's fragmented cultural and countercultural values coexisted in uneasy tension. Despite this, on leaving office, Bill Clinton was characteristically optimistic about the USA's future prospects. As he put it: "I still believe in a place called Hope."

Below: Monica Lewinsky (in blue) runs the media gauntlet following the revelation of her affair with the president.

THE INVENTION OF THE INTERNET

When *Newsweek* decided not to publish allegations of the relationship between Bill Clinton and Monica Lewinsky, the story was initially revealed on Matt Drudge's website. During the 1990s, the internet became a new and powerful medium of political communication. It was potentially democratic, allowing anyone to present their political views unmediated and unvarnished to a national and international audience.

On 11 September 1998, when Kenneth Starr's report containing details of the affair was first made available to anyone who had access to the internet, the website on which it had been posted received more than three million hits per hour. The internet, like the printing press, radio and television before it, ushered in a communications revolution. Politicians, including the president of the United States, have to adapt to a world where more and more people are part of the online network.

The way that the internet shapes the modern world has been the product of the interface between innovative technologies that have made personal computers an essential feature of everyday life. At the turn of the 21st century there were more than 45 million Americans subscribing to the internet. Bill Gates, the co-founder of Microsoft, which had developed the dominant operating system facilitating its use, had become the richest person on the planet.

For politicians, the internet has become an indispensable means of advertising themselves to potential voters. The White House website (www.whitehouse.gov) currently provides an official account of the public lives of the president, the first lady, the vice president and his wife. The impact of the internet has been felt particularly during elections, when it has provided candidates with innovative ways to

reach potential supporters and, just as importantly, more effective ways to raise money for campaigns.

The internet is potentially an ideal medium for democratic debate, allowing anyone to voice their opinions on the issues about which they are concerned. But issues remain. Are there limits to be imposed on freedom of speech, or on the actions of those who seek to influence others to embrace their

Left: Tim Berners Lee, changed the face of communications throughout the world when he developed the internet.

particular ideas, attitudes or prejudices? How trustworthy is the information available on individual websites?

In 1999, Al Gore, the then vice president, suggested that as a senator from Tennessee he "took the initiative in creating the internet", meaning that he promoted the use of the new technology. Unfortunately, his words as he prepared to run for the White House were easily altered by his opponents. They claimed that he said that he had 'invented' it: an inaccurate quotation that spread rapidly through cyberspace, making him the object of widespread ridicule. The internet has the potential to shape the popular images of aspiring presidents in new and possibly unanticipated ways.

Below: Mass access to the internet led to a communications revolution, allowing politicians greater opportunities to reach potential supporters and influence voters.

THE PRESIDENTIAL ELECTION
2000

The first presidential election of the 21st century was decided not by the American people but by the Supreme Court. George W. Bush, son of the former president, won the White House through the intervention of judges who had been nominated either by his father or by Ronald Reagan, after an election in which disputed votes in Florida, governed by his brother, were critical to the outcome.

The electoral college seemed a benign constitutional anachronism. It had worked throughout the 20th century. It was the first election of the new millennium that focused attention on the institution, which had, except on three previous occasions, avoided the political spotlight. Thomas Jefferson in 1800 and John Quincy Adams in 1824 had been elected by the House of Representatives. Rutherford Hayes had been awarded the White House in 1888 by an electoral commission composed of members of Congress and the Supreme Court. In 2000, it would be the Supreme Court alone that effectively decided the result.

Twelve years previously George H. W. Bush, then vice president, had defeated a state governor, Michael Dukakis, to become chief executive. Now George W. Bush, governor of Texas, challenged the incumbent vice president, Al Gore. The outcome was predicted to be close. Gore, who had served Clinton loyally, benefited from the economic prosperity that had marked the Democrats' eight years in the White House, but found it difficult to distance himself from the charges of corruption, in his case political rather than moral, that bedevilled the administration. Bush, who had won the nomination for his party after a hard-fought battle against his principal rival, Senator John McCain, pledged to restore "honor and dignity" to the White House, but his apparent lack of interest in the politics of the wider world led his detractors to doubt his presidential credentials.

On election night, the television networks correctly predicted that the

Left: George Bush and Al Gore contested one of the most controversial elections in presidential history.

Above: The 2000 presidential election result was subject to intense scrutiny.

key to victory would lie with the result in Florida. In their competition to be the first to report the outcome, the commentators agreed early in the evening that Bush had carried the state. They were wrong. After the results elsewhere in the country had been called, Gore telephoned Bush to concede defeat. Shortly afterwards, it became apparent that the Florida vote was in fact too close to call. The two candidates spoke again. Gore withdrew his concession.

FLORIDA

Florida state law required a recount. Then voting irregularities emerged. The ballot papers took the form of punch cards designed to be counted mechanically, and Americans became used to discussing the intricacies of 'butterfly ballots' and 'chads' that could be 'hanging', 'dimpled' or 'pregnant'. Arguments developed over how many votes were valid. The lawyers moved in. Courtroom battles decided to allow manual recounts and set deadlines for

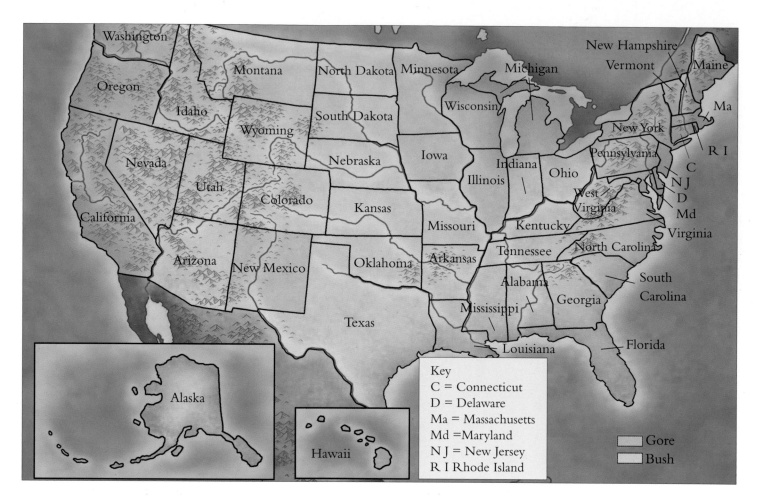

Key
C = Connecticut
D = Delaware
Ma = Massachusetts
Md =Maryland
N J = New Jersey
R I Rhode Island

Gore
Bush

Above: The result of the presidential election of 2000 was determined by the votes of one state, Florida.

their completion. On 26 November, 19 days after the election, Katherine Harris, Florida's secretary of state, certified the Florida result: Bush had won by 537 votes, out of the almost six million that had been cast. Gore disagreed.

SUPREME COURT DECISION

The legal arguments and the recounting continued while the Florida State Legislature met to consider how to select its electors in the event that the dispute remained unresolved. The Republican majority, supported by Governor Jeb Bush, would have been expected to endorse those pledged to support their party's candidate. It proved unnecessary when the Supreme Court delivered its verdict. On 12 December, by a 5–4 vote, it decided that the recounts were unconstitutional as they were not being conducted according to

a consistent standard in different Florida counties. They were stopped. The certification of Florida's result was endorsed. Bush had gained the critical one-vote majority he needed in the electoral college to win the election.

Overall, Gore had won the national popular vote but, like Samuel Tilden before him, he had lost where the outcome was decided: the electoral college had 'misfired'. Effectively, the Supreme Court had selected the president. The five judges who agreed the majority decision had been nominated by Republican presidents. Of the two justices appointed during his father's presidency, one, Clarence Thomas, sided with Bush. The other, David Souter, did not.

By involving itself in the partisan world normally inhabited by the executive and the legislature, the Court's reputation for independence was diminished. As one of those who dissented from its verdict, Justice John Paul Stevens, put it: "Although we may never

know with complete certainty the identity of the winner of this year's presidential election, the identity of the loser is perfectly clear. It is the Nation's confidence in the judge as an impartial guardian of the rule of law." On 20 January 2001, George W. Bush was inaugurated as the 43rd president.

BUTTERFLY BALLOTS AND CHADS

The 'butterfly ballot', with the names of the candidates' names down both sides separated by punch holes in the centre, was a design that potentially confused voters. 'Chads' are the paper waste made when a machine punches a hole in paper. A 'hanging' chad might have one corner still attached to the ballot; 'pregnant' and 'dimpled' chads were still fixed firmly to the ballot but with varying signs of indentation, possibly indicating an intention to vote for a particular candidate.

GEORGE W. BUSH
2001–2009

The defining moment of George Bush's presidency came on 11 September 2001, when terrorist attacks on the United States changed the face of domestic and international politics. His term in office was shaped by his reaction to the events of that single day. The attacks, which destroyed the twin towers of the World Trade Center in New York City, damaged the Pentagon, and threatened intended targets in Washington DC, led to his declaration of a 'war on terror'. Military action followed in Afghanistan. Then came Iraq. When the weapons of mass destruction that had provided the pretext for an invasion of Iraq proved elusive, the president's credibility crumbled. Saddam Hussein's regime in Iraq was toppled, but US troops were drawn into a prolonged conflict that eroded Bush's popularity. As his term in office entered its final months, his approval ratings were among the lowest ever recorded.

Born in 1946 and brought up in Texas, George W. Bush's journey into politics was the product of family expectation and tradition. He was not

Above: Contemporary approval ratings for Bush have been some of the highest and lowest ever recorded for a US president.

an outstanding student at Yale, although he enjoyed the social life of his fraternity. Service in the Texas Air National Guard, where he learned to fly, meant that he did not go to Vietnam. After graduating from Harvard Business School in 1975, he returned to Texas and a career in the oil industry.

At the age of 40, Bush gave up alcohol for sobriety. Encouraged by the Reverend Billy Graham, he dedicated himself to a life that would make him the most overtly religious occupant of the White House since Jimmy Carter. His public profile in his home state was raised by his part-ownership of the Texas Rangers baseball team. In 1994, helped by Karl Rove, his principal political strategist, he ran for governor of Texas. His landslide re-election four years later was followed in 2000 by his successful campaign for the Republican presidential nomination.

After the Supreme Court had settled the arguments and lawsuits that swirled around the Florida recounts, George W. Bush, like John Quincy Adams before

him, followed in his father's footsteps as he became the first president to take office in the 21st century.

11 SEPTEMBER 2001

After seven months in the White House, during which US foreign policy became more unilateralist – symbolized by Bush's refusal to sign the Kyoto Protocol on International Climate Change – his lack of popularity abroad was mirrored by low approval ratings at home. His vice president, Dick Cheney, who had served Bush's father as defense secretary during the 1991 Gulf War, was widely believed to be the driving force behind the administration's policies.

Then came 11 September. It gave Bush the opportunity to reinvigorate his presidency. His reaction, declaring a 'war on terror', and subsequently announcing the 'Bush Doctrine' in justification of pre-emptive military action to counter perceived threats to national security, provoked domestic opposition

Below: Pope John Paul II and President George W. Bush at the papal summer residence in July 2001.

Born: 6 July 1946, New Haven, Connecticut
Parents: George (b. 1924) and Barbara (b.1925)
Family background: Business, public service
Education: Yale University (1968), Harvard Business School (1975)
Religion: Methodist
Occupation: Business
Military service: First lieutenant, Alabama air national guard
Political career: Governor of Texas, 1995–2000
Presidential annual salary: $400,000 + $50,000 expenses
Political party: Republican

Above: Saddam Hussein's statue is toppled. Televised worldwide, this event symbolized the end of his regime, but the continuing insurgency has involved the United States in a protracted war with Iraq.

Above: The military campaigns in President Bush's 'war on terror' following the attacks of 11 September 2001 will remain his most controversial legacy.

and drained the reservoir of overseas sympathy in the aftermath of the terrorist attacks.

By the end of the year, the Taliban regime in Afghanistan, which had provided a base for Osama Bin Laden and Al Qaeda training camps, had been overthrown by a US-led coalition operating with United Nations approval. In his 2002 State of the Union address, Bush proceeded to identify an 'Axis of Evil' – Iraq, Iran and North Korea – which he suggested represented further threats to US security.

The next phase of the 'war on terror' fractured relations between the United States and the international community, with the notable exception of the United Kingdom. In 2003 Bush's dwindling 'coalition of the willing' invaded Iraq. Saddam Hussein was overthrown, and US troops remained in a hostile country where the political, economic and social infrastructure had been destroyed and there was no immediate prospect of its reconstruction. The war continued. Despite the controversy surrounding his actions, Bush won re-election in 2004. His second term was soon blown off course by the administration's inept reaction to the devastation caused when, in August 2005, Hurricane Katrina destroyed New Orleans. In the following year's midterm elections, the Democrats regained control of Congress, and the president's popularity reached its lowest ebb. George W. Bush ensured that the presidency remains the focus of national attention and that future occupants of the White House will have to confront complex and politically divisive issues of war and peace. Barack Obama, his Democratic successor, won the 2008 election, as the aftershocks of Bush's controversial eight years in the White House continued to shape the future of United States politics.

LAURA BUSH

Laura Welch was born in Texas in 1946. After graduating from Southern Methodist University in Dallas she became a schoolteacher. On gaining a Masters degree she worked as a school librarian. In 1977, she married George W. Bush. Their twin daughters, Jenna and Barbara, were born four years later. She is credited with playing an influential part in his decision to stop drinking in 1986. Uncomfortable in the political spotlight, as first lady she emulated her mother-in-law, Barbara Bush, and concentrated on supporting her husband and promoting education and women's health.

AL QAEDA

Al Qaeda, translated as 'the base', is a Sunni Muslim fundamentalist group, led by Osama Bin Laden, that grew out of the religious and political conflict in Afghanistan in the 1980s. After the 1991 Gulf War, the continuing presence of US troops in Saudi Arabia became a focus of its hostility towards the United States, ultimately leading to its organization of the 11 September attacks and prompting President Bush's 'war on terror'. Among the group's aims are an end to foreign influence in Muslim countries and the establishment of a new caliphate.

9/11/2001

The images are seared into the USA's historical memory. On the morning of 11 September 2001, television cameras recorded events as first American Airlines flight 11, which had left Boston en route to Los Angeles, and then United Airlines flight 175, scheduled to make the same journey, exploded into each of the twin towers of the World Trade Center in New York City. Shortly after those initial impacts, American Airlines flight 77 from Washington DC to Los Angeles slammed into the Pentagon. A fourth plane, United Airlines flight 93, which had been delayed taking off from Newark on its way to San Francisco, was the last of the hijacked airliners to crash: it came down in a rural area of south-west Pennsylvania without reaching its presumed target in the nation's capital. Nearly 3,000 people lost their lives. It was the worst terrorist atrocity that had ever been perpetrated on US soil.

President Bush, who was in Florida, made a brief announcement: "We have had a national tragedy. Two aeroplanes have crashed into the World Trade Center in an apparent terrorist attack on our country." Less than 20 minutes after he had spoken, airports were closed and commercial flights suspended across the country. As the full scale of the attacks emerged, the president flew first to Louisiana, where he vowed to "hunt down and punish those responsible for these cowardly acts", then to Nebraska, before returning to Washington. That evening, in a nationwide address, he proclaimed that the United States would "make no distinction between the terrorists who committed these acts and those who harbor them".

In New York, it was the mayor, Rudolph Giuliani, who took control of the situation in the hours following the attacks. The nation looked to its president to provide leadership. On 13 September, in a televised conference call with Giuliani and George Pataki, the governor of New York, Bush, who had initially not planned to visit New York that week, announced that he would fly to the city the following afternoon after attending a service at Washington National Cathedral. In his address to a congregation there that included three former presidents – his father, Jimmy Carter and Bill Clinton – Bush said: "This conflict has begun on the timing and terms of others. It will end in a way, and at an hour, of our choosing." The service ended with the singing of 'The Battle Hymn of the Republic'.

Later, in New York, he improvised the most effective three sentences of his presidency. Standing on a battered fire truck rescued from the wreckage of the collapsed buildings, Bush struggled to make himself heard as he spoke through a bullhorn. Someone in the crowd complained of being unable to hear him. The president, with his arm around the shoulders of a firefighter, responded: "I can hear you. The rest of the world hears you. And the people who knocked these buildings down will hear from all of us soon."

It was an image of defiance and resolve that was rapidly translated into substance. Osama Bin Laden, whose Al Qaeda terrorist network was immediately suspected of planning and executing the attacks, was held responsible: less than a week after 9/11, the president had announced that he was 'Wanted, Dead or Alive'. His sanctuary in Afghanistan would be the first target in the 'war on terror'.

As investigations continued into how the 19 hijackers had been allowed to enter the United States and take commercial flight training courses, national security became a major concern. In October, Congress passed the Patriot Act, increasing government powers to fight terrorism, which led to concerns that civil liberties were threatened. After the war in Afghanistan, suspected terrorists were taken to Guantanamo Bay, the US military facility in Cuba, where they were detained without trial. Osama Bin Laden's precise whereabouts remained unknown.

Left: The twin towers ablaze in New York. In his diary that night Bush recorded that "The Pearl Harbor of the 21st century took place today."

THE IRAQ WAR
2003

President Bush's 'war on terror' involved the United States in its most protracted overseas military action since Vietnam. From the end of 2001 onwards, the inconclusive conflict in Afghanistan was relegated to a sideshow as the administration turned its attention towards Iraq.

Iraq was the 'unfinished business' left over from the Gulf War of 1991. Its head of state, Saddam Hussein, was a dictatorial leader who defied the UN sanctions regime that tried to curb his abuse of power, who still had the potential to threaten neighbouring states in the Middle East and who, it was claimed, might also be stockpiling weapons of mass destruction. The Bush administration held him responsible for encouraging international terrorism, even though they could not establish that he had any obvious links with groups such as Al Qaeda. In January 2002, Iraq became a charter member of President Bush's so-called 'Axis of Evil'.

Five months later, in his speech at West Point, the president revealed that the ground was being prepared. In formulating the 'Bush Doctrine', he

Below: Saddam Hussein was deposed, captured and tried in Iraq.

Above: The US-led 'coalition of the willing' invaded Iraq, but found no weapons of mass destruction there.

warned that: "The gravest danger to freedom lies at the perilous crossroads of radicalism and technology. When the spread of chemical and biological and nuclear weapons, along with ballistic missile technology, occurs, even weak states and small groups could attain a catastrophic power to strike great nations. Our enemies … have been caught seeking these terrible weapons … Unbalanced dictators with weapons of mass destruction can deliver those weapons on missiles or secretly provide them to terrorist allies." He concluded that the United States needed "to be ready for pre-emptive action when necessary to defend our liberty".

The CIA supplied the intelligence. In December 2002, its then director, George Tenet, told the president that it was a "slam dunk case" that Saddam had concealed weapons of mass destruction. The UN weapons inspectors, who had resumed their work the previous month, would not be so confident about their existence.

The president was convinced, however, and on 28 January 2003, in his State of the Union address, he made a commitment: "If Saddam Hussein does not fully disarm, for the safety of our people and for the peace of the world,

we will lead a coalition to disarm him." The United States claimed that 40 nations were represented in a 'coalition of the willing' that supported action against Iraq, although only four – Britain, Poland, Denmark and Australia – contributed troops to the invasion force.

HOSTILITIES BEGIN

The war began on 20 March and Saddam's government rapidly collapsed. When US troops occupied Baghdad he was nowhere to be found. It soon became apparent that Saddam had bluffed. No weapons of mass destruction were discovered. On 13 December the former dictator was discovered, hiding underground in Tikrit. By then, Iraq was spiralling into violent conflict between militant Sunni and Shi'ite Muslims and Kurdish nationals, with the Americans and their coalition allies, among whom the British remained prominent, struggling to impose order. Optimism that, freed from dictatorship, Iraq would develop into a model liberal democracy were profoundly misplaced.

At the end of April 2004, the United States surrendered most of its remaining moral high ground in the court of world opinion when images of prisoner abuse at Abu Ghraib prison, Baghdad, were released. In June, political sovereignty was transferred back to Iraq, a country in which internal security had now collapsed into a maelstrom of militia rivalries, hostage taking and suicide bombings.

Saddam Hussein was executed on 30 December 2006, having been found guilty by an Iraqi court of crimes against humanity. His country's ordeal continued. George W. Bush's final months in the White House offered scant prospect of influencing the contemporary conclusion that his mission in Iraq remained unaccomplished. History's verdict remains to be drawn.

HURRICANE KATRINA

2005

Thomas Jefferson acquired New Orleans through the Louisiana Purchase in 1803. It was founded in 1718 by the French Mississippi Company, and was among America's oldest cities. Andrew Jackson established his military reputation there. In 1988 it hosted the Republican national convention that nominated George H. W. Bush for the presidency. Famous as the birthplace of jazz, for its Mardi Gras and its French Quarter, about half of New Orleans was built below sea level, and it is surrounded by water: the Mississippi River, Lake Pontchartrain and a system of slow-moving streams known as bayous.

On Monday 29 August 2005, the city became part of the lake. As Hurricane Katrina cut a swathe across Louisiana, Mississippi and Alabama, in New Orleans the levees that had been its defence against flooding were breached. As the waters continued to rise, a humanitarian disaster threatened in the wake of the environmental devastation.

The president was on vacation at his ranch in Texas. On the day before the hurricane's landfall, George W. Bush

Below: The impact of the hurricane was most severely felt in New Orleans, where the loss of life was greatest.

Above: Hurricane Katrina was one of America's worst natural disasters, displacing people and ruining lives.

spoke with Mike Brown, who was in charge of the Federal Emergency Management Agency (FEMA), the body responsible for responding to natural disasters. Bush told reporters: "We will do everything in our power to help the people in the communities affected by this storm."

As the storm's full impact became clear, he returned to Washington, flying over New Orleans on his way back to the White House. On the ground, conditions were deteriorating in the city's Superdome, where refugees from the

storm had been left stranded in its aftermath. In the city, law and order temporarily broke down as widespread looting took place.

Amid criticism that his administration was offering insufficient help, Bush toured the stricken area on Friday 2 September and expressed his confidence in FEMA's response to the disaster: "Brownie, you're doing a heck of a job." A week later Brown was dismissed from his job of managing the relief effort. He later resigned as FEMA's head.

It was those who had least who were the most dispossessed: those with cars left the city; the poor, elderly and homeless were left stranded. Hurricane Katrina exposed the disparities in US society between the rich and the poor, and between the white and black populations of the South. George W. Bush, beleaguered by the Iraq War, found his leadership once more in the spotlight of media attention, compounding the political problems caused by his controversial foreign policy.

BARACK OBAMA

2009–

On November 4th 2008, Barack Obama was elected president, the culmination of a remarkable personal and political odyssey. He was born in Honolulu, Hawaii, in 1961. His mother, Ann Dunham, was from Kansas, and his father, for whom he was named, was from Kenya. Their mixed-race marriage did not endure after Barack senior left to study at Harvard, and then returned to Africa. Obama's mother remarried and in 1967 took her young son to live in Jakarta, but after four years there, he returned to Hawaii to be brought up by his maternal grandparents.

In 1983 he graduated from Columbia University, in New York, and two years later moved to Chicago to be an organizer among the city's deprived and predominantly African-American South Side community. In 1988 he went to Harvard Law School, gaining national attention as the first black president of its law review. Returning to Chicago in 1991, he began teaching at the University of Chicago Law School.

The following year he married Michelle Robinson. In 1995 his autobiographical account of his search for identity, *Dreams from My Father* was published, and a year later Obama won election to the Illinois State Senate.

In 2004, now seeking election to the federal Senate, Obama's inspirational rhetoric was demonstrated in his keynote address at the Democratic National Convention, which nominated John Kerry for president. He won his Senate contest and just three years later entered the race for the Democratic Party presidential nomination, galvanizing his supporters in an insurgent primary campaign against the front-runner and heir apparent, Hillary Clinton. Obama's powerful message of generational and political change brought victory over the Republican candidate, John McCain,

Below: Barack Obama is the first African-American president in US history, and also one of the youngest presidents ever to take office.

MICHELLE OBAMA

Michelle Robinson was born in 1964 and grew up on the South Side of Chicago. A graduate of Princeton and Harvard Law School, and a successful career woman, she married Barack Obama in 1992. They have two daughters, Malia and Sasha, the youngest children to live in the White House since Amy Carter, 32 years ago.

in a hard fought, often bitter and increasingly negative election contest. During the campaign the American economy nearly collapsed and the wars in Afghanistan and Iraq rumbled on. Obama faces formidable domestic and international challenges as president, but his success affirmed to many not only the enduring promise of American life, but also 'the audacity of hope', as expressed in the title of the book he published in 2006, which, soon afterwards, would become the manifesto for his presidential ambition.

Born: 4 August 1961, Honolulu, Hawaii
Parents: Ann (1942–95) and Barack (1936–82)
Family background: Mother: anthropologist, father: public service
Education: Columbia University (1983)
Harvard Law School (1991)
Religion: United Church of Christ
Occupation: Public Service, Academic
Military service: none
Political career: Illinois State Senate (1996–2004)
US Senate (2004–08)
Presidential annual salary: $400,000 + $50,000 expenses
Political party: Democrat

INDEX

PICTURE CREDITS
Peter Newark's American Pictures: 1, 22, 23t, 28, 31, 35, 44, 48, 49, 50, 52 top, 54 bottom, 56, 63 bottom right, 64, 68, 72, 74, 75, 92, 138 top, , 140 top, 141 top, 142, 143 both, 144 top 144 bottom left, 145 top, 146 top, 147, 152 bottom, 153 bottom, 154, bottom left and right, 155 left, 155 centre right, 158 bottom, 160 top, 164 both, 165 both, 166, 167 top, 168, 169 top, 173 top, 174 bottom, 175 bottom, 176 bottom, 177 bottom, 179 both, 190, 194 top, 197 left, 198 bottom left, 200 bottom left, 208 top, 209 bottom, 216 217 top right, 221 both, 253 top and bottom, 254 top, 255 top.
THE BRIDGEMAN ART LIBRARY: Page 4 second from bottom, 30, 34, top, 36,66, 72 top, 80 bottom, 82–3, 90, 97 bottom, 98, 99 both, 102, 104 bottom, 113 top left and bottom, 115 all, 153 top, 158 top, 163 top, 203.
ALAMY: 4 second from top, 6 top, 9 top, 21 bottom, 25, 27, 37 bottom, 42–3, 43 bottom, 47 left, 53 top, 81 top, 103 left, 122 top, 126 bottom 198 bottom right, 235 bottom left, 236 both, 250 bottom.
NORTHWIND PICTURE ARCHIVE: 52 bottom, 54 top, 55 bottom.
CORBIS: 2, 3, 4 top, middle bottom, 5 all, 6 bottom, 7 both, 8 both, 9 bottom (both), 10–11, 12–13, 14 bottom, 15 both, 16 both, 17, 20, 21 top, 23 bottom, 24, 25 top, 26, 29, 32, 33, 34 bottom, 37 top, 40, 41, 42 top, 43 top, 45 both, 46 bottom, 47 top right and bottom, 49 bottom, 51 right, 53 bottom, 55 top, 58 left, 59 both, 60–1, 63 top middle, top right, bottom middle, 65, 69 both, 70 both, 71 top, 73 , 76, 77, 78 top, 79 top, 80 top, 84, 85, 86, 87, 88, 89, 90 top, 93, 94 both, 95, 96 both, 97 top, 100, 101, 103 bottom right, 104 right, 105, 106–7, 108 both, 109 both, 110 both, 111, 112, 113 top right, 114 both, 116, 117 top, 118, 119, 120, 121 both, 122, 124, 125 both, 126 left, 127 both, 128 both, 129 both, 130 all, 131 both, 132–3, 134–5, 136, 137, 138 bottom, 139 both, 140 bottom, 141 bottom, 144 bottom right, 145 bottom, 146 bottom, 148 both, 149, 150 both, 151, 152 top, 154 top, 155 top middle and bottom right, 156–7, 159 both, 160 bottom, 161, 162, 163 bottom, 167 bottom, 169 bottom, 170 both, 171, 172 both, 173 bottom, 174 top, 175 top, 177 top, 178 top and bottom, 180, 181 both, 182–3 184 both, 185, 186 both, 187 both, 188 top and bottom, 189 both, 191 all, 192 bottom, 193, 194 bottom, 195 all, 196 top, 197 top, 198 top, 199 both, 200 top and bottom right, 201 both, 202 all, 203 bottom, 204 top and bottom, 205 both, 206–7, 208 bottom, 209 top and left, 210 both, 211 both, 212, 213 both, 214 both, 215217 top left and bottom, 218 both, 219 both, 220 both, 222 both, 223, 224 both, 225 both, 226, 227 both, 228 both, 229 bth, 230–1, 232 both, 233 all, 234 all, 235 top and bottom right, 237, 238 both, 239 both, 240 both, 241 both, 242 both, 243 both, 244 both, 245 both, 247 both, 248 both, 249, 250 top, 251 both, 252, 254 bottom, 255 bottom, 256.
GETTY IMAGES: 67 top.

This edition is published by Hermes House, an imprint of Anness Publishing Ltd, Blaby Road, Wigston, Leicestershire LE18 4SE

Email: info@anness.com

Web: www.hermeshouse.com; www.annesspublishing.com

Anness Publishing has a new picture agency outlet for images for publishing, promotions or advertising. Please visit our website www.practicalpictures.com for more information.

Publisher: Joanna Lorenz
Editorial Director: Helen Sudell
Project Editor: Simona Hill
Designer: Nigel Partridge
Proofreading Manager: Lindsay Zamponi
Production Controller: Don Campaniello
All state flags illustrated by Alfred Znamierowski
All maps illustrated by Tom Connell
Indexer: Helen Snaith

ETHICAL TRADING POLICY

PUBLISHER'S NOTE